Educator's Complete Guide to Computers

Educator's Complete Guide to Computers

Theodore F. Swartz
Stephen M. Shuller
Fred B. Chernow

Parker Publishing Company, Inc.
West Nyack, New York

Library of Congress Cataloging in Publication Data

Swartz, Theodore F.
  Educator's complete guide to computers.

  Bibliography: p.
  Includes index.
  1. Education—Data processing. 2. Education—Computer
programs. 3. Microcomputers—Purchasing. I. Shuller,
Stephen M.   II. Chernow, Fred B.
III. Title.
LB1028.43.S92 1984   370'.285'4   83-19335

ISBN 0-13-240813-9

Printed in the United States of America

DEDICATION

To our parents:

John and Rena Swartz
Isadore and Florence Shuller

ABOUT THE AUTHORS

Theodore F. Swartz is the director of four schools for students with severe emotional and learning handicaps, under the auspices of New Jersey's Bergen County Special Services School District, where he has introduced the instructional use of computers. He has served as the New York Regional Contributor to *Classroom Computer News* and has spoken widely on the potential of the computer as a humanizing force in education. Dr. Swartz has authored several educational computer programs, as well as designed and implemented computer literacy courses for children and adults. Currently teaching computer programming in Basic and Logo for the Staten Island-based Richmond Educational and Computer Institute, which he directs, Dr. Swartz also serves as Adjunct Assistant Professor of English at the College of Staten Island. He received his Ph.D. in Educational Psychology from New York University in 1978.

Stephen M. Shuller is the director of Computer Outreach Services at Bank Street College of Education and an instructor in the Department of Languages, Literature and Social Studies in Education at Teachers College of Columbia University. While the director of the Center for Microcomputer Education in West Orange, New Jersey, Mr. Shuller was responsible for providing in-service education courses and technical assistance for 140 local school districts in northeastern New Jersey. In addition to conducting numerous courses and workshops for school districts, professional organizations, and institutions of higher education, Mr. Shuller has been a teacher at the elementary, secondary, and post-secondary levels. He holds a B.A. in Mathematics from Carleton College and an M.A.T. in Science Education from Harvard University.

Fred B. Chernow is a school principal on Staten Island, New York, where he has pioneered the use of computers in classrooms for gifted and for learning disabled youngsters. Currently an Adjunct Associate Professor of Mathematics at St. John's University, Mr. Chernow has written nine books in the areas of teacher training and school administration.

How This Book Can Help Answer Your Questions About Using Computers in Schools

The field of computer science and its implications for us as educators have grown at an unprecedented rate during the past few years. We must have at our fingertips the information and know-how that the new technology requires. It is fortunate that the most remarkable result of recent progress is that computers are now easy to use, inexpensive to buy and yet so powerful as to be a viable tool for workers in the most modest as well as the most elegant school settings. All that has been missing is a book such as this one, to guide educators step by step through an otherwise bewildering morass of technical jargon, high-powered sales pitches, and confusing arrays of similar-looking machinery.

As this new technology descends upon education, you need immediate answers to many important questions:

1. What options are open in terms of overall policy and equipment?
2. How do I get a model computer project initiated?
3. What steps are needed to sustain and enhance an on-going plan?
4. How can the power of the computer be harnessed to augment the delivery of educational services?
5. How can the overall functioning of a school be made more efficient and, at the same time, more joyful for all its various members through the use of computers?

This book answers all of these and many other crucial questions clearly and thoroughly. By breaking down the general areas of concern into a series of pinpointed issues, the authors generate a format that delivers easily located answers that can be immediately implemented by you. You will discover not only *what* to do to successfully harness and apply computer power in your school, but also *how* and *why*.

This book is written by educators who among them have more than twelve years' experience in implementing computer technology in a variety of learning environments. Their trials, spanning the pre-school through secondary levels, now provide you with proven methods for moving assuredly through every stage and level of utilization. Because they have already tackled situations like those you are now or will soon be facing, the authors put in your hands clear alternatives to help you save time and effort in making a multitude of necessary decisions. For example, to assist you in selecting appropriate funding sources, you are given an extended listing of potential sources, both public and private, along with names, addresses, and telephone numbers. Once you have earmarked prime targets, you merely turn to the appropriate section in Chapter 3 for detailed guidance in writing successful proposals.

Extensive research on your behalf underlies the whole of this book. In Chapter 2, tables of information are spread before you, giving you an easy-to-read analysis of the types of computer equipment you need, based on the uses you are helped to earmark. Hours of effort can be saved, along with many dollars, as you are presented with all of the information you need to determine at the outset which uses make the most sense in your particular school environment.

When faced with the question of how best to involve other school personnel, you can turn to Chapter 5 and find a fully detailed and documented plan, including advice on how to generate a climate of anticipation, suggestions on how to quickly make people feel "at home" with the equipment, a list of essential components of a basic training workshop, and a model feedback form for charting follow-up activities. When you need to know how to organize an ongoing teacher-training project, you will find that Chapter 10 provides you with a host of strategies, along with methods for maintaining the involvement of administrative personnel.

In addition to numerous and extensive tables, summaries, curricula, sample forms, letters, and reports, you are also presented with specific and tested techniques to serve in a wide variety of circumstances, including:

- twelve factors to consider before buying microcomputers
- three ways computers can help break bad learning habits
- five common blunders you should avoid when getting started
- two examples of using computers to stimulate instructional innovation
- seven ways to make the school's computers benefit the community

- four result-oriented suggestions for implementing that crucial first encounter between people and machine
- five tips for turning dissenters into supporters

When you want to know how the computer may be utilized to help solve learning problems, simply refer to Chapter 8. There you will encounter not only an easy-to-follow rationale, but also detailed suggestions for unlocking mental resources with computers and sample techniques for solving a persistent problem in writing. Also included is the inspiring account of a special education teacher who found that learning how to program microcomputers opened up exciting new possibilities for him and his students. You are provided with the listing of an actual, teacher-made, sample computer program that can be typed into a microcomputer and used to help students improve in their reading comprehension.

Extensive appendices, filled with information culled from literally hundreds of sources, serve to round out a presentation that is designed to serve all of your needs and to put you at the cutting edge of a bright new future. Technology should serve people; with this book, you can make computer technology serve the people in your school.

Theodore F. Swartz
Stephen M. Shuller
Fred B. Chernow

ACKNOWLEDGMENT

Theodore Swartz and Stephen Shuller express their profound indebtedness to Dr. Caleb Gattegno, for years of guidance, support, and tutelage in the area of human learning. The extent to which their writing is reflective of or contributing to a clear idea of how people exchange their time for learning is attributable, directly or indirectly, to Dr. Gattegno's pioneering efforts and research.

Contents

Educator's Complete Guide to Computers

1

What You Need to Know About Computer Hardware

1.1 WHAT IS A COMPUTER?

In a literal sense, a computer is nothing more than a complicated maze of electronic circuits in a plastic or metal case. If we were electrical engineers, we could look at these circuits in more detail to arrive at one kind of understanding of what a computer is.

There was a time when a circuit-and-wire understanding of computers was necessary. As recently as 1975, for example, the first microcomputers came as kits of electrical components. The only instructions available were schematic circuit diagrams. No wonder that only a few dedicated hobbiests were able to use these machines!

Fortunately, this level of understanding is no longer necessary or even helpful for most educators. For the most part, we will understand what a computer is in functional terms—by knowing what it can do and which component parts are best suited to various educational purposes.

Computers and Calculators

Computers are often thought of in comparison to calculators. Like calculators, computers can do arithmetic and print answers on paper or on a display screen. But most calculators require the user to key in one arithmetic expression at a time, after which the calculator produces the answer immediately.

To use a calculator for a job with several steps, such as balancing a checkbook, you need to key in many arithmetic expressions, one after another, working your way through the job one step at a time. To complete this job with a calculator, you must know every detail about the calculations in order to tell the calculator what to do.

On the other hand, computers can remember lists of instructions and then do them all at once whenever the user commands. These lists of instructions are called *programs*, and those who write them are called *programmers*. The computer itself and other electrical or mechanical components associated with it are called *hardware*. In contrast, programs for the computer are known as *software*.

Computers make possible a division of labor and expertise, wherein the programmer tells the computer how to do a job and the computer user merely places the program in the computer's memory and tells the computer when to start. Thus, to balance a checkbook with a computer, a programmer must know all the step-by-step details of the procedure, while the user does not. For users, then, computers can be powerful tools that allow them to do things they may not otherwise know how to do.

Many machines used in everyday life are "programmable," even though we usually do not think in these terms. For example, we place a particular time of day in the "memory" of an alarm clock that has been programmed to "go off" at whatever time we select. We set the thermostat for 68 degrees, thereby activating a program that makes the furnace go on and off as needed to maintain this temperature.

Alarm clocks and thermostats are not computers, however. These devices are very rigidly pre-programmed to do one specific task. Computers, in contrast, are flexible. They can be programmed to do a task, then ordered to forget that program and to learn a different one. An alarm clock is not a computer, but a computer can be programmed to be an alarm clock!

In recent years, some "programmable calculators" have appeared on the market. As might be expected, these calculators can remember some programs, which can be recalled and executed at will.

Is a computer just a programmable calculator, then? Perhaps yes—conceptually, this is a good place for an understanding of computers to start. Functionally, however, computers far outstrip calculators in power, speed, and flexibility.

Simply put, a computer can do far more than a calculator. Computers can process text as well as numbers, display information in a variety of ways, including graphics and sound, carry on interactive conversations that sound almost human, and many, many other things.

In summary, computers are highly flexible machines designed to store information and lists of specific instructions, called programs, which can be carried out on command. Their power and usefulness lie in their flexibility, and in the speed and accuracy with which they can execute their programmed instructions.

A Brief Historical Overview

Computers are so pervasive in modern life that it may be difficult to keep in mind how recent a phenomenon they are. The first commercially-available computer did not appear until 1951. It filled a large room with wires, electrical components, and 3000 vacuum tubes, the heat from which necessitated an elaborate air conditioning system. This computer was less powerful than today's desktop microcomputers, but cost millions of dollars. Fewer than 30 were ever sold, and manufacturers predicted that no more than a hundred computers would satisfy the entire world demand!

The first big breakthrough in computer technology came in the early 1960s, when transistors were successfully substituted for vacuum tubes in computer circuits. Transistors were an improvement because they were smaller and more reliable than vacuum tubes. As a result, two trends emerged:

1. The largest computers available became faster and more powerful for about the same cost.
2. Smaller computers—as fast and powerful as the original large computers—were developed at substantially lower cost.

Computers made with transistors were called "second generation" computers. The larger computers became known as "mainframes" or "maxi-computers," while the smaller ones became known as "minicomputers."

In 1968, another major breakthrough in electronics ushered in the third generation of computers. This breakthrough was a new circuit technology. Scientists were able to miniaturize electric circuits by photographically engraving them onto thin wafers of silicon called "chips." These integrated circuits made transistors and other discrete electronic components largely unnecessary.

Since much of the labor in building computers went into assembling and testing circuits, computers with integrated circuits were much cheaper to manufacture. As a result, the two trends outlined above—greater power and speed for the same price, and equivalent power and speed for a much lower price—continued and accelerated.

During the 1970s, chip technology continued to improve, so that first hundreds, then thousands, then tens of thousands, then hundreds of thousands of circuits could be engraved into silicon chips smaller than a dime. (See Figure 1–1.) These advances made possible faster and more powerful maxi-computers and, for the first time, microcomputers—computers low enough in cost for individuals and schools to afford, yet as powerful as some of the larger computers available in the mid- and late 1960s.

*Reproduced with permission of
Bell Laboratories*

Figure 1–1. UNIX Bellmac 32 Bit Chip

The technological advances that have produced large-scale integrated circuits continue, so that computer components get less and less expensive all the time. We can now see the day when the cost of internal computer components will become almost negligible compared to the cost of components like typewriter-style keyboards and television-like display screens. The day may be close at hand when computers are as commonplace as television sets, and most schools can afford to have a substantial supply of microcomputers for daily classroom use.

The Five Major Parts of a Computer

Any computer system, from the largest mainframe to the smallest microcomputer, is composed of the same five functional parts:

1. a Central Processing Unit (CPU)
2. internal memory
3. external memory or mass storage
4. input units
5. output units

These parts and their interrelationships are illustrated in Figure 1–2.

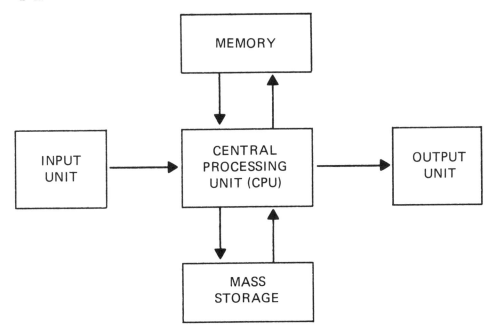

Figure 1-2. The Five Major Functional Parts of a Computer

Each functional part represents one or more physical components of the computer system. In the following sections, we will describe each functional unit and its major constituent parts.

In Chapter 2, we will describe the various educational uses for computers and discuss which features of each functional unit are needed for each educational use. In this way, you can use the information provided to select hardware specifications appropriate for the computers you will need.

1.2 UNDERSTANDING THE BRAIN OF THE COMPUTER: THE CENTRAL PROCESSING UNIT (CPU)

The CPU is the "brain" of the computer. It has two main components:

1. an arithmetic and logic unit (ALU)
2. a control unit

The ALU can perform calculator-type arithmetic operations and elementary logical operations. These logical operations are essentially comparisons of numbers or text. The ALU can determine, for example, whether two numbers are equal or which is smaller, and whether two words are identical or in alphabetical order.

The control unit directs the operations of the computer. It coordinates the workings of all the functional units and keeps track of which program step the computer is currently executing.

In reality, the computer knows nothing at all about arithmetic, logic, or program steps. It merely passes electrical pulses in and out of circuits designed to behave as though they were adding or comparing. The patterns of electric pulses form a code—somewhat like Morse code—that can be translated into numbers and letters for people to understand, and into electrical pulses for computers.

In Morse code, each letter and number is represented as a series of short or long electric clicks. For example, the letter S is three short clicks, usually written as three dots. The letter O is represented by three long clicks, usually written as three dashes. So, as the torpedoed ship sinks on the late movie, the telegraph operator frantically taps out "dot-dot-dot dash-dash-dash dot-dot-dot," the "SOS" distress signal.

If you look closely at Figure 1–3, you will see that up to six dots and/or dashes are required to specify each character. E and T need only one dot or dash, respectively, but all the punctuation marks require combinations of six dots and dashes. To a computer person, Morse code is a six-bit code, because at most six pieces or bits of information are needed to completely specify any character.

Computers use similar codes to store information and to move it inside the computer. Each bit represents either a pulse of electricity or the absence of such a pulse. We usually represent the pulses by the numeral one (1) and the time units with no electric pulses by the numeral zero (0).

Almost all computers use an eight-bit code to represent characters (letters, numbers, punctuation marks, and arithmetic signs). For

A	·—	M	——	Y	—·——	1	·————
B	—···	N	—·	Z	——··	2	··———
C	—·—·	O	———	·	·—·—·—	3	···——
D	—··	P	·——·	,	——··——	4	····—
E	·	Q	——·—	?	··——··	5	·····
F	··—·	R	·—·	;	—·—·—·	6	—····
G	——·	S	···	:	———···	7	——···
H	····	T	—	/	—··—·	8	———··
I	··	U	··—	-	—····—	9	————·
J	·———	V	···—	,	·————·	0	—————
K	—·—	W	·——	( )	—·——·—		
L	·—··	X	—··—	—	··——·—		

Figure 1–3. The International Morse Code

this reason, computer people have a special name for eight bits of information—a *byte*. Half a byte, or four bits, is called a *nibble*. (We will resist the temptation to make one or more terrible puns at this point, but be forewarned that most computer people are much more indulgent in this regard!)

Morse code is standardized throughout the world. Unfortunately, eight-bit computer codes are not. Most microcomputers, however, use dialects of one particular code called ASCII.

Figure 1–4 shows the ASCII codes for the letters of the alphabet. One job of the input and output units of computers is to translate between eight-bit computer codes and English characters.

A	01000001	H	01001000	O	01001111	V	01010110
B	01000010	I	01001001	P	01010000	W	01010111
C	01000011	J	01001010	Q	01010001	X	01011000
D	01000100	K	01001011	R	01010010	Y	01011001
E	01000101	L	01001100	S	01010011	Z	01011010
F	01000110	M	01001101	T	01010100		
G	01000111	N	01001110	U	01010101		

Figure 1–4. ASCII Alphabetic Codes

The CPU of a computer is characterized by how many bits of information it can process at one time. CPU sizes are generally multiples of eight bits; currently, the most widely used computers have 8-, 16-, or 32-bit CPUs.

In general, the more information processed at once, the faster the computer can work. Thus, other factors being equal, 32-bit machines are faster and more efficient than 16-bit machines, which are faster and more efficient than 8-bit machines.

One consequence of technological progress in large-scale integrated circuits is that CPUs can be produced on a single chip, containing more than 10,000 circuits. These single-chip CPUs are called *microprocessors*. A microcomputer is simply a computer that has a microprocessor for a brain.

Most microprocessors handle either 8 or 16 bits of information at a time. When processing speed is important, 16-bit microprocessors will be better than 8-bit ones. As chip technology improves, the trend will be towards more 16-bit microprocessors and even some 32-bit microprocessors as well. For most educational applications, however, 8-bit microprocessors are quite adequate.

Microcomputers and Time-Sharing Systems

Faster, more powerful computers have made possible increasingly flexible interaction with people. Until the mid 1960s, programs were usually submitted for processing on stacks of punched cards (of the "do not fold, spindle or mutilate" variety) or rolls of paper tape. A computer operator would feed the cards or tape into the computer and, when processing was complete, return the results on paper or other computer cards. To maximize efficiency, jobs were sorted by type and saved up until a number of similar jobs could be processed all at once. At most computer installations, the time from job submission to return—called turn around time—ranged from an hour or two to a week or more.

This system, called batch processing, was a disaster for education. Computer programming, like any skill, is learned to a great extent by making and fixing mistakes. Typically, a student programmer would write a program, submit it for batch processing, and get it back a week later with several "error messages," the computer's way of saying it could not do what was asked because it did not understand. After fixing the mistakes in the program, the job was resubmitted, and it was not unusual for three or four cycles of errors and revisions to occur before the program finally worked. Very little could be accomplished in computer courses under these conditions.

As CPUs became faster and more powerful, it became possible to replace most batch processing with time sharing. In time-sharing systems, the computer deals with several programs at once, switching so quickly from one to another that the human users cannot tell whether or not the computer is paying attention to them. Time-sharing systems permit highly interactive programming, in which results and errors are communicated almost immediately.

More than any other factor, interactive time-sharing systems spelled the beginning of the computer as a useful educational tool. As chip technology continued to develop, two educationally-promising computer systems emerged:

1. time-sharing systems, on which several students work simultaneously, using a large powerful computer

2. microcomputers which are, by and large, single-user systems, but highly interactive ones

Time-sharing systems and microcomputers each have advantages and disadvantages for educational uses. In Chapter 2, we will provide guidelines for deciding which is better for the educational applications you have in mind.

1.3 STORING INFORMATION INSIDE AND OUTSIDE THE COMPUTER: MEMORY AND MASS STORAGE

The memory of a computer stores programs and data, which are transferred to the CPU by the control unit as needed to execute each instruction of the program. It may help to think of the computer's memory as a collection of boxes or cells. Each cell has an address—like a post office box number—and room enough inside to store one byte of information.

Older-style computers have magnetic core memory, consisting of iron cores (shaped like donuts) wrapped with wire. These core units can be magnetized in two different directions, with the direction of magnetization of each core coding one bit of information.

Magnetic core memory has two very useful properties:

1. It is more or less permanent since the iron cores become magnets.

2. It can be erased and changed by reversing the direction of the current flow in the magnets.

Unfortunately, core memory is expensive for the same reasons that individual circuits are expensive: a great deal of labor is necessary to put the components together. Fortunately, chip technology has had as much (or more) impact on computer memory as it has had on CPU design.

Memory chip technology has improved so rapidly over the last few years that the same amount of money bought 64 times as much memory in 1982 as in 1977. As a result, both microcomputers and larger computers have increased dramatically in power while prices have continued to fall.

Unfortunately, memory chips that are both permanent and erasable are relatively expensive and unreliable. For this reason, two different kinds of memory chips are generally used in tandem: ROM chips, which contain permanent memory, and RAM chips, which are programmable and erasable.

ROM stands for "read-only memory." The computer can read what the memory cells have stored, but it cannot write new information into these cells. ROM memory remains intact when the computer is turned off.

RAM is "read and write memory." The computer can read what has been stored and can write new information into these cells. When the computer is turned off, however, the contents of RAM are lost.

Losing the contents of RAM is not necessarily a defect, however. One important characteristic of computers is flexibility—the computer can be programmed to be an alarm clock, a checkbook balancer, a game player, and thousands of other things. If computers could not forget, soon their memories would be full and this flexibility would be lost.

It may be worth noting, parenthetically, that forgetting serves an equivalent function in human memory. We are so used to seeing "forgetting" as a defect that we may not realize how essential forgetting is to preserving our mental flexibility.

Due to the nature of RAM and ROM, the following memory organization is used. Information that will be needed frequently when the computer is in operation, and information needed to get the computer started when it is powered up (turned on) is stored permanently in ROM. Specific programs are stored in RAM while they are being executed by the computer. When not needed by the computer, these programs are stored in permanent, secondary memory outside the computer.

The size of a computer's memory is measured in bytes. Since a byte is eight bits, and most computers use eight bits to store each coded character, it is convenient to think of a byte as the amount of memory required to store each character—digit, letter, punctuation mark, etc.—placed into the computer's memory. Computer people often use "K" as an abbreviation for a thousand. (For those familiar with metric measurement, this is the same K that stands for thousand in kilometer and kilogram.) Thus, a computer with 48K RAM has RAM memory sufficient to store about 48,000 characters of information.

When people talk about a 16K computer, for instance, they are referring to RAM. In general, the more RAM available, the more complex and sophisticated programs the computer will have room to store and execute.

Computer Languages

As previously mentioned, computers operate in terms of pulses of electricity. Even if we convert these pulses to patterns of ones and zeros, humans do not find it easy to communicate with computers in this "machine language." In the early days of computers, there was no choice, but in the mid 1950s, the concept of higher-level computer languages was invented.

A higher-level computer language consists of a limited set of words and a syntax (very specific rules for forming words of the language into grammatical sentences). Humans can understand ungrammatical sentences and frequently utter them in everyday speech, but computers cannot tolerate even the slightest departure from the syntax rules of the computer language.

To implement a higher-level computer language, one must write a machine language program telling the computer how to translate between the new language and machine language. This program is stored either in RAM or ROM memory. Thereafter, programs can be written in the higher-level language, and the computer will automatically translate the program into machine language in order to do what it says. Since 1955, hundreds of computer languages have been invented, and which is best for educational purposes is currently a topic of hot debate. (We will return to this topic in Chapter 6.)

Two types of translators are commonly used. One is a simultaneous translator, like those at the United Nations who translate line by line or sentence by sentence while the original speech is going on. In computer jargon, this line-by-line translator is called an *interpreter*. An interpreter translates each command to the computer just before it is needed, but does not save a copy of the translation.

The other kind of translator is a compiler, which does the entire job in advance. Like the translator who prepares a written translation of the whole text in advance, a compiler prepares a machine language translation of the program and stores it in the computer's memory, ready to be executed whenever needed.

Because their translations are done in advance and saved, compilers are more efficient than interpreters. In general, compiled programs can be executed more quickly than interpreted ones. Interpreters use less memory, however, and provide more immediate feedback about programming mistakes.

Some computer languages come with both interpreters and compilers; other computer languages, with one or the other. Microcomputers have tended to use interpreted, relatively simple versions of languages due to limited memory availability. As improved technology makes additional memory less and less expensive, more sophisticated languages for microcomputers are starting to become available.

Many microcomputers offer language interpreters in ROM, that is, on a ROM chip inside the computer. The language offered is usually, but not always, a version of a language called BASIC. Other microcomputers require language interpreters to be loaded into RAM after the computer is turned on. An interpreter in ROM is more convenient and does not tie up any of the available RAM, but this arrangement is less flexible because it is easier to load a new program into RAM than to replace a ROM chip.

When comparing computer memory size, it is important to consider which language will be used and whether that language is available in ROM. If not, from 8K to 16K of the available RAM will be needed to store a language interpreter or compiler.

Mass Storage

Mass (or secondary) storage is relatively inexpensive memory outside the computer. It is necessary to preserve the flexibility of the computer, so that programs and data that are not always used do not take up valuable memory space inside the machine.

Secondary storage uses the same technology as the tape recorder. A code similar to the computer machine language is stored magnetically, either on tape or on a magnetic film coated onto plastic or metal disks.

The least expensive secondary storage device is an ordinary cassette tape recorder using the same type of cassette tapes used for recording voice or music. The computer actually converts its code of electrical pulses into audible noises, which are recorded on tape just as your favorite song would be.

If you were to play a computer tape on a cassette recorder, you would hear a rapid pattern of high pitched noises. Perhaps you have heard noises like these in the background while talking on the telephone. If so, you were hearing two computers talking to each other (also known as high-speed data transmission).

Another device for mass storage is called a disk drive. This machine is something like a record turntable. Disks are placed inside, where they are rotated rapidly while a device resembling a record player tone arm moves across the disk surface, reading or writing magnetic signals on the coating of the disk. (See Figure 1–5.)

Courtesy of Apple Computer,
Inc.

Figure 1–5. Apple Disk II Drive

Unlike most turntables, however, the disk drive arm can move directly and precisely to any point on the disk surface. This means that the disk drive can read information from particular parts of the disk without having to search through the whole disk from beginning to end. This ability to find or write information pinpointedly is called *random access storage.*

In contrast, cassette tapes provide *serial access storage.* To find a specific piece of information on a cassette tape, it is necessary to search the tape serially, from the beginning to the place on the tape where the information has been stored.

Disks come in two types: (1) floppy disks, which are made from flexible plastic, and (2) hard disks, made from metal. Hard disk drives, also called Winchester drives, can store much more information and work more quickly and reliably than floppy disk drives. Unfortunately, the precision engineering required to reach these performance levels makes the Winchester drive mechanism expensive and delicate.

To protect the mechanism, hard disks are permanently sealed inside the drive. Floppy disks are somewhat sensitive to dirt and dust, but they can be moved in and out of the disk drive like phonograph records. Thus, the advantages of hard disk drives are speed and the convenience of a large storage capacity in one place. Floppy disk drives offer lower price and unlimited storage capacity on separate disks.

There are different sizes of disks available, though these sizes are standardized. The manner in which information is stored on the disk varies idiosyncratically from computer to computer, however. Under these confusing circumstances, it is best to compare disk drives in terms of storage capacity, which is measured in bytes, just like internal computer memory.

A few years ago, most microcomputers purchased for education used cassette mass storage, but there has been a trend towards increased use of disk systems. As microcomputer memory and power continues to increase, the inconvenience and slow speed of cassette systems are felt more acutely, making cassette players seem less and less desirable. Those who have never used disk drives do not usually mind cassette players, but once they experience the advantages of disk drives, chances are they will never want to use a cassette player again.

Perhaps a similar trend will emerge toward hard disk drives over the next few years. Disk technology is improving rapidly, and prices are falling at the same time as disk capacity is growing. At least for now, most hard disk drives are used either for large-scale administrative work or when several microcomputers can share a single disk drive for joint use.

Some microcomputers are designed so that cartridges containing ROM chips can be plugged into a slot in the computer. For these computers, cartridges are an additional form of mass storage. Once they are plugged in, ROM cartridges become part of the computer's internal memory, so they are much faster, easier to use, and more reliable than other forms of mass storage. As with other ROM, however, it is not possible to change the information stored on ROM cartridges, so this form of mass storage is a one-way street, more like a phonograph record than a recording tape.

The computer programs that are stored on cassettes, diskettes, or ROM cartridges are called software. Some software contains instructions for the operation of the computer system itself; for example, a computer language translator or a program containing instructions for the computer about operating the disk drives. These programs are called *systems software*. Other software contains programs instructing the computer how to perform specific tasks, such as balancing a checkbook or composing sonnets. These programs are called *applications software*.

1.4 COMMUNICATING WITH THE COMPUTER: INPUT AND OUTPUT

Input and output are two examples of computer jargon now part of everyday language. Chances are that you use both these words in your everyday speech and already know what they mean. For the record, however, the input unit of the computer gets information from the outside world into the computer, and the output unit takes information from the computer and presents it in a form humans can understand.

There are many different types of computer input and output devices. In fact, most of the choices confronting purchasers of computer hardware involve input and output devices and the particular computers that will or will not work with particular input and output devices.

For large computer time-sharing systems, the most widely used input and output device is a terminal. Some terminals look like typewriters or teletype machines. They are called hard copy terminals because they print input and output onto paper which can be kept for future reference.

Other terminals look like typewriter keyboards with television screens attached. These are often called CRT terminals. CRT stands for cathode ray tube, the kind used for picture tubes in television sets. CRT terminals display input and output on the screen, but no permanent record is made. Time-sharing systems with CRT terminals usually have one or more printers available to produce "hard copy" of computer output when needed.

One important factor affecting terminal performance is the rate at which the terminal can transfer data to and from the computer CPU. Computer people use "how many bits of information can be transferred per second" (or baud) as a unit of measure to compare the relative speeds of terminals, other input/output devices, and mass storage devices. For example, some terminals transfer data at 120 baud, or 120 bits per second. Since 8 bits make a byte, 120 baud is 15 bytes or 15 characters per second.

Now, 120 baud is slow for a computer, but 15 characters per second would make for a very fast typist—well over 100 words per minute. So, even slow computer terminals will not have any trouble keeping up with even very fast typists.

Baud rate becomes important for output, however, because typical terminal transfer rates are not fast enough to enable time-sharing computers to generate elaborate graphics or animation on terminal screens. The moral of the story is: if you want to do fancy, interactive graphics, use microcomputers rather than time-sharing systems.

Most microcomputers use a typewriter-style keyboard as an input unit and a video display (television) screen as an output unit. Some microcomputers have separate physical components for each unit. Most have keyboards built into the computer unit and some have screens and mass storage units built in as well, as shown in Figure 1–6.

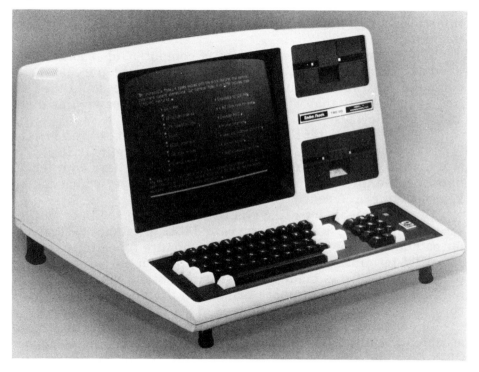

TRS-80 is a trademark of
Radio Shack Division of Tandy
Corporation.

Figure 1–6. A Microcomputer with Built-In
Keyboard, Screen and Mass Storage Units

There are many, many options in input and output units, both in types of units and in styles of individual units. Some of the choices are a matter of personal taste and should be decided by trying out the various options. Others are more clearly related to particular educational uses, and will be pointed out below.

Keyboard Input Units

Keyboard input units function more or less like typewriter keyboards, allowing computer users to type information into the computer. The input is displayed on the video screen as it is being typed, so that the user can see what he or she is doing. This procedure is called *echoing*.

Keyboards come in many different arrangements—some like typewriters, others like traditional computer terminals, and still others hybrid. The arrangement of alphabetic keys generally follows the typewriter standard, which is good for touch typists and not so good for hunt-and-peckers. Number keys are either similar to a typewriter keyboard, on a separate numeric keypad (usually found at the right of the keyboard), or a combination of both.

Computer programmers generally use only upper case letters for input, so many computer keyboards only allow input of upper case. Even if there is a standard typewriter keyboard with a shift key, it is not necessarily possible for the keyboard to differentiate upper and lower case when it sends input to the computer CPU.

Other keyboard variables include the size of the keyboard, the key "action," and the number and type of keys. Keyboard size is either standard typewriter or a more compact design, which can feel cramped.

There are three main types of keys: typewriter style, calculator style, and pressure sensitive. Calculator-style keys are generally smaller than typewriter keys and have a different feel. They are usually spaced out on the keyboard, a feature that makes touch typing more difficult.

Pressure-sensitive keys are not really keys at all, but a flat membrane on which key shapes are embossed. When the appropriate area of the membrane is touched, the keyboard responds as though a key had been pressed. Most adults seem to dislike membrane keyboards, although children do not seem to mind. Membrane keyboards may prove more durable than more mechanical keyboards unless the keys are pressed with sharp objects (like pencil points).

Key action refers to how the keyboard responds to the user. Some keyboards are "bouncier" than others. Some automatically repeat a key when it is held down; others have separate repeat keys for the same purpose. Key action is an area where personal taste is the most important factor to consider.

Some keyboards have special keys that command the computer to perform commonly used functions with a single press. Such keys are convenient in that they save typing in a longer message on the keyboard. Some keyboards also feature special keys for graphic symbols that can be displayed on the screen.

A good quality keyboard should have the following features as well:

1. Rollover: The computer remembers keystrokes that come very quickly in succession.

2. Buffer: The computer remembers keystrokes that are typed when the computer cannot process them, and sends them to the computer as soon as it is ready.

3. Debouncing electronics: The computer encodes signals from the keyboard in a way that eliminates echos, which could cause mistakes.

All of these features are standard in the most widely used computers and only need be considered when buying a lesser-known brand.

Video Output

Video output units—also called VDUs (video display units), CRTs, and monitors—look basically like television sets. Some are built into the computer unit and some are separate. As in the case of other input and output devices, there are several types of video units available.

Video units can be divided into two broad categories: video monitors and television sets. Video monitors depend on receiving a special signal from a computer or video tape recorder in order to work. In North America, this signal is called NTSC composite video, or composite video for short. Other parts of the world have different systems, so we will assume that we are talking only about North American microcomputers and video units.

Microcomputers with built-in video displays and many designed for separate video units have a socket, or port, that sends out a composite video signal. Depending on the computer, this signal may be black and white or color. If color is available, the number of colors and the quality of the color picture depend on video display ROM chips inside the computer.

Video pictures and text characters are actually composed of many small dots of light on the screen. The more dots that can be placed on the screen at once, the less grainy the picture looks and the more readable the text material. Composite video monitors and American television sets can display about 500 rows with about 500 dots in each row. In other words, the maximum resolution of a composite video monitor or television is about 500 x 500.

Most microcomputers do not use the full resolution of the video screen. The maximum number of dots each computer can place on the screen varies from computer to computer. In general, the finer the resolution, the better the graphics possible with that computer.

Some computers can control each screen dot independently, whereas others control only clusters of dots at a time. A computer that controls screen dots individually will have maximum flexibility to create graphics on the screen. It is possible, however, to have relatively high flexibility with relatively poor overall resolution, or vice versa.

Even though all composite video monitors have the same resolution, the clarity of the image on the screen can vary widely from one type of monitor to another. In particular, color monitors vary from less expensive versions, which are approximately equivalent to similarly priced color television sets, to much more expensive models that are quite noticeably superior in clarity of screen image. The difference in clarity is particularly evident when text material is displayed on the screen.

For computer applications requiring a great deal of text output, green or amber monitors are recommended. These monitors display green or amber characters on a dark background with good resolution. They tend to cost mid-way between the price of conventional black-and-white monitors and the least expensive color televisions.

To use a television set for video output from a computer, the composite video signal must be changed into an imitation television signal that can be received by the television and changed back into a composite video signal inside the set. This convoluted procedure is accomplished by a device called an RF modulator, which comes built into some microcomputers, generally those designed primarily for home use. You may already have an RF modulator on a video game player or a video cassette recorder. If a microcomputer does not have a built-in RF modulator, it is usually possible to add one on.

Due to the roundabout process of getting video output from a computer to a television set, the picture is generally not as good as with a monitor. Compared to a lower-priced color monitor, a color television picture will look about the same, but the difference between a television picture and that of an expensive color monitor will be quite noticeable.

In the last few years, a new type of video display monitor, called RGB, has been developed. RGB (short for red, blue, green) monitors have separate mechanisms for displaying red, blue, and green dots on the screen. The result is a much clearer picture, with much finer resolution than anything possible with composite video.

Some computers have RGB ports built in. With others, an electronic component can be added to translate the computer output into signals appropriate for RGB monitors. At present, RGB monitors are quite expensive compared with other available options, but where spectacular color graphics are important, RGB is definitely the best choice in video displays.

In the near future, flat display screens will also become available. These screens will enable the microcomputers to be even more compact and portable than they are at present.

Text on the Screen

Every microcomputer can display text characters on the screen by generating patterns of dots that look like letters. The number of characters per line, number of lines on the screen, and actual design of the characters vary from computer to computer. Some computers can display both upper and lower case. Some can display text in different sizes, different type styles, or foreign alphabets. Some computers even allow the user to design new type styles.

Screens that display 32 to 40 columns of characters on each line are acceptable for general programming and educational uses, and are legible on most monitors and television sets. When each line displays as many as 80 characters, however, the clarity of the display is very important, and a green or amber monitor, or an RGB color monitor, would be advisable.

Other factors that determine the legibility of the display are the number of dots that make up each character (the density of the dot matrix) and the design of the matrix. Some lower case letters like "g" and "p" go "below the line" in ordinary print, requiring what computer people call descenders. If the dot matrix is designed without descenders, these lower case letters will look like they are up in the air, and the text on the screen will be harder to read.

1.5 EXTENDING THE COMPUTER'S CAPABILITIES WITH PERIPHERALS

Peripherals are input or output units that supplement the main input/output units of a computer. In this section, we will provide you with an understanding of how peripherals can be connected to computers, and survey some of the most popular and innovative ones.

Input/Output Interfaces

An interface is a device that permits two pieces of equipment to be connected together functionally. Computer interfaces are channeling devices that take pulses of electricity inside the computer and send them to an output device, or take pulses of electricity from an input device and transfer them into the computer.

Some input and output devices require translation of their signals before they can communicate with the computer. For example, keyboards must turn pressure on mechanical keys into electrical signals the computer can understand. Similarly, computers must turn their electrical signals into a composite video signal before sending it to a video display unit.

Other input and output devices use the same kinds of signals used internally by the computer. For these devices, the only problem is channeling the information in a form and at a speed the device can accept. There are two types of interface which do this job:

1. Serial interfaces send one bit of information at a time, Morse code style.
2. Parallel interfaces send several bits of information at a time.

Parallel interfaces provide for faster data transfer; but since there are several possibilities for how to organize the information being transferred, there are several types of parallel interface. Serial interfaces are slower, but more easily standardized. Most input or output devices that need a serial interface use one called RS232.

Printers

Printers can be added to most microcomputers to produce a permanent, written record of computer output. There are two types of printers in widespread use at present: dot matrix and daisy wheel.

Dot matrix printers put text on paper in a manner similar to the way video displays put it on the screen—with arrays of dots. Instead of dots of light on the screen, dots of ink are pressed onto paper by rows of tiny hammers pressing against an ink ribbon. Dot matrix printers vary widely in print quality. Basically, the more dots used to create each letter, the clearer and easier to read the letters become.

Dot matrix printers come in many different styles, from giant line printers that print an entire line of text at once, to much slower, smaller, and very economical models about the size of a telephone book. Print quality ranges from barely legible to what the manufacturers call "correspondence" quality, which is almost as good as an electric typewriter with a cloth ribbon.

For letter quality printing, daisy wheel printers are used. The daisy wheel is a circular arrangement of type elements that spins and presses against a film ink ribbon in a manner similar to that of an IBM typewriter ball. Daisy wheel printers are slower and more expensive than dot matrix printers, but the quality of the print compares to that of the finest office electric typewriter with a film ribbon.

Other types of printers that can electronically set type or print letter quality documents at lightning speed through laser technology are available. But most likely, these are beyond both the needs and the means of educators.

When buying a printer, care must be taken to match the printer and computer through an appropriate interface. Not all printers can be connected to any computer, so care should be taken that the proper interface is available before purchasing a printer.

Other Input Devices

Although most computers use keyboard input for most purposes, a variety of other input devices are available.

1. *Light Pens.* These instruments look like large metal pencils attached to the computer with a cord at the eraser end. (See Figure 1–7.) When touched to the computer display screen, they send a signal to the computer specifying where on the screen they are touching. The computer can use this information to simulate drawing on the screen with the light pen. This device can also be used to allow users to respond to the computer by touching particular areas of the screen, rather than using the keyboard at all.

2. *Touch-Sensitive Screens.* The last mentioned use for the light pen can also be accomplished with a touch-sensitive screen. At present, light pens can pinpoint the exact position of touch more specifically, but light pens are also more delicate and somewhat less reliable than touch-sensitive screens. The technology in this area is improving rapidly, however, and both devices will undoubtedly improve in quality and drop in price over the next few years.

Figure 1–7. Example of a light pen

3. *Game Paddles and Joysticks.* Game paddles and joysticks are widely used to play arcade-type games on the computer. They usually allow a player to steer some sort of representation on the screen. Most of these devices also have buttons that can be used to send a signal to the computer. Game paddles and joysticks can have educational uses by providing an alternative to the keyboard for young children or students for whom use of keyboards is difficult. These devices have also been used with handicapped children.

4. *Speech Recognition Units.* As their name implies, these devices can recognize human speech and use it as input to the computer. This technology is still in a developmental stage, and units usually must be set up in advance to recognize the speech of specific individuals, while the speech of others may not be recognized. Still, these units have already proven valuable in helping paralyzed individuals use computer-controlled mechanical devices such as wheelchairs.

5. *Optical Scanners and Card Readers.* These devices can sense patterns of light on printed material or paper. One application of optical scanners is the device that reads universal product codes at supermarket checkout counters. Another is a card reader that can

read pencil marks placed on test answer sheets. Card readers can be very effective labor-saving devices to keep track of information like test scores or school attendance records.

Other Output Devices

In addition to video displays and printers, computers can send output to a variety of other devices.

1. *Plotters.* Plotters draw on paper with pens to create graphs, charts, and other graphics, sometimes in several colors.

2. *Speech Synthesizers.* These devices produce voice output, permitting the computer to actually speak. Some synthesizers store actual speech samples and produce a limited amount of high quality speech. Others store syllables and phonetic features. These speech synthesizers can produce virtually unlimited amounts of speech, though the quality is not always good.

3. *Music Synthesizers.* These devices produce electronic music of good quality. They facilitate experimentation with various aspects of musical expression in a way not possible without computers.

4. *Robots.* These creatures are currently used to perform repetitive, assembly line tasks, and to perform some types of scientific experiments. The possibilities in this area, however, are just starting to be explored. One robot that has made its way into the classroom is the Logo turtle, a cybernetic, child-controlled creature which will be described in Chapter 6.

Electronic Communication Devices

A final input/output device that deserves some mention is a modulator-demodulator or modem, which enables a computer to be attached to another computer through telephone lines. In this way, a microcomputer can receive input from and send output to another computer anywhere in the world. Through modems, microcomputers can serve as terminals in a time-sharing system. Modems also permit microcomputers to be used as parts of electronic communications networks, through which microcomputers can tap into large-scale information banks, electronic mail and teleconferencing systems, and the like.

When attached to a larger computer through a modem, a microcomputer is a "smart terminal," in contrast to ordinary time-sharing "dumb" terminals. Microcomputers are "smart" terminals because they are computers in their own right and do not depend completely on their attachment to a host computer.

Using a smart terminal to communicate with a larger computer can save time and money. For example, suppose you are using an electronic mail system. With a smart terminal, it is possible to compose a letter on the microcomputer and then call up the electronic mail system, sending the letter right away. In this case, the time-sharing system charges only for the time required to send the letter, and not the time spent composing it.

Networking

Sometimes microcomputers are linked to each other rather than to a larger computer. Through this procedure, called networking, microcomputers can share input and output devices such as printers and disk drives, minimizing the cost of providing these options for a number of microcomputers in the same room. Networking also facilitates communication and software sharing among microcomputers on the same network.

Several different types of networks are available, and an increasing number of new systems are coming on the market. Each system has advantages and limitations, so careful shopping is necessary. In Chapter 2, we will discuss educational uses for microcomputers that will benefit from network systems and provide some guidelines for their purchase.

2 | Getting the Most for Your Money

2.1 PRELIMINARIES TO CHOOSING THE BEST COMPUTER FOR YOUR SCHOOL

Educators often ask, "What is the best computer to buy? Are microcomputers better than mini-computers? Which brand is the best for school use?" Unfortunately, these questions do not have simple answers.

The fact is, there are several well-engineered, well-supported, widely-used computers on the market, with promising new entries appearing almost weekly. None of these computers is clearly superior to the others for all purposes. Each computer has strengths and weaknesses, however. For any particular set of educational needs, there will be a relatively small number of "best choice" computers with just the right strengths for the tasks at hand.

The best place to start the process of purchasing computers is with the question, "What do we want to do with the computers once they are here?" When the projected uses of the computers are clearly defined, hardware and software choices are usually not difficult.

A Four-step Planning Process for Computer Acquisition

1. *Develop a rationale.* Why are microcomputers needed? What will the school do with them? These questions must be answered at the outset, preferably by a broad-based group representing all constituencies affected by the new project.

2. *Conduct a needs assessment.* Given the rationale and goals for the computer project, what will be needed in terms of equipment, facilities, and staff development?

3. *Develop an implementation plan.* How can available resources best be used to provide for the staff, facilities, and equipment specified in the needs assessment? Most schools and school districts do not have the resources to do everything they would like to do in one year, so formulate both long- and short-term implementation plans.

4. *Acquire hardware and software.* After steps one through three have been completed, hardware and software can be purchased. In some cases, availability of particular software will determine the hardware choice.

The balance of this chapter and Chapters 4 through 6 examine this implementation process in more detail, and provide practical advice about how to put these steps into effect.

2.2 FOUR COMMON CONCERNS ABOUT IMPLEMENTING A SCHOOL COMPUTER PROJECT

Won't the computers we buy today become obsolete too fast to make purchase worthwhile?

Not really. The computers you buy today will always be able to do what they do now. As long as the purchasing decisions are well thought out, the present-day computers will make their intended contribution to your computer project.

Yes, next year, computers are likely to be more powerful and less expensive, but this trend only means that it will be progressively easier to find the resources for your long-range computer implementation plan. It is important to plan carefully and to proceed cautiously, but not at the expense of not starting, because computer power will continue to expand and prices continue to drop for the foreseeable future. Waiting until next year can become a vicious cycle.

Why not rent computers instead of buying?

The answer to this question really depends on what sort of computer system you decide to use:

• If you decide to use a mainframe computer system: Very few schools systems have the required expertise or financial resources to even consider purchasing the hardware. Only a very large school district, a regional consortium, or a state educational agency could consider purchasing such a computer system. For most educators, rental of equipment and services is the only viable option.

• If you decide to use a mini-computer based system: The merits of rental and purchase are about even. If financial and technical resources in the school district are sufficient, money can be saved by purchasing equipment. On the other hand, rental arrangements covering technical support and maintenance of equipment can eliminate headaches and make it easier to upgrade equipment as technology changes.

• If you decide to use microcomputers: Purchase will almost always be the correct decision. Most of the major manufacturers offer lease/purchase agreements, but these typically cost 40% to 50% of the equipment purchase price per year, only two thirds of which is credited towards purchase at the end of the lease. These agreements typically do not cover maintenance and repair, which can add another 10% to 20% of the purchase price to the annual cost. Under these circumstances, very few schools will find it economical to rent microcomputer equipment.

By the way, many dealers will provide "loaner" microcomputers to schools which are considering purchases. Thus, it is usually possible to try out microcomputers without committing any funds.

How do we decide among microcomputers, minis, and mainframes?

Micros, minis, and mainframes differ substantially in features that affect educational uses of computers. Just as different brands have strengths and weaknesses which make them well suited for some purposes and poorly suited for others, micros, minis, and mainframes all have their place. Once again, we need to start with the question, "What do we want to do with the computers when we get them?" Once this question is answered, it will be possible to choose hardware wisely.

The next three sections of this chapter will provide a step-by-step decision-making process for hardware acquisition to help you answer this question for your particular needs and circumstances.

Should we consider buying hardware first or software first?

Most people's inclination is to buy hardware first and then look around for software. This procedure can spell disaster if appropriate software for important applications turns out later to be unavailable for the computer which has been purchased.

For this reason, many computer experts have given the advice: look at software first, and then buy the hardware to run the software you have selected. But this advice is somewhat simplistic. For some educational applications of computers, software is a very important consideration, but for others, it is not important at all. Once again, the best procedure is to first decide what uses will be made of the computers. This decision will help determine whether or not it will be important to look at software before deciding which computer to buy.

2.3 AN OVERVIEW OF EDUCATIONAL USES OF COMPUTERS

By now it should be clear that we have to know what we want to do with computers before deciding which one to buy. For this reason, let's take a brief tour of the world of educational computing. Each of the topics surveyed below is covered much more extensively later in the book, but this overview will provide a basis for looking at the hardware options discussed later in this chapter.

Our tour will have four parts. We will consider the computer as: (1) teacher; (2) tool; (3) learner or student; and (4) object of instruction. In practice, these categories sometimes overlap, as do the category subdivisions which will be introduced below. Even so, we have found this framework very useful in providing a working overview of computer use in education.

The Computer as Teacher

When a computer is used as a teacher, it is programmed to provide an appropriate learning experience for a student or group of students, who need only minimal computer-related skills to participate. The computer generally functions either as "instructor" or as "learning environment," though mixtures of these two modes can occur.

The first mode, which we call "Computer as Instructor," has its roots in behaviorist psychology and the instructional strategy of programmed instruction developed in the 1950s. In this approach, a content area is broken down into a large number of small steps. Traditionally, the instructional pattern consists of cycles, starting with an explanation of a particular step, followed by questions to test whether the step has been mastered, and finally some reinforcement. If mastery has been achieved, the next step in the

```
COMPUTER AS TEACHER
    COMPUTER AS INSTRUCTOR
        DRILL AND PRACTICE
        TUTORIAL
    COMPUTER AS LEARNING ENVIRONMENT
        SIMULATION
        EDUCATIONAL GAMES
        "MICRO WORLDS"

COMPUTER AS TOOL
    STUDENTS' TOOL FOR:
        PROBLEM SOLVING
            CALCULATIONS
            STUDENT-WRITTEN PROGRAMS
            DATA ANALYSIS
        INFORMATION RETRIEVAL
        ELECTRONIC MAIL/TELECONFERENCING
        WORD PROCESSING
    TEACHERS' TOOL FOR:
        COMPUTER MANAGED INSTRUCTION (CMI)
        RECORD KEEPING
        GENERATION OF INSTRUCTIONAL MATERIALS
        TESTING

COMPUTER AS LEARNER
    PROGRAMMING

COMPUTER AS OBJECT OF INSTRUCTION
    COMPUTER AWARENESS
    COMPUTER LITERACY
    COMPUTER SCIENCE
    DATA PROCESSING
    COMPUTER OPERATION AND REPAIR
```

**Figure 2-1. Educational Uses for
Microcomputers**

sequence is taught; otherwise, the current step is reviewed and retested.

Reinforcement activities range from simple feedback about the acceptability of the student's answers, to phrases of encouragement, often personalized with the student's name, to elaborate graphics and sound displays. Recently, a number of instructional programs have incorporated arcade-style video games as reinforcement activities.

Two types of computer programs use the computer as instructor:

1. Tutorial programs provide instructional material, test questions (usually in a multiple choice format), and reinforcement.
2. Drill-and-practice programs provide only sequences of test questions and reinforcement.

Most of the educational software on the market today consists of tutorials or drill-and-practice programs.

When used appropriately, this type of educational software can:

1. help individualize instruction
2. free the teacher for other aspects of teaching for which human sensitivity is more crucial
3. provide an unlimited supply of randomly-selected practice problems
4. provide automatic scoring and immediate feedback to the students who are practicing
5. motivate students to engage in tasks they might otherwise find repetitive and boring

To be effective, it is crucial that "computer as instructor" software be closely matched to the educational needs of the students and the instructional activities taking place in the classroom as a whole.

The title of the second type of "teaching" educational software— "Computer as Learning Environment"—is meant to convey a different philosophy of instruction, one rooted in humanistic psychology and the principles of discovery learning. In this approach, the learner is seen as actively constructing his or her own learning. The job of the teacher is to facilitate this learning process by providing a rich environment and intervening only when necessary. Three types of programs that attempt to provide such environments are simulations, educational games, and "Microworlds."

Simulations are slices of reality modeled by the computer. For example, NASA uses computer simulations to give astronauts pseudo-experience in flying spacecraft. The computer controls a mock space capsule, modeling the behavior of a real capsule in response to programmed "outside conditions" and the astronauts' actions.

Simulations have two striking advantages as educational programs:

1. They can compress time, modeling in a few minutes events that might take much longer in the real world.
2. They can bring into a classroom (or some other suitable place), experiences that would be unavailable to classroom-bound students without the computer.

With simulations, students learn by doing. They test hypotheses by getting feedback from the computer about the consequences of their actions.

Educational games are structured activities with rules and a goal. Students play against each other or the computer, which acts as scorekeeper, referee, and generator of the activities of the game.

Some games are simulations as well. For example, a program called "Geography Search" (McGraw-Hill) is a simulation game in which participants are ship captains. The activity is a game because it has the goal of getting back to home port with the richest cargo, but the playing of the game is a simulation of events that require a knowledge of navigation. Students who play the game learn geography by suffering the consequences of their mistakes, and then playing again.

Other educational games include strategy games like chess or checkers, games that have educational content like hangman, and quiz games. The latter are similar to drill-and-practice programs in that the computer asks randomly selected questions. In some quiz games, the goal is simply to get a high score or to complete the game in a short time. In others, the quiz is imbedded in another activity, such as a baseball game. The players determine what happens in the outer activity (here, the baseball game) by how well they answer questions put to them by the computer.

The term "Microworld" is used to describe computer environments deliberately set up to provide specific types of educational experiences. Microworlds are very much like simulations, except that they may simulate "mathland" or "musicland" rather than a real-world model. Microworlds allow students to pursue even traditional academic subjects in an exploratory educational environment. Proponents forecast revolutionary changes in education as a result of their use.

The term "Computer-Assisted Instruction," or CAI, is often used to describe uses of computers as teachers. Other terms such as Computer Augmented Learning (CAL) and Computer-Based Instruction (CBI) are sometimes used as well. Those who favor using the computer as a learning environment generally use the term CAI only in reference to tutorial and drill-and-practice programs. Others use CAI to refer to all the uses of computers as teachers.

The Computer as Tool

Computers can serve teachers and students as tools that extend their capabilities and enable them to work more quickly and efficiently. There are so many applications of computers as tools that we will only focus on a few of the most prominent.

For teachers, computers can be a useful tool for computer managed instruction (CMI), for record keeping, for computer-generated materials development, and for testing.

In computer managed instruction, the computer performs several record-keeping, testing, and assignment-making functions for the teacher. Let's consider briefly a CMI system for mathematics instruction as an example.

Each student comes to the computer individually and "logs on," giving his name and perhaps an identification number or password. The computer looks up its file on that particular student, and selects a test at an appropriate level. The computer administers the test and, on the basis of the student's responses, makes an assignment in a text or workbook. The computer stores a record of the session in the student's file, so that when he returns, it can test the student on the material assigned and proceed accordingly.

Typically, CMI systems keep elaborate class records so that the teacher can see at any given time how each student is doing at his or her level. Some CMI systems are coupled with CAI systems; in these cases, the computer can provide instruction and practice as well as testing. Some advocates of coupled CAI/CMI systems feel that such systems can replace teachers. They envision schools of the future as places where students mainly interact with computer terminals. The evidence on the effectiveness of such systems is mixed at best, however, and many educators see a much different future for computers in education, one in which computers help teachers rather than replace them.

Computers can also be used for record keeping without the instructional management functions of CMI. For example, there are electronic gradebook programs that can store class records and, in addition, compute student grades, class averages, and other useful statistics. All of this information can be printed out in several choices of format.

Computer-generated materials development refers to the use of computers to produce worksheets, posters, and other classroom materials. For example, a computer can develop a hidden word puzzle, embedding a set of teacher-selected vocabulary words in an array of random letters, and then print out the puzzle on a spirit duplicating master. Using the computer for such purposes can save teachers a great deal of materials-preparation time.

Computers can be used in testing in a variety of ways. CMI programs test students to determine placement and mastery of assigned material. Computers can also be used to store item banks— long lists of questions from particular content areas and particular levels within these areas—along with statistical information about the items. Tests can then be constructed by selecting from the item bank items that will give the test characteristics selected by the teacher.

Computers can also be used to provide more efficient and reliable achievement tests by using the student's response to each question to determine which question to ask next. This "tailored testing" procedure is not yet widely available, but seems promising.

Students can also use computers as tools in many ways. Computers can be a powerful aid to many problem-solving activities, for example. For problems that require relatively simple calculations, the computer can function as a calculator. To solve more complex problems, students can write computer programs or use existing data analysis programs to eliminate many tedious calculations and save a great deal of time.

Using the computer as a problem-solving tool can dramatically affect the kinds of problems that can be given to students in mathematics, science, social science, and other courses. Interesting, real-world problems too complex to be solved without a computer can now be substituted for the simplified examples presently used in many courses.

Information retrieval is another promising area for student use of computers. Students can learn to use data base systems—electronic filing cabinets—to store and retrieve information, and to search through the stored information to formulate and test hypotheses.

Large, computerized data banks now available store information on almost everything imaginable, from current events to literature to history and so on. Using telephone lines and modems, the data banks stored in large computers can be accessed by microcomputers and time-sharing terminals. With access to a powerful information retrieval system, a student could, for example, call up on a display screen the front page of *The New York Times* on January 20, 1861, to see how the press of the day reacted to Lincoln's inauguration as president. The possibilities for putting information at our fingertips are almost endless.

The same large computers currently used for storing data banks usually also provide facilities for electronic mail and teleconferencing. In these systems, each computer user has an account and some storage space on the computer. Electronic mail is a procedure through which any user of the computer system can place a message in another user's storage space. Teleconferencing is a procedure through which public storage spaces—like electronic bulletin boards—are set up so any user can read or write material for anyone else interested in the topic of the conference.

One of the most promising areas for use of the "computer as tool" is word processing. Here, the computer becomes a combination typewriter and editor, enabling great flexibility in composing, editing, and revising text material.

Teachers of writing generally experience difficulty getting students to edit and revise their work, partly because the process of re-copying text is so time consuming and monotonous. Despite the time-honored plea to "make a rough draft first," few students actually do so.

Word processing takes the drudgery out of editing by making it very easy to change text on a computer display screen. The computer can print out as many revisions as are necessary, quickly and painlessly.

Many of the computer applications cited above are useful for student, teacher, and administrator alike. Furthermore, as computers achieve a larger and larger place in the everyday work world of most people, these "computer as tool" skills become essential vocational skills for most people. Clearly, the computer as tool will have a growing role to play in our schools for some time to come.

The Computer as Learner

Programming a computer is, fundamentally, a process of teaching the computer how to do something it could not do before. As calculators, computers may be more than a match for any human, but as learners, computers cannot compare to even the most limited humans among us. Teaching a computer, then, is no small task. It demands qualities the development of which may provide much more learning for the programmer than for the computer.

That teaching is a good way to learn should not surprise any educator. Most teachers have had the experience of enriching their own understanding of a particular subject area by trying to teach it to others. Programming has this to offer children and adults alike.

Teaching programming to children has three major benefits:

1. fostering procedural thinking
2. fostering thinking about thinking itself
3. engaging children in active, creative learning

Procedural thinking is the sort of thinking required to move step by step through a complex activity. Each step must be clearly defined and related to the steps that come before and after it. Developing the skills necessary to break down programming tasks into steps a computer can understand and to assemble a set of steps into a well-defined procedure is a cognitive task of some complexity. This process develops cognitive skills that are valuable in a context much wider than computer programming per se.

In order to teach a computer or a human, we must be clear on just what it is we are teaching. Particularly in the area of skills, we tend to "know how" without much awareness of just what we are doing. For example, few adults who know how to read can say with any degree of precision just what they are doing when they read.

To teach a computer, then, a necessary first step is "thinking about thinking"—looking into what we know how to do to discover just how we do it. This kind of introspection can pay large and often unexpected dividends of insight, which can enrich and deepen understanding.

Finally, computer programming is an active, creative form of learning. Since the most fundamental learnings derive from the process of programming itself, the content of the programs make little difference. Students can learn a great deal while programming arcade games, for example, no matter what the educational value of the finished product.

Thus, a fundamental issue in the educational use of computers has emerged: Should the computer teach the students, or should the students teach the computer? A few years ago, the unquestioned assumption was that computer programming belonged in high school or even in college. Now, some educators are involving children as young as five and six in programming activities. It appears that these activities have the potential to enrich the education of these children in ways not possible before computers were available. Still, this work has not been going on long enough or extensively enough to be sure what its potential impact on education can be.

For those who decide to teach programming to students, a second issue is the choice of computer language. To program a computer, one must learn to communicate with it through one of several computer languages. No one computer language is best for all purposes, and it is not entirely clear which languages are most appropriate for the various programming courses offered in schools.

The computer language most frequently taught in schools is called BASIC. This language was designed to be easy for beginners to learn, and it has become so popular that it is built into the ROM of most microcomputers. BASIC was invented in the mid-sixties, however, and lacks several important features of more modern languages. As a result, languages other than BASIC are used for most "real world" business and computer science applications.

For high school students interested in computer science, the current language of choice is Pascal. The College Board's Advanced Placement Examination in computer science is given in Pascal, and this is the language most often required for graduate school admission in computer science. For those who would like to find employment in the business world, the most commonly used language is called Structured COBOL.

Recently, a language called Logo has become available for several microcomputers. Logo is a sophisticated, modern language that was designed to be very easy to learn, even for very young children. It features "turtle graphics," a system of built-in commands that allow users to create striking, complex graphic designs very soon after they start programming.

The issue of which language to teach will be explored further in Chapter 6. For now, let's summarize as follows:

1. To introduce programming to children up through the middle elementary school grades, Logo is clearly superior.
2. For high school students who want to study computer science, Pascal is essential.
3. BASIC can be taught successfully to students starting at the upper elementary school grades.
4. In general, it is helpful to know more than one computer language, for the same reasons it is helpful to speak more than one natural language.

The Computer as Object of Instruction

As computers become more and more important in our daily lives, schools must meet the challenge to provide appropriate computer education. Depending on the ages of the students, their interests and their career goals, several different options are possible for computer education.

It seems inevitable that soon each school will provide every student with at least a minimal exposure to computers. This computer awareness may include a sense of what computers are, what they do, and how they impact our daily lives. Many schools will provide each student with hands-on computer experience and at least some computer programming.

For those students interested in careers working with computers, courses in data processing, computer science, computer operation, and computer repair must be available.

Administrative Applications

By now it must be obvious that computers can do a great deal to expedite the myriad administrative tasks confronting a school administrator each day. Figure 2–2 provides a list of school administrative and other non-instructional tasks to which a computer can be applied. Chapter 9 will present detailed information about how to use computers to considerably ease the burden imposed by these tasks.

ATTENDANCE RECORDS AND PROJECTIONS
SCHEDULING OF STUDENTS, TEACHERS, TRANSPORTATION
BUDGETING
INVENTORY CONTROL
SCHOOL RECORDS AND DATA FILES

LIBRARY CIRCULATION
ELECTRONIC CARD CATALOGS

STUDENT FILES
GUIDANCE INFORMATION
COLLEGE AND VOCATIONAL COUNSELING

PERSONNEL FILES
MAILING LISTS, FORMS, FORM LETTERS
WORD PROCESSING

**Figure 2–2. Non-Instructional Applications of
Microcomputers**

2.4 KEY POINTS IN DECIDING BETWEEN
MICROCOMPUTERS AND TIME-SHARING SYSTEMS

Now that we have explored in some detail both the inner workings of computers and the main applications of computers to education, we are in a better position to reconsider the issue of microcomputers versus time-sharing systems. As might be expected, each type of system has advantages and disadvantages. Once educational use priorities are established, however, one best choice usually becomes clear.

At the core of most time-sharing systems is a large mini-computer or a mainframe, consisting of a central processing unit, a memory unit, and mass storage. This computer is connected to several terminals, which act as input and output devices for the system. The terminals may be wired to the main computer within a building or campus, or they may be connected to the main computer via telephone lines only when they are in use.

Time-sharing systems may be purchased intact, or terminals may be connected to a time-sharing system owned by someone else. In the latter case, the owner of the CPU keeps track of how much "computer time" is used by each organization, and bills them accordingly. In the long run, this arrangement is generally more expensive than owning the entire system—particularly with heavy use—but it also places the burden of system maintenance and technical expertise on the CPU owner rather than the school system. For this reason, renting time and either buying or leasing terminals is the most attractive time-sharing option for most schools.

In many parts of the country, larger school districts, state agencies, or consortia of smaller school districts own time-sharing systems and sell computer services to schools in their area. These organizations often offer lower prices and more extensive school-related services than commercially oriented time-sharing systems or service bureaus.

The main advantages of time-sharing systems are those of the larger computers: extensive memory and processing power, access to extensive mass storage facilities, and, usually, availability of more than one powerful computer language.

The CPUs of large time-sharing computers are usually much faster than those of microcomputers as well. This speed is a great advantage for processing large amounts of data. It does not help much for interactive programming and graphics, however, because the low baud rate of most terminals negates the superior processing speed of the CPU.

The main advantages of microcomputers are generally lower cost, flexibility, and availability of educational software. The cost issue is difficult to disentangle because different ways of assessing costs produce different results. For example, consider depreciation. Microcomputers are so new that no one really knows how long they will last in heavy, everyday use. Depreciating microcomputers over three or more years makes a big difference to an overall cost comparison. On the other hand, it should be pointed out that time-sharing systems achieve optimal cost when several terminals are purchased at once. If a school will be using only a handful of computers at a time, or if the school computer program must be phased in gradually, the cost of microcomputers will be invariably much lower than that of comparable time-sharing systems.

Speaking in general terms, it appears that most microcomputer installations will cost from slightly less to two or three times less than time-sharing systems. Furthermore, time-sharing system costs are ongoing, and likely to increase with greater usage and inflation.

Microcomputers are more flexible than time-sharing systems in several ways, including portability and greater variety in available input and output devices. Time-sharing systems also "crash" from time to time, that is, the main computer becomes inoperative, rendering all the terminals inoperative at once. With microcomputers, an equipment breakdown almost always affects only one unit, leaving all the other microcomputers functioning normally.

The final advantage of microcomputers is availability of educational software. Developing educational software for time-sharing systems is costly and difficult due to the cost of the computer equipment and the large number of different models in widespread use. Even though much of the available microcomputer software is of questionable quality, good quality software does exist, and the market for microcomputer software is large and growing.

This point must be qualified somewhat, because some time-sharing systems have a great deal of software available, although most do not. Many of the educators who feel that computer assisted instruction is the wave of the future point to the PLATO system, developed at the University of Illinois and currently owned by Control Data Corporation, as the foremost example of a well-developed time-sharing system with a great deal of sophisticated educational software already developed and tested. Systems such as PLATO are a great deal more expensive than microcomputers at present, but may still be an attractive option for districts interested in well-done CAI of this type.

In summary, time-sharing systems should be strongly considered for the following purposes:

1. an extensive district- or schoolwide computer assisted or computer managed instruction program using mainly tutorial and drill-and-practice programs

2. uses that require extensive internal memory, such as large-scale data processing and data analysis, information retrieval, testing, and large-scale administrative applications

3. sophisticated computer programming applications, requiring access to several powerful computer languages

For most educational computer users, however, microcomputers will be the better choice for the reasons mentioned above. As microcomputers become more and more powerful, the advantages of time-sharing systems will diminish and the trend in educational computing will be increasingly towards the smaller, independent units.

The remainder of this chapter will be concerned mainly with establishing guidelines for choosing and purchasing microcomputers. Due to the vast array of different mainframes and minicomputers on the market and their technical complexity, we will not further pursue this topic here, except to offer the following advice:

1. *Look at software before buying hardware.* Each brand of computer will have different software available, so it is vitally important to know that the computer can do what you want it to do before investing in expensive hardware.

2. *Use independent, expert consultant help.* Computer equipment is so technically complex and so expensive that very few people can keep up with all the latest developments. A specialist is necessary, and representatives of the various manufacturers may not be unbiased in their judgment.

3. *Visit current users of the systems you are considering.* Try out the software, talk to the administrators and teachers, and learn from their experience.

4. *Don't be a pioneer.* The latest technology almost always has "bugs" when it first comes out. The newest may not be the best, and you will have no way of knowing until it is too late. Be cautious.

2.5 HOW TO SELECT THE MICROCOMPUTER FEATURES YOU NEED

In the remaining sections of this chapter, we will describe in detail a three-step microcomputer hardware selection process. In this section, we will consider the first two steps in this process:

1. Specify how you plan to use microcomputers in your school.
2. Pinpoint which microcomputer features are necessary to put these plans into action.

In Sections 2.6 and 2.7, we will show you how to obtain the hardware information necessary to match the features you need against the available microcomputers. Usually, this process narrows down the field considerably, so that the final hardware decision is not difficult.

Specifying Projected Microcomputer Uses

In Section 2.3, we surveyed the various uses of computers in education under four broad categories: the computer as teacher, tool, learner, and object of instruction. Cutting across this classification, we can consider the uses of computers in the instructional process—that is, by students and teachers in classroom or laboratory settings—and non-instructional uses of computers by other school personnel.

Within the instructional use category, the first question to be addressed is: To what extent will the students learn to program computers, and to what extent will they use computers as teachers or tools to learn material in the existing curriculum?

If programming will be included in the school computer project, the following questions must be decided:

1. How important is programming versus use of the computer as a teacher or tool?
2. Which language(s) will be taught?

```
CHECKLIST: CURRICULUM AREAS FOR COMPUTER USE

___ LANGUAGE ARTS
    ___ READING
    ___ SPELLING
    ___ GRAMMAR
    ___ WRITING

___ MATHEMATICS

___ SCIENCE

___ SOCIAL STUDIES

___ FOREIGN LANGUAGES

___ ART

___ MUSIC

___ HEALTH

___ HOME ECONOMICS

___ PHYSICAL EDUCATION

___ BUSINESS EDUCATION

___ INDUSTRIAL ARTS

___ VOCATIONAL EDUCATION
```

Figure 2–3.

3. Will the computers most likely be housed in a central computer lab or distributed among regular classrooms?

The answers to these questions will help pinpoint the features you need in the microcomputers you purchase.

If computers will be integrated into the curriculum as teachers and tools, use the following procedure to pinpoint which educational uses are most important.

1. On the checklist in Figure 2–3, identify the curriculum areas in which you would like to use computers.

2. For each curriculum area you checked, specify how you will use computers, in terms of the categories in Figure 2–4. Enter this information on a chart like the one shown in Figure 2–5. If you need detailed information about the educational uses of computers in the various curriculum areas, see Chapter 6.

CHECKLIST: CATEGORIES OF COMPUTER USE IN THE CURRICULUM

—— DRILL AND PRACTICE

—— TUTORIAL

—— EDUCATIONAL GAMES

—— SIMULATIONS

—— MICROWORLDS

—— PROBLEM SOLVING

—— DATA ANALYSIS

—— INFORMATION RETRIEVAL

—— WORD PROCESSING

—— TESTING

—— COMPUTER-MANAGED INSTRUCTION (CMI)

—— MATERIALS GENERATION

Figure 2–4.

3. Look over the "Use Categories" you have written in the right column of your "Computer Use Planning Chart." Use the checklist in Figure 2–4 to specify in priority order the use categories you need to accomplish your computer project goals.

Curriculum Area	Use Categories
Social Studies	Simulations, Information Retrieval
Mathematics	Microworlds, Educational Games, Drill and Practice

Figure 2–5. Sample Computer Use Planning Chart

If you want to do many different things with computers and you will be purchasing more than one, divide the designated uses by computer, and make a separate list of required educational uses for each. You may find it best to purchase more than one type of microcomputer, according to what is best to satisfy the needs of different parts of your project.

To determine your needs for non-instructional uses of computers, use the checklist in Figure 2–6. (Further information about non-instructional uses of computers in schools is discussed in detail in Chapter 9.) Note whether any of the computers will be used for both instructional and non-instructional purposes.

Matching Microcomputer Features with Selected Uses

This section reviews the major microcomputer hardware options in terms of the requirements for different educational uses of computers. Four categories of hardware options will be considered:

CHECKLIST: NON-INSTRUCTIONAL USES OF COMPUTERS

__ LIBRARY OR MEDIA CENTER
    __ INFORMATION RETRIEVAL
    __ CARD CATALOG
    __ BORROWING RECORDS
    __ INVENTORY

__ ADMINISTRATIVE OFFICE
    __ WORD PROCESSING
    __ RECORD KEEPING
    __ BUDGETING
    __ SCHEDULING
    __ GRADE REPORTING

__ GUIDANCE OFFICE
    __ SCHEDULING
    __ CAREER INFORMATION
    __ COLLEGE INFORMATION
    __ APTITUDE TESTING

__ NURSE'S OFFICE
    __ HEALTH RECORDS
    __ ILLNESS ABSENCE MONITORING

__ CAFETERIA
    __ NUTRITIONAL ANALYSIS
    __ MENU PLANNING
    __ ORDERING
    __ INVENTORY

__ CUSTODIAN
    __ INVENTORY
    __ ENERGY USE MONITORING

Figure 2–6.

memory, mass storage, keyboard and display screen features, and peripheral input/output devices.

Most microcomputers currently in use contain RAM memory ranging from 3K to 48K bytes, although 64K machines are becoming the standard, and 128K and 256K machines are beginning to appear. With only 3K of memory, very little can be done except introductory programming in a language that is in the ROM memory of the computer, and using the computer as a calculator for simple problem-solving activities.

With 8K or 16K of RAM, many drill-and-practice programs, tutorials, and educational games can be used, as well as problem-solving activities using student-written programs. A few very primitive word processors will run with 16K of memory, but more memory is recommended for these activities.

With 32K to 48K, more sophisticated tutorials, games, and simulations will run on microcomputers, including programs with extensive use of graphics. Better quality word processing is possible, as is computer managed instruction, record keeping, generation of instructional materials, testing, and some administrative applications. (See Figure 2–7.)

Even more memory is useful for most administrative applications, data processing, sophisticated data analysis, information retrieval, and advanced programming using computer languages not stored in ROM memory.

When buying a microcomputer, look not only at the amount of RAM memory, but at RAM expandability as well. Memory chips are

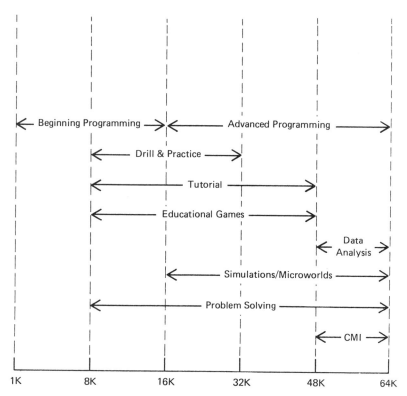

**Figure 2–7. RAM Memory Needed for Selected
Educational Uses of Microcomputers**

rapidly decreasing in price, so it will be quite inexpensive to upgrade an expandable system if more memory is needed in the future.

Mass storage is available through cassette recorders and disk drives. The latter are generally preferable because they are a much faster and more reliable means of storing information. Disk drives are crucial for most administrative applications, computer managed instruction, record keeping, testing, word processing, and information retrieval. In addition, they are very helpful for any other computer activity in which programs are going to be saved in mass storage and loaded into the computer's main memory with any degree of frequency. Thus, disk drives are also recommended for programming beyond the introductory stages.

Most of the keyboard features noted in Section 1.4 are matters of good design or personal preference. A few are important for some applications, however. For example, a numeric keypad is helpful for applications such as data processing or administrative programs requiring many numbers to be typed in. Upper and lower case is very important for word processing, and can be useful for CAI programs in language arts as well. For applications that require relatively a lot of typing, full-sized, typewriter-style keyboards are preferred over smaller keyboards, or those with membrane or calculator-style keys.

The appearance of text material on the screen is important for all applications except possibly calculations, some data analysis, and very elementary programming. For word processing, an 80 column-wide screen is best. All applications that require reading a great deal of text material benefit from clear characters and an amber or green display screen.

Graphics and color capabilities enhance most types of computer assisted instruction, and may be considered almost essential for these areas, especially for younger children. Although graphics are not necessary to teach programming, students are generally quite interested in graphics, so availability of sophisticated graphics capabilities is very helpful in programming courses as well. For most purposes, composite video displays suffice, but for applications that require extremely clear color graphics, RGB display units should be used.

Among other input and output devices, printers are the most frequently needed. Printers are essential for word processing, advanced programming, instructional materials generation, record keeping, and most administrative applications; in general, anywhere a permanent record of the computer output is needed. For most purposes, dot matrix printers suffice, but daisy-wheel printers should be used for word processing and administrative activities that would require film-ribbon electric typewriter quality printouts.

Educational Use	Mass Storage[1]	Keyboard Features	Video Display Features	Useful Peripherals[4]
Drill and Practice	C or D			
Tutorial	C or D		color, graphics	speech synthesizer
Educational Games	C or D		color, graphics, sound	joystick, game paddles, lightpen
Simulations/ Microworlds	C or D		color graphics, sound	
Problem Solving	C or D			
Data Analysis	D	numeric keypad		printer, lab instrument monitoring devices
Information Retrieval	D			printer, modem[3]
Word Processing	D	upper and lower case	60-80 column display, green or amber screen	printer, daisy-wheel printer
Testing	D			
Computer Managed Instruction	D or 2D			printer
Materials Generation	C or D			printer
Programming in BASIC	C or D		graphics, color, sound	printer
Programming in Logo[2]	C or D		graphics, color, sound	printer
Programming in Pascal[2]	D		graphics, color, sound	printer
Non-Instructional Applications	2D or H	upper and lower case, numeric keypad	60-80 column display, green or amber screen	printer, card reader

NOTE: Items underlined are required; others are recommended.
[1]C = cassette, D = disk, H = hard disk
[2]Not available on all microcomputers
[3]For connection to large computer data base
[4]Printers are dot matrix unless otherwise specified

Figure 2–8. Hardware Needed for Educational Uses of Microcomputers

Previous discussion of other input and output devices in Section 1.5 indicated in general terms when these peripherals may prove useful. It may not be possible to specify in advance all peripheral needs, so it is useful to buy microcomputers for which a wide selection of peripherals is available. In general, microcomputers that have both serial and parallel interfaces built in—or provisions for adding on these interfaces later—are more flexible, and therefore better to have. (See Figure 2–8.)

2.6 TWELVE FACTORS TO CONSIDER BEFORE BUYING MICROCOMPUTERS

In this section, we will summarize the most important factors to consider when buying microcomputers. In Section 2.7, we will use these factors as the basis for a microcomputer hardware selection procedure. The relative importance of the factors depends on how the microcomputers will be used, so you will need the plans you have developed in Section 2.5 to weigh the factors appropriately for your school.

Factor 1: Cost

Comparing the cost of microcomputers is difficult because the base prices of different brands include different features. Since many different configurations of equipment are possible, the only safe way to compare costs is to list all the features you want, and then price all the equipment to make each brand do what you want it to.

Beware of comparing base prices. Manufacturers of many lower-priced microcomputers have recently adopted the strategy of selling stripped-down models at very attractive prices, with many add-ons available for later purchase. Schools that have opted to buy stripped-down models in an effort to obtain as many microcomputers as possible often find that they cannot do what they would like with these machines, or that expensive additional equipment is necessary.

The cost of maintaining the equipment should also be considered before purchasing microcomputers. Some manufacturers offer service contracts—either on site or carry in—as do many dealers. Prices are generally a percentage of equipment cost (retail), ranging from 8 to 12 percent per year for carry-in service, and up to 20 percent for on-site repair.

Factor 2: Reliability

Rating the reliability of microcomputers is difficult because they are so new. Most of the widely-used microcomputers appear to be quite reliable, however, and the manufacturers generally correct design problems as they crop up.

From a reliability standpoint, beware of new models. They almost inevitably contain minor design flaws, and there may be periods of frustration when no one has yet figured out why the computer will not do what it is supposed to do. As a rule of thumb, once a model has been in the field for a year or so, most of these problems are either solved or well enough known so that you can make an intelligent decision.

All of the major brands of microcomputers carry a factory warranty but most are in force for only 90 days. Some manufacturers offer extended warranties at additional cost, while some dealers offer their own extended warranties as well.

Although microcomputers seldom need service, the manufacturers vary widely in the quality, speed, and convenience of their service operations. If you buy a computer from a manufacturer with a poor service record, it is vitally important to buy from a dealer equipped to service the equipment without manufacturer support.

Factor 3: Software Availability

Unlike records and tapes, computer software cannot be interchanged among different brand machines. For this reason, it is important to know that the software you need is available for the particular brand of microcomputer you buy. In some cases, you will need to shop for software first and base your hardware purchase decision mainly on the availability of the software you prefer.

In other cases, software is widely enough available so that this need not be a primary consideration. If you plan to use microcomputers exclusively for programming and related problem-solving activities, software is not necessary—except for the computer language itself, which is sometimes available as software. (See Factor 7: Languages Available.)

Shopping for software before hardware is most crucial in areas where the software is complex and specialized, including most non-instructional applications, business and industrial education, and less widely-used applications such as prosthetics for the physically handicapped. In most instructional applications, on the other hand, the general availability of software for a particular brand of microcomputer is a good indicator of what you will find in specific categories.

Another good indicator of software availability is popularity of the particular brand in schools. If many schools are buying it, you can be sure that many people will write software for it. If you have very specialized needs or you are interested in a less widely-used brand, however, be sure to check out available software before you buy.

Factor 4: Documentation

Documentation refers to the instructions that tell you how to operate the computer. Documentation should be clearly written, comprehensive, and well organized. It should include material appropriate for non-technically-oriented users who are just starting out, but also thoroughly cover all the features specific to that model of computer. There should be tables summarizing important information and a comprehensive, accurate index.

If your school computers will be used by people with relatively little computer experience, the availability of good quality documentation is a necessity. If an experienced computer specialist is available, however, the readability of the documentation is less important.

Factor 5: Memory

There are three major memory considerations: amount of ROM, amount of RAM, and RAM expandability. In general, computers with relatively more ROM have greater "built in" capabilities—a BASIC language interpreter, for example, which might otherwise take up space in RAM—but computers with relatively less ROM and more RAM are more flexible.

Microcomputers differ markedly in how much RAM comes "standard" with each unit, and how much can be added on. Figure 2–7 in Section 2.5 shows approximate RAM requirements for the various educational uses of computers. In general, it is best to purchase microcomputers in which the memory can be expanded, because these machines will be the most flexible as the trend towards larger capacity but less expensive memory chips continues.

If you are identifying software first, and then purchasing microcomputers on which it runs, be sure to check how much memory is needed for each software package. If additional memory is required, the purchase price of the computer may be considerably more than the base price.

Factor 6: Microprocessor

The microprocessor is the brain or CPU of the microcomputer. Nearly all of the microcomputers used in education have 8-bit microprocessors. This means that the brain of the computer can process eight bits, or one byte, or one character at a time. In comparison, business microcomputers often have 16-bit microprocessors, with 32-bit machines appearing soon. In general, the more information that can be processed at once, the faster the computer can operate. Thus, 16- and 32-bit machines are generally faster than 8-bit machines.

For most educational purposes, 8-bit microprocessors are quite adequate. Nevertheless, for applications that require a great deal of data processing—preparing student schedules or analyzing a great deal of experimental data—a 16-bit processor can be advantageous.

Factor 7: Languages Available

Most microcomputers come with BASIC "built in"; that is, a BASIC language interpreter is part of the computer's ROM. Some computers require BASIC to be loaded into RAM from a disk, or plugged into the computer on a ROM cartridge. Most microcomputers use a reasonably comprehensive version of BASIC developed by the Microsoft company, and include it with the computer in one form or another. Some microcomputers have less comprehensive versions of BASIC, however, and some do not include the BASIC interpreter in the base price of the computer.

Other languages besides BASIC are available for most microcomputers, either as plug-in ROM cartridges or on a disk that can be loaded into RAM. If you are interested in a disk-based language, be sure to check how much RAM is required to use it.

As mentioned above, not all versions of any given computer language are equivalent. The best way to choose among different versions of the same language is for someone who knows that language to try out the various versions. As a rule of thumb, however, the amount of memory required for the language interpreter or compiler will provide a general indication of how comprehensive that language version is. For example, an 8K BASIC interpreter will be less comprehensive than a 14K one.

Also note that the way a computer handles languages affects how much usable RAM memory you have left. A 48K RAM computer that uses 14K for BASIC is really much more comparable to a 32K RAM computer with BASIC in ROM than to a 48K RAM computer with ROM-based BASIC.

Factor 8: Mass Storage

Almost all microcomputers provide two options for mass storage: cassette player/recorders and disk drives. The former are more economical and adequate for most instructional uses of micrcomputers (see Figure 2–8 for details). The latter are generally faster and more reliable.

Disk drives vary in size and capacity. Both cassette and disk units vary in speed of data transfer and reliability. Of all these factors, reliability is the most important. Be sure that reliable mass storage of the type you want is available on the microcomputer you select.

If you are considering large-scale administrative or business applications, check to see if a hard disk drive is available. If you will be using a number of microcomputers in a laboratory environment, check to see if it is possible to network or cluster the microcomputers together to share disk drives. Often, disk sharing can provide substantial financial savings over buying a disk drive for each individual machine.

Factor 9: Keyboard Features

Keyboards are generally similar to typewriters, but there are many different types and features to consider. Most choices are a matter of individual preference, so those who are going to use the computers should try out the various keyboards before a final decision is reached. The main factors to consider are:

1. type of keyboard—pressure sensitive, calculator style, or typewriter style
2. arrangement of keys—each model has a somewhat different arrangement; some have numeric keypads or special keys to input graphics or special commands
3. key action—rollover (computer "remembers" keys pressed in rapid succession); anti-bounce electronics (key will not repeat when pressed normally); repeat function (mechanism to repeat any key without multiple pressing)

Two other factors should also be considered: cursor control and upper/lower case. A cursor is a character-sized shape placed on the display screen wherever the computer will place the next character typed. The computer user controls where the computer will type on the screen by moving the cursor to the appropriate place. Some computers make it easier than others to move the cursor around the screen.

Unlike typewriters, most computer keyboards usually place upper case letters on the screen. Some keyboards allow both upper and lower case to be used, a feature almost essential for word processing and very handy for some other applications.

Factor 10: Screen Display Features

Several questions regarding screen display features should be considered before purchasing a microcomputer.

1. Is a display screen included with the computer or must a separate unit be attached? A built-in display screen means fewer components and wires, but also less flexibility.
2. If the microcomputer must be attached to a separate display screen, what kinds of units can be attached? Microcomputers have one or more of the following: RF Modulators (for television), composite video output (for video monitors), and RGB output (for RGB color monitors).
3. How is text displayed on the screen? Factors that should be considered are the number of characters per line, number of screen lines, and the density of the dot matrix from which the screen text characters are created.
4. What types of graphics are available? Factors to consider are resolution, color, capacity for animation (sprites or multiple screens), and special graphics characters.
5. Some microcomputers can generate sounds through the video unit speakers, so this feature is included here even though some microcomputers generate sound in other ways.

Factor 11: Interfaces

There are two types of interface—parallel and serial—and a most common form for each. The more or less standard parallel interface (especially for printers) is called a Centronix parallel interface. The standard serial interface is called an RS232. Most microcomputers either include these interfaces or contain slots for plugging them in.

Computers without facilities for adding interfaces should be avoided, because it will be very difficult to expand them or to add peripherals. Computers with built-in interfaces make it somewhat easier and considerably less expensive to add peripherals like printers, modems, etc.

Factor 12: Available Peripherals

Even though many peripherals, such as printers, can be made to work with several brands of microcomputers, generally some software or hardware modifications are necessary, and many peripherals are machine-specific. If you need specific peripherals other than a printer, consider only microcomputers for which these peripherals are available.

In general, you will have greatest flexibility with a computer for which a large variety of peripherals is available. As with software, independent suppliers tend to produce peripherals for the most popular microcomputer models. If you purchase one of these models, you will very likely be able to find whatever peripherals you need.

2.7 HOW TO BUY MICROCOMPUTER HARDWARE

There are two basic approaches to buying microcomputer hardware. One is to specify the types of features you want in microcomputers, leaving the actual choice of equipment up to the suppliers who respond to your bid request. The other is to specify particular brands of equipment.

The former procedure is used mainly by large state or regional agencies as a basis for collective purchasing agreements. At this level, bids usually come directly from manufacturers or distributors, and represent a competition among the various brands to provide cost effective microcomputer systems to do what the bid specifications say.

The second procedure—specifying particular brands—works much better for most schools and school districts. Even though you have to do more work initially to pinpoint exactly what you want, in so doing, you have much better control over the purchasing process. For this reason, we will focus the remainder of our discussion on a purchasing procedure starting with making a particular choice of equipment.

Choosing the Equipment You Need

If you now know what you would like to do with microcomputers in your school (see Section 2.3) and you have identified the features you need (see Section 2.5), you are now ready to choose equipment. Figure 2–9 is a chart designed to help you collect the information

Factor	Needs	Micro 1	Micro 2

1. Cost
    Initial
    Maintenance			

2. Reliability
    Warranty
    Service			

3. Software
    Availability
    Quality			

4. Documentation			

5. Memory (RAM)
    Size
    Expandability			

6. Microprocessor
    Word size
    Execution speed			

7. Languages Available			

8. Mass Storage
    Types available
    Reliability
    Storage capacity
    Loading speed			

9. Keyboard features
    Upper/lower case
    Editing features			

10. Display screen features
     Text: clarity, columns
     Graphics
     Color/Sound			

11. Interfaces
     Serial
     Parallel			

12. Peripherals Available			

Figure 2–9. Hardware Selection Worksheet

you need. The left-column reproduces the twelve hardware selection factors discussed in Section 2.6. The second column, labeled
"Needs," provides space for you to specify your needs in each

category. The remaining columns provide space to enter information about particular microcomputer models as you conduct your investigation.

The first step is to fill in the "Needs" column. In each box in the column, specify the features you need which are related to that hardware factor. For example, in the box for "Software Availability," specify the kinds of software you need. You will probably find little or nothing to write in some of the boxes. This is merely an indication that these factors are less important in your selection process.

Leave the "Cost" box for last and use it to summarize the hardware components you need. Then, as you look at various models of microcomputers, be sure to obtain cost figures that include all of those components. (Figure 2–8 provides a checklist of equipment that may add extra cost to the base price of the microcomputer unit.)

When you have clearly defined your needs, you are ready to begin investigating microcomputers. To the right of the "Needs" column, add one column for each brand of microcomputer you are considering. Write its name at the top of the column.

We did not choose these microcomputers for you or fill in the other columns of the comparison chart for two reasons:

1. There is a great deal of volatility in the microcomputer market. New models are introduced, prices are changed (mostly lowered), refinements are made to existing models, and new software is released all the time. The only way to be sure your information is current is to investigate at the time you will be making your purchases.

2. There are so many possible configurations of equipment that any prepared chart is likely to oversimplify and thereby distort information vital to your decision. Price comparisons, for example, are only accurate if they reflect the specific configuration of equipment you need at the prices currently available in your area.

We can, however, offer some suggestions of microcomputers to investigate and some strategies for gathering useful information.

A Brief Survey of Microcomputers in the Schools

The overwhelming majority of microcomputers in the schools today come from three manufacturers: Apple, Commodore, and Radio Shack. The models most prevalent in the schools are the Apple II and II Plus, the Commodore PET series, and the Radio Shack TRS 80 series. Because of their popularity, a wide range of software and peripherals are available for all of these models. It is not evenly distributed, however, so individual school needs should still be investigated before buying.

Radio Shack and Commodore also make lower-priced computers, the Color Computer and the VIC 20 respectively, both of which were originally designed for the home market. Commodore released a promising new educational computer in 1982, called the Model 64, featuring sophisticated sound and graphics, and a great deal of memory at an attractive price. Both Apple and Radio Shack upgraded their most popular educational computers in the first quarter of 1983. The Apple IIe, the TRS-80 Model 4 and Commodore 64 all now feature 64K of RAM.

Two other manufacturers that have been especially active in the educational field are Atari® and Texas Instruments. The Texas Instruments Model 99/4A is not widely used in schools at present, but recent price reductions and the availability of Logo make it worth considering for some applications. The Atari® 400 and 800 are more recent entries into the educational market, and seem to be gaining a following, based on advanced design, sophisticated sound and graphics output, and an expanding base of software and peripherals. In the fall of 1983, Atari® released four new models which offer expanded memory and features while competing with Commodore and Texas Instruments at the low end of the price scale.

None of the more than 50 other microcomputer manufacturers has made much of an impact on the educational market through the 1982-83 school year. Schools tend to be conservative, and new machines start without the software and peripherals base which make the current leaders attractive for many educational applications. For these reasons, we expect that the companies mentioned above will continue to be the main suppliers of microcomputers to education for some time to come.

Perhaps a few names should be added to the present list. IBM is starting to market the Personal Computer to educational institutions, and is putting its considerable weight behind the development of educational software. Those primarily interested in non-instructional applications will find a large range of quality business microcomputers in addition to the ones listed above. Here, the key to selection is to start by looking for appropriate software and local dealer support. In the fall of 1983, IBM announced a new lower-priced version of its PC.

Apple's overwhelming popularity has encouraged several manufacturers to produce Apple clones. Two of the most common are the Franklin Ace 1000 and the Basis 108. These models are "hardware and software compatible" with the Apple II Plus; that is, software and peripherals for the Apple will work in the Franklin or Basis. The clones offer some hardware improvements over the Apple II Plus, but they are not completely compatible with Apple's newest model, and prospective buyers face the unknowns of dealing with small, new companies without track records or extensive service organizations.

Finally, a maverick British engineer named Clive Sinclair has been producing some amazingly inexpensive microcomputers that may have an impact on American schools. Already available is the Sinclair Z81, also known as the Timex Sinclair 1000, a miniaturized but authentic computer for less than $100. A more sophisticated model called the Spectrum was expected in 1983. Recently, Spectravideo and Coleco have followed Sinclair's lead, offering feature-laden new entries at extremely attractive prices.

Gathering Information about Hardware

Appendix J contains a selected listing of names and addresses of hardware manufacturers. By writing to each, you can obtain descriptive information about their microcomputers and a list of local dealers.

Computer periodicals (see Appendix A) are also an excellent source of information about hardware, from advertisements, new product announcements, reviews, and articles comparing features of different models. Leafing through a few of the educational computing periodicals will also help you keep up to date on current trends in this fast-moving field.

Once you have identified a microcomputer you would like to investigate, contact a local dealer. If your potential order is large enough, many dealers will bring machines to your school for a demonstration, or even loan one to you for a trial period. Either of these two options, or else a hands-on session in the dealer's showroom, is strongly recommended to give you a feel for the microcomputer, especially for keyboard and screen features that may be largely a matter of individual taste.

Ask colleagues and dealers for contacts among area educators who already have computer projects similar to the one you are planning. Talk with them about their experiences with their microcomputer hardware, and observe their projects in operation, if possible. Their feedback will be especially valuable about the quality of support from local dealers.

In many areas of the country there are independent microcomputer centers with demonstration collections of hardware and software, information, and consultants available to answer your questions. Ask around to find out if such a center is near you.

While you are investigating microcomputer hardware, bear in mind the following five points:

1. Move cautiously. Allow at least two to three months to complete your investigation and reach a hardware decision.
2. Be prepared with specific questions, such as the ones suggested in our discussion of hardware selection factors.
3. Give yourself time to digest the information you receive, and do not hestitate to return to dealers or projects you have visited to clarify points.
4. Be wary. Check out information you receive. Even though there are many honest, reliable dealers, there are also many unscrupulous people selling microcomputers. The honest people will only benefit from your efforts to check their information.
5. Do not buy anything you have not actually seen. If a product "will be out next month," it does not exist. If it is in the catalog but not in the showroom, it does not exist. Microcomputer manufacturers are generally well intentioned, but terribly overly optimistic about when products will be finished and what they will be able to do.

When you are comparing the cost of various configurations of hardware, the following points may be helpful:

1. Do not compare base prices. Some microcomputers offer many more standard features than others, so such comparisons are almost meaningless.
2. Since substantial educational discounts are available on almost all microcomputers, avoid comparing list prices. Radio Shack offers a flat 20% educational discount, but other discounts vary with local dealers. Ask colleagues and local dealers to determine appropriate prices for comparison.
3. Many states have collective ordering agreements or "state contracts" on various brands of microcomputers. Note, however, that some states permit either state contract or competitive bid purchase, so state contract prices are not necessarily the least expensive.

Purchasing Your Microcomputers

Once you decide which microcomputers and peripherals you would like to buy, you will probably need to prepare a request for bids. The following pointers may help:

1. Specify each item exactly, using identification numbers from the manufacturers' catalogs whenever possible. This practice will prevent any possible "misunderstandings" about what items you want.

2. Allow no substitutions to the items specified in the bid specs (if your state law permits), but allow bidders to specify substitute items and prices in addition to the items in the specs. This practice will provide you with maximum flexibility—you can buy what you originally wanted but you can also take advantage of alternatives if you so choose.

3. Specify that partial contracts can be awarded. In practice, you will probably not want to do so (because of possible complications in service and dealer support), but this feature will prevent a dealer from cutting the price of one item drastically to get the bid, but charging too much for other items.

4. Consider specifying a longer warranty (perhaps a year) than that offered by the manufacturer (usually 90 days), including provisions for loaner equipment if repairs cannot be completed within two working days.

5. Specify that the bid prices must be quoted as a percentage discount from current list price, good for 90 or 120 days. This feature means that, if the list price drops within the period specified, the quoted price drops accordingly. In a period of sharply falling computer prices, this feature will provide you with some protection.

6. Consider placing a geographical restriction (for example, number of miles from the school) on prospective bidders if you are concerned about a non-local "carton mover"-type dealer underbidding everyone but not providing service or support.

7. If you have identified particular software which you know you are going to purchase, consider placing it in your bid specs. Dealers generally receive a larger markup for software than for hardware, but they usually sell software for list price. In order to get the hardware bid, dealers may sell you the software at a cheaper price than you would ordinarily receive.

8. If you need help in setting up the equipment and providing in-service training to your staff, consider putting these services into the bid specs. If you do not need these services, however, specify that they will not be required. Many dealers will then quote you a lower price.

If you prepare your bid specifications with these points in mind, you should be able to obtain the equipment you want under quite favorable conditions.

If you are not required to go through a formal bidding process, the points mentioned above can still serve as guidelines for conducting price negotiations with local dealers. Generally speaking, you will have a decision to make between a very low price with little or no dealer support and somewhat higher prices with dealer support. Your decision should depend mainly on your own expertise and the degree to which adequate service can be obtained independently of the dealer from whom the equipment is purchased.

3 | How to Fund a Computer Project

Funding any innovative educational project usually requires initiative, patience, energy, discipline, and, as often as not, good luck. It is fortunate for those who want to fund a computer project that two factors are working very much in their favor.

Public Interest in Computers and Their Applications Is Constantly Intensifying

Computers and news about them abound. Tiny computers are now commonly found in automobiles, kitchen appliances, high fidelity and video equipment, and, of course, toys. The pre-programmed little machines will continue to proliferate and make their presence more deeply and widely felt in our everyday lives simply because they allow our time to be continuously freer from concerns about trivial matters and thus, increasingly available for matters which more vitally concern us at the various stages in our lives. Furthermore, more powerful and flexible computers are presently in hundreds of thousands of homes, either because of arcade-like games that can be played on them, or because of their curiosity value, or their strength as teaching devices, or their potential as an exciting, open-ended hobby, or their help in managing finances or accessing huge sources of information and knowledge, or for some combination of these and other reasons. Longstanding uses of larger computers—in the entertainment and travel businesses or in educational or financial institutions, for example—combined with the newer, more diverse applications of their smaller counterparts have drawn intense public attention and interest. In addition to school board members, other officials in education or in positions affecting education, share that interest, thus making computers and their educational applications timely, school-related issues. Funding for computer projects is therefore generally less difficult to obtain than is funding for other projects related to subjects, perhaps equally deserving, but less in the limelight.

Getting a Computer Project Initiated Does Not Necessarily Involve Spending Substantial Sums of Money

We have reached a point where a viable pilot project can be undertaken with an expenditure measured in hundreds, rather than thousands, of dollars. While it is often true that more can be accomplished more quickly with more money, it is nevertheless a fact that many school situations dictate a more gradual, deliberate and carefully planned introduction of computers. In such circumstances, limited funding at the beginning may very well be advantageous in the long run. Many schools and school systems, therefore, find themselves in the fortunate position of being able to begin integrating computers into the educational environment with funds extracted from the regular tax-levy budget.

In those situations where a more ambitious project is called for or where even several hundred dollars cannot be carved from the regular budget, schools and school systems have a number of fruitful alternatives open to them. This chapter is devoted to helping put those alternatives at your disposal.

3.1 IDENTIFYING MAJOR FUNDING SOURCES

There exists a number of major sources of funding for a computer project. Identifying them, however, may not be an easy or obvious process. This section will aid you in that process.

Public Sources

On July 1, 1981 Congress passed legislation that significantly changed longstanding procedures and sources for public funding of educational projects. The legislation, called the "Educational Consolidation and Improvement Act of 1981," represents an attempt on the part of the federal government to accomplish two major objectives at the same time: (1) to substantially reduce the federal role in terms of fiscal responsibility, and (2) to significantly limit its regulatory role, thereby giving to states and local districts greater autonomy in planning, maintaining, and monitoring their educational programs. For those persons seeking to identify public sources for funding a computer project, the changes have significant implications.

Two of the three chapters that comprise the Educational Consolidation and Improvement Act are immediately relevant. Chapter 1 basically represents a reworking of the now defunct ESEA Title I. While funding in this category has been substantially reduced, local educational agencies are less restricted in how they might utilize what they will be receiving. It seems clear that monies forthcoming under the new Chapter 1 could be earmarked for a variety of computer projects.

Chapter 2 of the Act far more profoundly affects procedures and sources of funds. By consolidating most federal education programs, it, in effect, eliminates a number of public sources that have been tapped over the years by educational agencies for the funding of computer projects. For example, categorical programs such as "Improvement in Local Educational Practices" (ESEA, Title IV-C) and "Education for Gifted and Talented Children & Youth" (ESEA, Title IX-A) no longer exist. They, along with many others, have been replaced by state formula grants, which allocate a greatly reduced total amount of money to individual states, mainly on the basis of school age population data. Such "block grants" filter down to local districts and schools, where they may be used at the discretion of local authorities, with few strings attached. Clearly, the specified categories of activities that may be funded through the block grants—special projects, basic skills, support services, educational improvement—leave adequate leeway for the utilization of the funds for virtually any imaginable computer project. In fact, it is likely that some local schools and districts, which did not try or were otherwise unsuccessful in competing for funding from previously categorical programs, may find themselves with more federal money for innovative activities. On the whole, however, fewer strings attached will mean fewer dollars, and those educators who find out first how to compete for the remaining competitive funds will be in a far better position.

To obtain an updated listing of the major public funding sources that remain competitive, a letter, such as the one shown in Figure 3-1, should provide the information you need.

The letter should be sent to the appropriate person at your State Education Department (a phone call there will reveal the name you need). The information you receive should include the following, at least:

1. Federal or state title of program
2. Authorizing legislation

(School or District Letterhead)

Dear   :

We are currently exploring a variety of avenues for
implementing a computer project in our school (or
district). Toward that end, we are in need of any
information you can provide regarding appropriate state
and federal funding sources. Thank you.

Sincerely yours,

Figure 3-1

3. Name of contact person, with address and phone number
4. Total amount of funding during previous and present fiscal
   years
5. Total amount of funding allocated to projects using computers during previous fiscal year
6. Brief description of program's mandate

Private Sources

Relevant major private funding sources are those foundations
that provide financial support to educational institutions for activities that in one way or another "enhance" education. While
everyone has heard of the Ford or Carnegie Foundations, many
educators do not realize that, while such large foundations may very
well be good sources to tap, major wells of funding exist in the form
of thousands of smaller foundations. Each one of those less well-
known sources welcomes worthy proposals, and although they may
have considerably fewer dollars to dole out, they have far fewer
competitors applying for them. Furthermore, while there is a tre-
mendous degree of variability in the type of activities any one of the
smaller foundations may be prepared to fund, many of them may be
willing to provide money for computer projects in schools.

One easy way to identify appropriate private funding sources is
to examine the *Foundation Directory*, found in many public and most
postsecondary school libraries. This thick volume, which is updated
annually, lists the name of virtually every private foundation in the

country, along with information you would need to determine whether you should contact them regarding your computer project. Any one of the following persons in a school can easily select a considerable number of names of private foundations that might fund your computer project, simply by leafing through the pages of the *Foundation Directory*:

- an assistant principal or department chairperson
- one or more volunteer teachers (perhaps the best bet, in terms of long-range planning)
- a secretary or clerical assistant
- one or more students (thereby providing, at the appropriate grade levels, a valuable research project)

The *Directory* is published by an organization called the Foundation Center, which provides a wide range of other resources to anyone seeking private funding sources. In a brochure, the Center describes itself as "an independent, nonprofit organization established by foundations to provide information to grantseekers."

The Center maintains two comprehensive national library/service centers (one in Washington, D.C., and one in New York City) and two major field offices (one in San Francisco and one in Cleveland, Ohio). In addition, regional collections are located throughout the United States. Some of the services and resources available through the regional or major offices are:

- computer printouts of reported grants of more than $5,000, indexed by subject
- annual reports published by many foundations, describing their programs in detail
- sample application forms and guidelines
- books and periodicals on proposal writing and fund raising
- workshops and special orientations
- Internal Revenue Service information on virtually every foundation in the country

In order to contact the regional collection nearest you, simply call (800) 424-9836, a toll-free number, for a complete and updated list of their addresses and phone numbers.

Once you have compiled a set of addresses of private sources of funding which appear viable, either by tapping the *Foundation Directory* or another of the Foundation Center's publications or services, a letter, such as the one in Figure 3-2, should be sent.

(School District Letterhead)

Dear   :

It has come to our attention that the (name of foundation) may be willing to support schools (or school districts) in implementing projects utilizing modern instructional technology, in particular, computers. We are in the planning stage of such a project.

We would deeply appreciate receiving, as soon as possible, all particulars relevant to our applying for funding for our project through your foundation.

Sincerely yours,

Figure 3-2

3.2 PROVEN TIPS FOR SELECTING FRUITFUL SOURCES

A number of options are open to you for zeroing in on the most fruitful sources of funding. They each involve information gathering and, therefore, require a little time and effort; however, the sources of information you will be tapping are ones you will want to be in contact with anyway, at some time further down the road.

In pursuing each of the six options below, your two-fold goal is the same:

- Find the names of schools and school districts that have computer projects.
- Obtain from those schools or districts specific information on how and where they obtained their funding.

The specific information you will be obtaining includes:

- name and address of funding agency, with phone number and contact person
- scope of project, including personnel and budget
- specific equipment and/or software involved
- precise project objectives, along with means of evaluating them

• complete copies of proposals for funding, where possible (especially useful)

See Figure 3-3 for a questionnaire to send out in order to obtain the information.

Any of the following information you can provide about your school's or district's computer project will be appreciated. Please use additional sheets as necessary and mail completed questionnaire to:

> (Your name and title
> Your school, district or agency
> Your address)

1. How was funding obtained?

   If you applied for funding to a particular federal, state or private agency, please fill in:

   Name and address of agency:

   Name of contact person:

   Phone # of contact person:

2. Brief description of scope of project, including personnel and budget:

3. Specific equipment and software involved:

4. Project objectives and means of evaluation:

5. Please attach full copy of proposal you may have submitted for funding.

Figure 3-3. Computer Project Questionnaire

Option 1: Read Relevant Magazines/ Journals/Newsletters

A large number of publications often contain articles that provide the names of schools and/or districts that have successful computer projects (see Appendix A for extended listings of "Publications Specific to Educators" and Appendix B for "General Interest Publications with Educationally Relevant Material"). These magazines and journals can be obtained through sufficiently well-equipped libraries or by direct subscription.

Option 2: Attend Relevant Lectures/ Workshops/Conferences

Notices abound these days of meetings at the local, state, or national levels that address issues directly relevant to the implementation of computers in schools. These notices can be readily found in the publications listed in Appendices A and B (especially those specific to educators), in the average school administrator's daily stack of mail, as well as on the bulletin boards of teacher colleges and universities with teacher-preparation programs.

Attend such meetings yourself or through a representative, with the following objectives clearly in mind:

- to meet people who have obtained funding for a computer project
- to find out from them where the money came from and how they got it

Do not feel reluctant to request such information. Most people who are engaged in educational computing are seeking support and allies in their efforts. Your interest in their project represents colleagueship in a shared vision. It will most likely be welcomed.

Feel free to bring along copies of your Computer Project Questionnaire, such as the one proposed in Figure 3-3. It can be distributed in either of the following ways:

- Find out if the meeting's organizers would be prepared to distribute it for you, along with other materials handed out to each of the participants as they enter or leave the meeting area. Perhaps a special announcement could even be made to draw people's attention to your request.
- Individually hand out the questionnaire to people you meet, thereby gaining the opportunity to make a personal request on an individual basis. If you are not comfortable in such a role, send a representative to the meeting who would be.

Option 5: Join One or More Appropriate Organizations

The selection of fruitful sources of funding can often be facilitated through your linking with organizations of people dedicated to the promotion of effective uses of computers in education. Scores of educationally oriented groups involved in computing exist and can be identified by examining the publications listed under Option 1 above. Furthermore, "user groups," which are often devoted to one or another of the more popular brands of microcomputers, are proliferating. Most have among their members educators who may be able to point you in productive directions. Lists of user groups can be obtained through equipment manufacturers or local computer stores.

Refer to Appendix C for a core sampling of the larger, educationally oriented organizations you may want to join.

Option 4: Conduct an ERIC Search

An up-to-date and comprehensive computer printout of schools and districts involved in research on the implementation of computers in education is easily obtained through an ERIC (Educational Resources Information Center) search. Contact the reference desk of any nearby university for information on how to conduct one.

Option 5: Obtain a Copy of the Microcomputer Directory

The Gutman Library at Harvard University publishes the *Microcomputer Directory: Applications in Educational Settings*. Listed in it, by state, are brief descriptions of hundreds of educationally relevant computer projects, along with names, addresses and phone numbers of contact people. This valuable directory is available for a nominal fee from:

> The Gutman Library
> Graduate School of Education
> Harvard University
> Cambridge, MA 02138

Option 6: Solicit Advice from Sources in a Nearby College or University

Colleges and universities usually have on their faculties at least several persons who are very much up to date in terms of research in areas that may be directly related to using advanced technologies in education. They will most likely be eager to share with you their knowledge, experience and certainly their advice. Some may be interested enough to help you gather the information you seek (or to help write your proposal and perhaps even to submit a joint proposal of some sort).

Many of the larger postsecondary institutions also have a grants director or officer. That person could be an ideal source of information for avenues you might explore, regardless of the age of the student population you serve.

3.3 HOW TO MAKE PARENT AND CIVIC GROUPS EAGER TO CONTRIBUTE

Generally, two criteria prevail among parent and civic groups in their reaching decisions for funding school projects:

1. Will it really help my children?

2. Can it really be accomplished with limited resources?

It should not be too difficult to convince any parent or civic group that a computer project can most definitely meet both criteria well.

Depending on the particular project you design, one or more of the following arguments will provide you with a sound basis for showing how computers will help the students:

- Computers used as vehicles to assist teachers in direct instruction have been shown to result in a significant decrease in time students need to master basic skills.

- Computers used as objects of instruction provide students with an opportunity to directly and thoroughly understand how the new technology presently and in the future will profoundly affect society as a whole and their lives individually.

- Computers used to manage instruction or other essential school record-keeping activities result in a freeing of teachers and other school personnel to provide more direct, personal contact, thereby helping to promote a humanizing and supportive atmosphere at all levels of interaction.

- Computers used to enhance learning experiences can open doors to worlds of active mental exploration, problem solving and decision making, which are difficult if not impossible to access through other modes of instruction.

As to whether or not the limited financial support that most parent and civic groups are able to provide can actually contribute significantly to a viable computer project, the following reasoning should suffice.

For an investment of several hundred dollars, equipment and software can be purchased that will provide all of the following:

- remediation for a group of students in basic skill areas
- basic programming skills for groups of average and advanced learners
- enhanced educational experiences for gifted students

For an outlay of several hundred more dollars, peripheral material and equipment would make available:

- increased opportunities in each of the three areas specified above
- more efficient and possibly more effective management of school finances, data management, record keeping, word processing, and scheduling

To further ensure that you will generate an eagerness among parent and civic groups to contribute, the following tips should help:

- Make your proposals brief and specific, leaving out all technical jargon and concentrating on meeting both of the prevailing criteria specified above.
- Try to organize some sort of group experience, with a vendor, a teacher, or better yet, a parent or civic group member making a short presentation with a computer on hand. Demonstrate at least one of its more dramatic uses.
- There is a very good chance that some members of an appropriate parent or civic group are in some way involved in the use of computers. Invite them to take an acitve role, both in the planning and presentations stages of your proposal.
- If some students are already involved in computing, incorporate them in your proposal. They will make your best spokespeople of all.

3.4 HOW TO TAP THE SELF-INTEREST OF THE BUSINESS COMMUNITY

Large corporations tend to have formal foundations for distributing funding, which can be tapped through procedures covered in Section 3.1. Here we will be concerned with those small, local business enterprises that will be more than willing to support your endeavors once they recognize it is in their interest to do so. Depending on your particular school situation, one or more of the following three benefits will accrue to the businessperson who provides financial support for your computer project.

Excellent Public Relations and Advertising

The possibilities here are limited only by the imaginations of those involved. Basically, the fact to keep in mind is that the business that has contributed funding for computer equipment to a school has performed an extremely important public service. Handled tastefully by the school and the business, that fact can legitimately bring the business's name more prominently before the public, thereby directly or indirectly leading to significantly increased numbers of customers. Here are a few examples of what steps might be taken:

- A plaque can be placed on the computer or near the computer station, boldly identifying the source of funding.
- An announcement can be made at one or more public meetings (especially one held for the PTA), thanking the contributors for their support.
- A representative from the business could be invited to formally present and dedicate the equipment at a public meeting or a specially scheduled assembly to which the public is invited.
- A printed announcement in the school's newsletter or a more lengthy article could feature the nature and source of the support.
- A specially prepared handout could be sent home with each child, describing the contribution, its sponsors, and its impact.
- A poster could be displayed in the school and/or at the place of business to help inform the public.
- A press release to local newspapers is entirely appropriate and especially effective when accompanied by a photograph of the key persons involved.
- Any on-going news of how the equipment is being utilized could be sure to include a reminder of the initial source of funding.

Reduced Costs

For small businesses that currently implement or are considering to implement a microcomputer to facilitate their operations, having funded a computer project in an elementary or secondary school or a community college can lead to the following use of the school's equipment:

- Students studying programming or other areas of computer literacy can be given class or homework assignments that call for solving a programming or system design problem unique to the business that has supplied the school's equipment. Custom software packages could even be developed.
- Students studying word processing can be involved in preparing letters, documents, reports and announcements that are needed to support and enhance the functioning of the business donor.

Using the school's resources to provide such cost-reducing support to a contributing business is not only a way to encourage contributions, it is also completely sound pedagogy. There is no better way to help prepare students for careers in the real world of business than to have them working on real-world business projects. Their close contact with an actual business and its daily problems and challenges will go far in refining their understanding and skill.

A Reliable Source of Part-Time Employees

School teachers and administrators are in a unique position in being able to recommend or refer applicants to fill a small business's need for part-time help. It is almost inescapable that the needs of the business clearly supportive of a school's efforts in an area as exciting and future-oriented as computing would be prominent in the minds of the school's professional staff when responsible, qualified students are seeking part-time employment. By referring top-notch students, school officials are acting not only in the business's interest, but clearly in those of the students and their families as well. A business that has demonstrated its concern for a school by providing money for a computer project is likely to provide, as well, the type of environment that would be supportive and nurturing to part-time employees.

In contacting local businesses to solicit funding, the school representatives—be they students, parents, teachers, or administrators—should find themselves well armed with a knowledge of these three benefits They should keep foremost in their minds that several smaller contributions from a variety of businesses may be easier to obtain than one single, larger donation. For example, one hundred dollars each from ten small businesses should not be too difficult to obtain, and the thousand dollars gathered is certainly sufficient to launch a viable pilot project.

3.5 STRATEGIES FOR WRITING SUCCESSFUL PROPOSALS

You will significantly increase your chances of successfully obtaining funding for your computer project it you adopt the following strategies:

1. *Stress the long-range implications and the fact that what you do is potentially beneficial to many other school programs.* Funding agencies are intensely interested in seeing that as much benefit as possible can be squeezed out of each dollar they allocate. It is therefore incumbent upon you that you spell out:

- how many students will directly benefit both immediately and—just as importantly—in the future from the project you will be implementing
- how others might be able to replicate your successes in a variety of different environments

2. *Be certain that you demonstrate a need for computers, per se.* Every worthwhile proposal has some sort of statement of need. Your strategy in that section of your proposal must be to delineate clearly one or more needs that can be only or, at least, best met through the implementation of the computer equipment for which you are seeking funding. Some examples of such needs would be:

- to maintain or increase student achievement in one or another academic area, despite cutbacks in personnel
- to provide students with the appropriate knowledge and skills to meet their futures adequately in an increasingly computerized society

3. *State unambiguous, specific objectives that are carefully correlated to the defined needs.* Your statement of clearly spelled-out objectives is the most critical section in your proposal (except perhaps for the budget breakdown). Unless you manage to delineate

unequivocally those things you expect to accomplish through your proposed computer project, it is very likely that your request of funding will be unfavorably looked upon by reviewers. Of course, the specificity of the objectives will vary according to the nature of the proposed project and the requirements of the particular funding source.

For instance, the following objective may be specific enough for a local civic organization:

- To provide students with fundamental skills in computer literacy.

However, one of the larger private foundations might require a more refined breakdown:

- Students will specify ten major uses of computers in modern society.
- Students will delineate at least five legal and moral issues associated with the widespread use of computers.
- Students will write original programs in BASIC computer language, which are adequate for solving any problem in long division.
- Students will produce a diagram representing the memory structure of a popular brand of microcomputer.

In any case, whether more or less specific, the objectives must be stated with such clarity that they are amenable to assessment, which brings us to the next strategy.

4. *Obligate yourself to evaluate the degree to which each of your objectives is achieved.* Again, your handling of this section of your proposal will be dictated by a variety of factors; however, if you are asking someone or some agency to give you money to pioneer the utilization of computers to help meet perceived educational needs in your particular circumstances, you must provide them with some specifics regarding evaluation. Among these specifics, you should include:

- when the evaluation will be conducted, for example, continuously, at regular intervals, once at the culmination of the project
- who will conduct it, for example, teachers, administrators, outside consultants, the participants themselves
- what measurement of assessment devices will be employed, for example, questionnaires, checklists, standardized tests, criterion-referenced tests, formal or informal observation

• what the proposed criterion is for attainment of an objective, for example, percentage of correct answers, number of hours devoted to a particular activity, grade level equivalences

Here is an example of how one of the objectives listed under 3, above, could be evaluated: "As each of the students completes the computer literacy course, he or she will be asked by the teacher to submit in written form a computer program in BASIC, which will solve any long division problem. At least 90% of the students will produce such a program."

5. *Be precise with regard to how much money you are requesting for each component of your project, and do not ask for too much OR too little (but don't forget inflation!).* Some funding sources may require far less precision than others in the budget section of your proposal. However, as a reliable strategy, the more clearly you have defined in your proposal criteria for precisely identified budget items, the greater the likelihood your project will be considered favorably. This fact holds particularly true for proposals that implement computer technology, since the sources, prices, and the effectiveness of both computer hardware and software are subject to continuous and sometimes dramatic change. Here, especially, you must do your homework carefully, since it is too easy to come across as improperly prepared. At the same time, it is not difficult to demonstrate a relative expertise, since you are entering a new and changeable field. For example, be precise as to the specifications of the particular machines, software packages, and peripherals you feel are needed, making sure that they relate back to the needs, objectives, and methods you will use. You must have criteria for using each dollar requested! Do not include in your budget section a 48K color computer with a dot-matrix printer, unless color, that much memory, and hard copy are all clearly called for in how you will meet the specified objectives.

On the other hand, if, for instance, there is a need to rapidly access large data bases in order to achieve one or more of the objectives, then be sure to go beyond listing a "modem" with an estimated cost. Instead, specify a manufacturer, a model name/number, and include all necessary cables and software, along with exact figures.

Often, those who seek funding for a computer project tend to go to one extreme or the other in terms of the total allotment they request. While it is foolhardy to assume that the budget can be overly "padded" to protect one's ignorance of the real costs involved, it is perhaps even more dangerous in the long run to have underestimated the financial resources required to achieve one's objectives.

In such cases, an unpleasant choice might eventually have to be made: to have the project fail or to unduly drain other resources.

Both pitfalls—overestimating and underestimating—are easily avoided through prudent planning.

3.6 A SAMPLE ILLUSTRATED PROPOSAL

The following sample proposal is fictitious. It is offered not so much as a model, since the formats and requirements of proposals vary so widely, but rather as an illustration of how the strategies offered above can be integrated into a cohesive presentation.

Proposed Title: Reading Fundamentals Through Computer-Based Instructional Strategies

Statement of Need

The XYZ School serves the educational needs of students who present a wide variety of learning, developmental, and emotional problems. Educational and/or medical diagnosis include such terms as: attention deficit disorder, learning disability, neurological or perceptual impairment, emotional disturbance, hyperactivity, minimal brain dysfunction, etc. A pervasive problem of students characterized by such etiologies, and one that is revelant to a significant portion of our student population is the inability to sufficiently sustain on-task behaviors to thoroughly master the basic fundamentals of reading through traditional and even most non-traditional means.

Many of the students require a method of presentation that is repetitive but not boring, so that it might capture their attention for at least brief periods of time, even though they may have gone through it on numerous previous occasions. At the same time, the presentation must be rich enough in terms of what can be learned from it, so that more and more can be learned each time.

Goal and Objectives

It is the overall goal of the proposed project that the children in the XYZ School will master the basic fundamentals of reading by the age of seven.

There are three specific objectives:

1. The students will maintain on-task behaviors while engaged in learning activities designed to provide them with a mastery of the fundamentals in reading.

2. The students will acquire knowledge of a restricted set of sounds and spellings that is sufficient for reading a large number of meaningful words, sentences, and short passages.

3. The students will master those fundamental skills of reading that underlie the process of transforming print into meaningful language.

Implementation

Microcomputers provide a medium of presentation of basic reading fundamentals that is uniquely well suited to the needs of the pupil population with which we are concerned. An appropriate computer program exists and is ready to run on the ABC Brand Microcomputer in cassette form. Called "Read Well," this computer program consists of 20 short, self-contained, yet interrelated modules, each of which provides a sufficiently rich presentation of motivating material in a format that is easily reactivated as many times as necessary. Children interact individually with the computer program through a device called a "light pen," which the child simply presses against a section of the computer's video display unit to indicate his responses. A microcomputer station will be set up in a back corner of our first-grade classroom to be used by one child at a time, directly or indirectly supervised by a teacher or teacher-aide, who may need to be available to certain students to help them load the program into the microcomputer.

The ABC Microcomputer, linked to a "light pen" and loaded with the "Read Well" program, appears to offer a viable format for presenting the following reading fundamentals in a manner that can be repeated many times without being boring and with new possibilities for further mastery on each occasion.

1. Skills

   a. associating sounds with letters or groups of letters
   b. left-to-right progression
   c. speed, phrasing, intonation
   d. carefulness

2. Knowledge

   a. five short vowel sounds, each with at least one associated spelling

    b. the "schwa" sound, with two associated spellings: "a" and "e"

    c. thirteen consonant sounds, each with at least one associated spelling in the initial, medial, or final positions: t, p, z, s, m, n, f, v, y, l, w, and th (both hard and soft)

Print materials, coordinated with the content of the computer program, will be utilized to ensure transfer of learning from the electronic to the print medium, as well as for purposes of evaluation.

Evaluation

Assessment of progress will be on-going from the start for each student. Data will be collected in two forms: observational and criterion referenced.

To test whether Objective 1 is achieved, either a teacher or a teacher-aide will observe on a regular basis students' interacting with the computer program to gather data on:

    a. percentage of time students visually attend to the video display unit. It is expected that students will visually attend at least 50% of the time.

    b. percentage of audible vocalizations. It is expected that at least 50% of students' audible verbalizations will be appropriate to the content of the computer program modules with which the students interact.

At least 80% of the students will meet both of these criteria for on-task behaviors.

To test whether Objective 2 is achieved, the students will be individually evaluated by a teacher or a teacher-aide for their mastery of the particular sounds and spellings presented in the computer program. The testing will be accomplished in the print materials and will be administered whenever students are observed during their interaction with the program to have apparently achieved mastery of another sound or spelling. A student will be considered to have mastered one of the sounds or spellings when he or she reads words presented with that sound or spelling (in combination with others for which mastery has been established) with 80% accuracy. At least 80% of the students will meet this criterion.

To test whether Objective 3 is achieved, students will be individually evaluated by a teacher or a teacher-aide for their mastery of the four fundamental skills specified earlier under the heading

"Implementation." A scale of 1 to 5 will be used to rate the oral reading achievement of a student in the print materials for each of the skills, but only after the student has demonstrated mastery of all the sounds and spellings covered by the program. A student who achieves a rating of 4 or better in each of the four skill areas will be considered to have mastered the fundamental skills of reading. At least 80% of the students who are so evaluated will meet this criterion.

Budget

Personnel

> To be supplied by the XYZ School through its regular budget. No special costs for personnel are involved.

Equipment and Supplies

1 ABC Brand Microcomputer with 16K Memory	$795.00
1 ABC Brand Cassette Recorder with cables	49.00
1 Light Pen	45.00
1 "Read Well" Interactive Computer Program on cassette, requiring 16K memory	85.00

3.7 A SURVEY OF PRIME SOURCES OF FUNDING

In Appendix D you will find an extensive listing of prime sources, meaning they are reported to be those that educators have used most frequently for purchasing microcomputer equipment and support materials. However, it must be strongly emphasized that funds are not available to purchase computer equipment unless proposals clearly define problems that can be addressed through the use of such equipment. Also, please note that:

- The list is by no means exhaustive. It is not meant to replace the efforts suggested in the first two sections of this chapter, but only to give you some initial direction.
- You should use the telephone numbers provided. A phone call can help you further define and select those sources that are most likely to be interested in the particular project you have in mind.

- Manufacturers of computers commonly used in schools may themselves have special funds for innovative computer projects.

If you want additional information about prime funding sources, the following two resources are recommended:

- A short video or filmstrip program entitled "The Coming Changes in Federal Education Programs," available from the Atlantic Educational Corporation, 420 C Street, N.E., Washington, D.C. 20002 (202/546-7334)

- The Block Grant Center for Media and Technology, 1101 Connecticut Avenue, N.W., Suite 700, Washington, D.C. 20036 (202/857-1195)

4 | Initiating a Successful Computer Project

4.1 HOW TO MOBILIZE PARENT SUPPORT

How do you view parents in your school? Do you see them as an obstacle to be circumvented or as a valuable resource that can benefit your computer project and your pupils? Each school situation is different and the degree of parent involvement will vary. You should, however, mobilize the parents into a support system—morally, financially, and philosophically.

You have the ability to turn otherwise minimally concerned parents into VIPs (Vitally Interested Parents) in many different ways. This section will give you some new ideas as well as some new twists to strategies you have no doubt put into practice in the past.

• Involve parents in the initial planning. If you are serious about seeking parent support for your computer project, you must involve them from the start. Parents, as much as anyone else, are turned off when presented with a final proposal and then asked to support it as written by others. Have a group of parents join in the early days of planning, being sure to include them in visits to other schools already using computers. They will have some ideas worth hearing. Some of them have had first-hand experience in industry using computers. Others have friends or relatives in schools where computer projects have succeeded or flopped. They are taxpayers and will be counted on as fund raisers for equipment and software, and as such they have a right to be involved from the ground floor. Early involvement and your taking their suggestions seriously will guarantee their loyalty, support, and commitment. Be sure to capitalize on this readily available resource.

• Parents can be a real asset when you're ready to shop for and purchase computer equipment and supplies. Mothers and fathers

103

have connections through their work or friends in the computer field. In most districts, the schools are free to make their own purchase arrangements for basic equipment and, in virtually all districts, peripherals and software can be bought locally. Discounts on new equipment and good quality previously-owned equipment frequently become available through parent contacts.

• Set up a Parent Advisory Board. These parents can have input into such important matters as space for the computers, selection of personnel, and scheduling for computer use. While these decisions are for the administrator to make (and we are not suggesting that she or he abdicate), there is room for parent suggestions. They are feeding back the feelings and perceptions of their children who are your consumers and should be heard from.

• Publicity is an excellent parent project. Who has greater credibility in the community than the parent of a pupil in the computer program? You will need a lot of publicity at first to generate financial and moral support for the new project. Recalcitrant teachers have been known to wake up to the computer age when prodded by an enthusiastic parent, even after an optimistic supervisor has failed. Because of their contacts in the local press and service and civic clubs, you have a great PR unit right in your parent association. Be sure to tap it.

• Hold a formal dedication of your new Computer Lab. Use parents to help make the necessary arrangements: invitations, refreshments, displays, publicity. By getting your computer project into operation with a bit of fanfare, you will enhance not only parental support, but pupil interest and teacher enthusiasm as well—two vital ingredients of a successful project.

• Parents can also be of great help in two less glamorous areas—repairs and security. In your parent group you may find a parent who has the skill and who will make the time to repair your equipment, thus reducing any "down" time or expense. In a like manner, there must be a police officer or security officer in your parent body who can give you some free advice on how to best secure your expensive equipment, especially during holiday and summer vacation time.

• Use your cadre of parent advisers to reach the hard-to-reach parents who rarely come to school. You will need the support of a growing number of parents if you want to expand your computer project next year. Here's how one school used a small group of parents to radiate support for its fledgling computer project, now the largest and most sophisticated in the district:

1. Bilingual letters went home to explain the project.
2. When pupils were admitted to the school in mid-year, a two-page letter explaining the project went home with the child.
3. School buses picked up parents living farthest from the school to attend the computer room dedication.
4. A mini-course was given to parents on the use of the computers.
5. A speaker from industry spoke at a PTA meeting about the growing need for pupils trained in computer programming.
6. Parents with computer training were invited to assist the teachers in individualizing pupil instruction on a regular basis.

• The evaluation of your school's computer project is the responsibility of the professional staff. However, you should include some parent component. They see and hear their children at home discuss and display their computer skills. Their perceptions should be made part of your on-going evaluation.

4.2 HOW TO HANDLE THE SKEPTICS

In seeking support for your project, you are liable to encounter some skeptics, so you ought to be prepared to handle them. Hopefully, the following typical, skeptical comments, along with suggested answers, will help prepare you to respond successfully.

Comment: "Computers are dehumanizing and therefore have no place in education."

Response: The outdated notion of a behemoth machine, far removed from the ordinary people whose lives it somehow maliciously controls, lingers in some people's minds. Such an idea of what computers are and what bad things they can do to people, by reducing them to a set of identifying numbers, for example, is reinforced by infrequent, yet widely publicized reports of errors made by large, computerized operations, such as large financial institutions.

The computers that the school (or district) will be using are no bigger than a standard typewriter. They are controlled by the people in the school, to do whatever they are capable of doing and whatever the people want them to do. The equipment is like any other tool used in education. It is no more dehumanizing or dangerous than a piece of chalk or a movie projector or an index card file. On the contrary, by freeing teachers, administrators, and other school workers from many time- and energy-consuming record-keeping chores, the small, yet flexible and powerful computers of today contribute to an increasingly humanized school environment.

Examples abound:

- The assistant principal who can devote more time to helping teachers enhance direct instructional services because a microcomputer has reduced by more than 50% the time needed to prepare regular attendance reports.
- The guidance counselor who has access to computerized information on college and vocational options and can therefore now spend much more time helping students solve school or interpersonal problems.
- The teacher who has discovered that the time-consuming chore of keeping track of grading can be handled more efficiently and accurately by a microcomputer. The teacher now has the time to give additional attention both to students in need of remediation and those who should be given extra incentive because of special talents.

Comment: "Computers cost too much money."

Response: A microcomputer, adequate for enhancing instruction, teaching computer literacy, and basic computer programming, costs about as much as a good electric typewriter.

Comment: "Small computers just have a bunch of games that distract kids from their studies."

Response: While it is true that most microcomputers are very well suited to such applications, arcade-like games cannot be played on the computers unless the computers are programmed to play them. The computers in our school(s) will be just as well suited to an overwhelmingly huge number of solid educational applications. It is also true that some of the games themselves can be put to good pedagogical use under the judicious guidance of a teacher who is sensitive to their motivational potential and their applications in the exploration of problem-solving techniques.

Comment: "Computers are just a fad—they will soon be in closets gathering dust."

Response: It is true that in some schools where computers have been purchased, they are only too soon relegated to the "supply closet wasteland." When that happens, it is simply the result of poor management and planning.

In our school(s), the introduction of the equipment will be accompanied by a carefully orchestrated overall plan for their use, which will be formulated by administrators, teachers, and other interested persons. Staff training and appropriate schedule adjustments will insure proper and continuous usage.

To blame inadequate implementation on the computer's being simply a passing fad is absolutely contraindicated by evidence seen all around us on a daily basis. Computers are a fact of life in our society. Besides an increasing reliance on computers on the part of businesses of all sizes, millions of homes will soon have multipurpose microcomputers. Educational institutions will literally be forced into assimilating computers into their programs, if for no other reason, because of the mushrooming knowledge explosion, presently estimated at six million new facts each year! The printed page is inadequate to contain so much information, and electronic storage devices, accessible through computers, are unavoidable.

Computers will more and more play an integral part of civilized life, in much the same way that telecommunications do today. We can turn our backs and eventually be hit from behind or we can more boldly face the future straight on, right now.

4.3 SPECIFIC TIPS ON DETERMINING WHEN YOU NEED AN EXPERT AND WHERE TO FIND ONE

A number of situations dictate the advisability of enlisting the aid of an expert. For example:

1. You simply do not have the time, patience or inclination to delve deeply enough into the area of educational computing yourself.

2. You remain unable to decide which hardware will best suit the needs of your school program.

3. You have as a priority one or more of the relatively complicated and/or technical applications (for example, voice input, complex bookkeeping, sophisticated data base management, advanced statistical packages).

4. You dearly need to cover all bases.

5. You are just getting started and want that extra support to help ensure the optimal first moves.

If you do determine that you need an expert, where will you find that person? Common sense suggests that you begin by looking closest to home and radiate your search outward only as far as necessary.

• Begin by surveying the people with whom you work on a daily basis. You may be pleasantly surprised to find that someone spends hours each weekend in the dark recesses of his or her basement, excitedly exploring the possibilities of a home computer system.

• Several of the school's parents are undoubtedly involved in some application of computers in the business world.

• The school district office is likely engaging the services of a computer specialist, if only on a part-time basis and strictly for financial, personnel, and data management applications. Don't be surprised to find that a person with expertise in instructional applications is already or soon to be on staff.

• Local businesses use computers for many purposes, some of them directly applicable to education.

• Computer clubs abound. Most have members eager to proselytize, and what better way than through the local school system!

• Regional education and/or teacher centers are increasingly adding to their services support for those entering the world of educational computing.

• Computer stores are cropping up everywhere. Some boast at least one person with true savvy and interest in applications relevant to school environments.

• Representatives of equipment manufacturers often know their business inside and out, and can provide very useful criteria if questioned carefully.

• By now, probably every large and many small colleges and universities have educational computing specialists on their faculty. Demonstration facilities and computer resource centers are often open to the educational public.

• Any educational consulting company worth its salt nowadays has at least one knowledgeable computer specialist on call.

• Educational computer consortiums, research centers, and thinktanks are becoming more numerous and more highly visible.

4.4 FIVE COMMON PITFALLS YOU CAN AVOID

If you order the wrong French books and they remain in the book closet unused, you waste a couple of hundred dollars. If you implement a computer project that is wrong for your school, you may waste a lot more money, alienate the staff, parents and students, and miss a golden opportunity to do something great for your pupils.

The woods are full of dangers and we cannot protect you from every misstep. However, we are in contact with many educators who have been involved in initiating a computer project. They have shared their problems, challenges and near misses, which we have grouped under five broad headings: Simple Simon, Trivial Tripe, Excuse-All, GIGO, and Sub Teacher.

1. *Simple Simon.* Too many school people are quick to accept the common claim that the best computer system is the easiest to operate, so they wind up with the most pre-recorded, canned programs. In no time at all, the students outgrow the school's equipment and justifiably brag that they have a better set up in their home basement. You never heard a youngster brag about a better biology lab, gymnasium, or language lab at home. While you don't necessarily want the latest state-of-the-art sophisticated equipment that requires 1,000 hours of background before you press the first command button, do be sure that you can acquire "add-ons" as they become necessary. As noted in Chapter 1, these may include: musical tones, synthetic voices, elaborate game panels and controls, and microphones that allow you to give verbal commands to the computer.

2. *Trivial Tripe.* Sadly, many teachers use the computer as an expensive, electronic workbook. They design or buy programs that are nothing more than repetitious drill exercises. With some encouragement, they might program the computer to act as a calendar, a notebook, a board game, or a filing cabinet full of files; however, in many situations, the newly acquired computer won't do the tasks significantly better than the desk calendar, the looseleaf, the chess game, or an index-card filing cabinet. It will just be something the teacher will be able to explain to the uninformed pupil. The great potential for discovery and problem solving will be lost to those caught up in such trivial uses.

3. *Excuse-All.* Still others will use the computer as a crutch or scapegoat. They'll have it remember things that they are perfectly capable of remembering on their own. The administrator of a small school project who has the school secretary spending time to "store"

pupil information already easily available in three other places is an example of this misuse. Other people will fall into the pitfall of using the computer as an excuse. They will blame the computer for their own misjudgments or shortcomings, for example, when projected enrollment figures do not pan out.

4. *GIGO.* This stands for "Garbage In, Garbage Out." It is the computer's special failing. Unless you feed it correct information and a program that does exactly what you think it does, the computer is likely to subvert all your intentions and produce nonsense—impressive nonsense, but nonsense nonetheless.

5. *Sub Teacher.* A computer, no matter how elaborate, cannot take the place of a teacher. There are many functions of a teacher that it can perform, but certainly not all. We have pointed out how routine drill exercises can be programmed. But the deepest affective components of learning that a teacher provides transcend the capabilities of even the most sophisticated multi-million dollar computer. The computer is best used as a tool to help teachers and students in their work, not as a replacement for the teacher. Used correctly, the computer can magnify the teacher's skills, assist the pupil in learning new ideas and techniques, and help both work more efficiently, creatively, and enthusiastically.

4.5 PROCEDURES FOR ESTABLISHING PRIORITIES

Think about the most important aspect of your job. Whether you are a classroom teacher or a district superintendent, it is setting priorities. A successful computer project is dependent upon the thoughtful establishment of priorities and the adherence to them. The teacher may set as his or her goal a simple tutorial situation, drill and practice, dialogue, problem solving, games, simulation exercises or inquiry situations. She or he can't do something "different" every day. Teachers must first set up their priorities and work towards their goals.

Likewise, for example, an administrator must first decide if he or she wants the students in the department, school or district to learn *about* computers or learn *with* computer support. Will it be computer-assisted instruction or computer-managed instruction?

What are your goals or objectives for your computer project? What steps have you taken this year to implement your plans or goals? Many school people seem to have trouble planning because they regard it only as "thinking," which all too often is translated into either "staring into space" or "daydreaming." They need to make a more concrete task out of planning. Our experience tells us it is much better to think of planning as "writing" rather than as "thinking."

Get out a large sheet of lined paper. Write down the three or four big things that you would like to accomplish through your computer project. Write down broad objectives or goals, such as: teacher training in computer use, improved programming skills for seniors, better parent understanding of the computer project. Number each objective you write down. Next, turn your paper over and list the staff members in your school who can help you achieve these goals. Write their names under each number.

In the back of your mind, you have been thinking of your long-range goals. But simply thinking about them is quite a different experience from writing them down. Unwritten goals often remain vague dreams. Writing goals down tends to make them more concrete and specific and helps you probe below the surface of the same old clichés you've been telling yourself for years.

Through a careful reading of your thoughts committed to paper, you gain a valuable new perspective because you can then examine them more closely. Once they have an independent identity, you can scrutinize them better. They can be analyzed, refined, updated, pondered, and changed.

Turn your paper over; notice how you listed certain people under your goals. You may never have thought of enlisting the guidance counselor as an agent of change in moving your school into the computer age. By including her here, your mind will now be drawn to specific ways in which she can help teachers individualize instruction or talk to classes about career opportunities in computer science.

You can't perform goals or priorities. Short-term planning as well as long-term planning is needed. Short-range planning requires specific activities. You can perform activities. These activities are steps along the way to goals.

In all your planning with teachers and administrators, you make a list and set priorities. Remember: all the items on the list are not of equal value. Train yourself once you have reduced your priorities to paper to number them in order of importance. No list is complete until it has been numbered according to priority—use just three numbers: 1, 2, 3.

Place a "1" to the left of those items on the list that have a high value—the "must accomplish" items. Use a "2" for those with medium value, and a "3" for those with low value. Get the most out of your time by doing the 1's first and saving the 2's and 3's for later.

Train yourself to take a few minutes each morning to jot down the things you want to accomplish that day. Write them down in any order that comes to mind. This may take two or three minutes. Then take another two minutes deciding which are 1, 2 and 3 priorities.

This is most important! You don't want to get caught up in a lot of 3's day after day and let the 1's slide by undone. These extra two minutes will let you reap maximum benefits from minimum time investments.

Check your daily or short-range lists periodically. It is best to keep them in a little memo book or on a calendar. In this way, you can look back at yesterday's list to see if there is anything undone. It may take several days to accomplish a 1 priority task. Keeping it in your pocket calendar or memo book will prevent you from conveniently forgetting about it. Try this system for two weeks and you'll be hooked.

4.6 SUGGESTIONS ON WHERE TO PLACE THE COMPUTERS

Placing the computers in the best location in your school is worthy of careful planning. The degree of access can spell the difference between a successful project and a failure. Some obvious considerations are: What kind and amount of equipment are you talking about? What are your current long- and short-range plans? How is your school building laid out? Are there limitations caused by personnel, maintenance, or security considerations?

Your prime concern should be ease of access. Here you come to a fork in the road: Do you want central or decentralized locations of the machines? There are advantages to each approach. Read this compendium of suggestions and then decide, along with involved others, which one best suits your school's needs.

1. No matter where the computers are used, there should be one place where they are stored when not in use. This room or closet can be fitted with secure locks, sealed windows, alarms, etc. This computer storage area should also house the many manuals, magazines, software, and peripherals you'll accumulate.

2. The location of the central computer lab or storeroom should be within the general traffic pattern of the school, such as the library or media center. If only a storeroom, it should be near the classrooms most likely to utilize the equipment. A more significant factor might be a location least likely to be penetrated by vandals.

3. The school library or media center, by tradition and procedures, is a place where AV and other materials are stored and retrieved. It usually has continuous adult supervision. Many schools check out the terminals and software to teachers just as they do books. The library would need to be open as many hours as possible.

4. Computers-on-wheels might be the best arrangement for you. If secured to permanent carts the same height as desks, they could be easily moved from classroom to classroom. See Section 4.8 for in-depth discussion of this option.

5. Computers must be kept dust-free and relatively cool, so they should be placed away from the chalkboard or heating vents. Locations near windows are bad because of dust and security problems.

6. Decisions on physical locations should take into consideration available electrical outlets and pupil distractibility. The machines are usually best placed where the screen is not visible by the whole group of students but only by the pupils using it.

7. The guidance office or teacher's room should not be overlooked as storage areas. The availability of locked steel file cabinets make overnight and weekend storage of software and possibly the hardware a cinch.

8. The dilemma of priorities raises its head when you consider gifted and talented students as opposed to the learning disabled or those otherwise in need of extra support as prime computer consumers. Here your school philosophy and goals will contribute heavily to the decision of placement. Sharing equipment with both groups usually works.

9. Utilization may extend beyond ordinary schoolroom placement. Where feasible, pupils may be given access anytime during the school day (lunch, study period) or even after school. You might even try allowing pupils to sign out microcomputers on weekends. Some schools encourage interested teachers to sign out computers during holiday and vacation time. This accomplishes two purposes: most break-ins to schools occur at that time and the teacher is motivated to develop his or her computer skills.

4.7 FACTORS TO CONSIDER IN DESIGNING A COMPUTER LAB

Central computer facilities in schools are housed in a variety of places, from former classrooms to former closets. Newer buildings have multi-media centers or computer labs designed by an architect. Other buildings utilize whatever space is available.

A basic consideration is the availability of sufficient electrical outlets. You don't want to overload a single receptacle with multiple, octopus-like, double sockets. Your next concern should be for adequate ventilation since the equipment generates heat. A good source of light, artificial or natural, completes our list of three basic considerations.

Just as important is adequate security of the room or center. Here we come to a dilemma: the room should be secure with a solid door and a paucity of windows. At the same time, it should be accessible to adult scrutiny and supervision, even when an adult cannot be physically present. This arrangement is usually accomplished by having a solid reinforced door that is kept open when students are present and is locked at all other times.

Furniture is an important consideration. While most of the available school desks will suffice, there are other considerations. A traveling Computer Center requires wagons, carts, or other wheeled devices, but where hardware will be used in one place, wheels tend to be a disadvantage. Devices that anchor the keyboards and monitors, at least, should be purchased as a precaution in case of illegal entry and also to keep some overeager student from knocking valuable equipment off a desk top.

What was once thought of as standard furniture designed to "fill up" a school building does not always lend itself to a computer center. Your design and furniture should define space, make students comfortable, and help provide the acoustical and aesthetic environment necessary for learning.

The following six guidelines will help you through the morass of catalogs and advertisements that flood your mail:

1. Durability. Look for easily cleaned surfaces, solid construction, and easy repair.
2. Simplicity. Watch out for the stuff with a dozen uses and a thousand pieces and extraneous gadgets that fall off.
3. Usefulness. Can it be used for just one type of hardware? Can it do the job better than something you already have?
4. Flexibility. Can students of different sizes and shapes get their legs under it? Is the chair compatible with the height of the keyboard?
5. Movability. Can it be moved by students? If there are wheels, do they have brakes? Is there a rail to keep the equipment from falling off?
6. Compactness. Is the piece too big? Does it take up more space than necessary?

You will probably want dividers or partitions to separate the clusters of pupils using each computer. It used to be that walls, dividers, and partitions merely separated one space from another. Today you are better off defining space rather than dividing it. Define the spaces as large or as small as necessary and maybe in alternative parts of the room. Remember, a wall that doesn't do anything isn't functional and should serve as something more than a divider. Furniture that fills these requirements are called space definers, and they come in a variety of styles and uses. One popular yet often overlooked item is a steel, locked, four-drawer file cabinet. It's high and deep enough to define a work area and its drawers can be used to secure software that is not in use. Some keyboards can actually be locked in these drawers on weekends.

Other space definers can be chalkboards, bulletin boards, projection screens, bookcases, two-door cabinets, and even pupil lockers.

Space definers should not be permanently fixed in place. Storage racks, basket bins, and display partitions are all available on wheels or skids, or they are simply lightweight enough to pick up and move.

Independent study has made carrels common in schools at all levels of education, and are no longer restricted to libraries. They provide about six square feet of work surface and a degree of visual privacy. Often, they include storage space, a light, and shelves. For the purpose of the computer lab, they must be "wet," that is, with wiring and electrical connections. "Wet" carrels are often designed with accoustical paneling to reduce sound transmission.

As part of the design process, you should involve a representative from your local telephone company. Even if you are not ready now, you will eventually want a modem and telephone line so that you can become involved in networking (see Chapter 7) or tap the software resources of the district office or some other off-campus location. It's better to plan for telephone hook-ups now rather than more hardware later to accommodate the phone lines.

A final word—modularity. In your design, seek component parts designed on a modular basis. For example, carrels can be clustered to make use of fewer components, such as, two carrels side by side needing only three side pieces, not four.

4.8 HOW TO SET UP A UNIQUE TRAVELLING COMPUTER CENTER

As noted earlier, there are situations that dictate the movement of one or more computers from one work location in the school to another. Carrying the equipment by hand is definitely not advisable because it is cumbersome, time consuming, and likely to lead to broken or damaged machinery sooner or later. The one viable alternative is to set up a travelling Computer Center, which turns out to be a rather straightforward affair.

Essentially only two problems need to be resolved:

1. What means should be used to transport the equipment?
2. How can users be provided with up to date and easy access to appropriate software?

The only reasonable way to transport a microcomputer along with its monitor and any peripherals is on a portable cart of some sort. These may be inexpensively obtained by utilizing appropriate old furniture like the following, making any adjustments or modifications, as necessary:

- refitted typewriter stands
- old lunchroom wagons
- unused TV stands
- double or single pupil desks with casters added

Such adaptions are certainly financially attractive, and since commercially manufactured portable carts may end up costing almost as much as some low-cost computer systems, they may be the best answer in many situations. However, the more expensive, specially designed carts have a number of important features that, in the long run, are likely to justify their initial cost (see Figures 4-1 A and B). In selecting such carts, we suggest you consider the following questions:

- How sturdy are the legs, the table, and the fittings that connect them together?
- Is it possible to incorporate casters that are at least two and preferably three inches in diameter?
- Is there a shelf for fan-folded computer paper and a slot in the table top or some other convenient way of feeding paper into a printer?
- Is there adequate room on the table top or a built-on shelf for a monitor or for such common peripherals as a printer, a cassette recorder, or a disk drive?
- Is there provision for bolting the keyboard and other equipment onto the table top or shelf?
- Is there provision for bolting on a strip of outlets, so that all wires are kept neatly out of the way and only one plug ever needs to be put in and out of a wall outlet?
- Is the height of the table top adjustable, to accommodate users of various sizes?

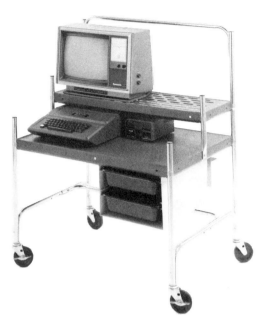

Figure 4-1A. Example of Commercially Available Cart

Figure 4-1B. Example of Commercially Available Cart

The solution to the problem of providing users with easy access to software stored on cassette tape, disks or cartridges is more time consuming to establish, but well worth the effort in terms of the number of hours eventually saved in choosing and obtaining software from the growing selection that will be available in your school. It involves cataloging the computer programs and wedding the actual storage medium with any accompanying documentation and other printed support materials.

An implementation of such a solution has worked well in a hospital-based school program run by the Special Services School District of Bergen County, New Jersey, where the microcomputers have actually been wheeled from one building to another through an underground tunnel system. Teachers interested in utilizing one of the computers arrange for the equipment to be delivered to their classroom by an aide. They select software first by thumbing through a set of index cards that is readily available to each of them.

On each of the cards, there is a very brief description of one of the school's computer programs, along with other relevant data (see Figure 4-2). The cards are organized according to topics within each of the traditional subject areas.

Language Arts

Topic: <u>Spelling</u>

Program Name: <u>WORDFORM</u>

Disk #<u>123</u>   Computer: <u>TRS-80</u>

Grade Level: <u>2nd-6th</u>

Brief Description: Students must visualize and then type in a complete word when shown a part of it. Students control the presentation of clues.

**Figure 4-2. Sample Index Card for Organizing
Software Collection**

**Figure 4-3. Binder for Holding Software and
Related Print Material**

The teachers, having initially screened programs of their choice through perusing the index card catalog, then obtain the disks they intend to use for previewing at some appointed time. Each disk is numbered and placed in its accompanying sleeve, which has been stapled to the inside front cover of a three-ring binder. (Where cassette tapes or cartridges are used, inexpensive plastic bags or other containers can be fixed to the covers in place of the sleeves.) The outside of the binder displays a label that shares

---

Program Name: _____

Disk #: _____   Side #: _____

Specific Topic: _____

Type: _____   Grade Level: _____   Reading Level: _____

Graphics: _____   Sound: _____   # of Students: _____

Description:

Performance Objectives:

1.

2.

3.

4.

5.

Prior Knowledge Required:

Response to Mistakes:

Response to Correct Answers:

Special Equipment:

Special Alerts:

**Figure 4-4A. Sample Sheet Kept in Binders to
Provide Additional Criteria for
Choosing Appropriate Software
(Front)**

Evaluative or Other Comments	Your Name	Date

**Figure 4-4B. Sample Sheet Kept in Binders to
Provide Additional Criteria for
Choosing Appropriate Software
(Back)**

the same number as the disk it houses (see Figure 4-3). In the binder, along with printed material to accompany each program on the disk, is a sheet for each program, which provides additional criteria for the teacher in deciding which programs to use (see Figures 4-4 A and B). The binders themselves are kept on a portable set of shelves, so that the whole library of software can be transported should the need arise. More often, only the easily identified binders housing the chosen programs are transported along with the equipment.

4.9 A CHECKLIST FOR SAFEGUARDING VALUABLE EQUIPMENT AND SUPPLIES

At meetings of administrators, a frequent topic of conversation is "break-ins." More and more schools in large and small cities as well as suburban and rural areas are plagued with intrusions. These range from harmless pranks to psychotic vandalism to sophisticated burglaries. The addition of computers to a school's inventory dramatically increases its chance of a break-in.

While we can't prevent vandalism and burglary, we can make it more difficult for thugs to rip-off our computer equipment and supplies. Through bitter personal experience and interviews with other school people, we have come up with the following checklist:

1. At point of delivery (stockroom, general office, principal's office) open cartons promptly, check contents against orders and either store the original cartons or destroy them. Leaving them outside with the trash merely advertises to the world at large that the school just received some valuable equipment.

2. Record all serial numbers in at least two places for safekeeping. Maintain an inventory card for every computer item. If items are stolen and later recovered by the police, you probably won't get them back unless you have the serial numbers.

3. Brand all equipment and supplies with an electric stylus. These are available for about ten dollars. Etch in your school name and phone number. This practice makes recovery easier if an item is found. More importantly, it discourages removal by burglars.

4. Anchor computers to desk tops with steel bolts. Your custodian can do this or you can purchase special anchor devices from audio-visual and business machine catalogs. Many thieves are discouraged if they can't easily get the equipment off the table.

5. Keep the computer room lit up all night. The minor expenditure for electricity is a small premium to pay in the way of burglary insurance.

6. Classrooms with computers should be on upper floors or with their windows modified with blocks that don't allow them to be opened more than six inches.

7. Classroom doors with glass windows should be covered with tempered masonite or steelplate. Likewise, transom windows should be covered.

8. Store supplies and software in locked, steel, two-drawer file cabinets. Diskettes, tapes, and other software should be locked in these file drawers when not in use.

9. Supervise the computer area during the school day. In certain situations, it is advisable to require that pupils check their book bags and knapsacks before entering the computer room.

10. Change locks on the doors of computer rooms. These should be "off" the school's master key. Restrict keys to as few staff members as possible.

11. Safeguard equipment from daily abuse. Keep paper clips, soda cans and other extraneous material far away.

12. Keep room keys locked away during weekends and holidays. If all the teachers hang their keys in one wall cabinet, enterprising burglars can have a field day.

13. Maintain a good working relationship with your police precinct or department. This will assure their complete cooperation if you have a break-in. They can also give you some security tips.

14. Have the custodian check to see that everyone has left the building before he locks up. One common modus operandi is for the burglar to hide in the building before it is secured for the night. This saves him the trouble of breaking-in.

15. Solicit the cooperation of neighbors who live near and around the school building. Too often they adopt a "see no evil, hear no evil" attitude about the school building after hours. Your sincere solicitations of their help can turn them into watchdogs.

4.10 OPTIONS IN SCHEDULING THE USE OF THE EQUIPMENT

Before you begin to schedule the use of the computers, you must recognize the fact that doing work on a computer often requires larger blocks of time than are needed for most other educational tasks. It is not uncommon to spend two or three hours, or even all night, working through a problem. In large schools, teachers are enslaved by the program clock and the ringing of period bells. Even though there are times when it is appropriate to encourage students to do their thinking away from the computer, it is usually far more productive, if you have a generous pupil-computer ratio, for the students to be at the machine receiving continuous feedback on their ideas and work.

Since most schools cannot luxuriate in generous computer-pupil ratios, there is a need to explore other options to maximize the use of available equipment. Different attitudes toward computer use will affect how you schedule the use of your hardware. Some schools feel that students should be scheduled for computer use only if they are enrolled in computer courses; others insist on high academic achievement as defined by the math teacher or guidance counselor; still others schedule only students in specially funded programs.

Some of the options available to you include:

1. Issue a "Disk-Driver's License" as they do in a Los Angeles middle school. Only after students have mastered the use of the disk drive are they given a "license." With this license they can sign up on a wall schedule mounted in the library to use the equipment.

2. Station a lunchroom aide in the computer room during the lunch period. She or he can schedule up to twenty pupils to use the equipment during the lunch period.

3. Schedule a zero period before the first period of the day. During this early part of the school day, the eager beavers can use the computers. There seems to be a high positive correlation between computer enthusiasts and early risers.

4. Extend the school day to accommodate pupils who are not dependent on bus transportation to stay one hour later after the regular school day.

5. Offer a mini computer workshop. During the twenty-minute homeroom, study hall or assembly periods, allow groups of pupils into the computer room.

6. Make arrangements with staff members to supervise the computer room instead of engaging in administrative duties like hall patrol or lunch duty. Don't leave out non-teaching personnel who have some interest or background in computers.

7. Supplement computer room staff with community volunteers, parents, or retired senior citizens.

8. Assign older students, or students with a knowledge of computers, as computer room aides. Peer tutoring frequently brings about startling results.

9. Set up a scheduling team. It should be small enough to be functional yet large enough to be representative. It should represent all elements of the staff (grade and/or subject) and students. A number somewhere between three and six people is advisable, depending upon the size of the school. Such a team will insure fair and maximum use of the computer equipment.

10. Include all facets of your school in the scheduling. Excellent results have been obtained when learning disabled, former truants, acting-out, and shy, withdrawn students have been given the opportunity to be part of the computer schedule.

5 | A Complete Action Plan to Involve School Personnel

This chapter will help you successfully initiate and carry out a critical phase in the implementation of a computer project in any school environment: the productive involvement of school personnel. At the very least, the ease with which computers are integrated into the daily life of a school depends on how well this matter is handled; at most, the eventual success of the whole project may hinge on the effectiveness of your plan to actively involve persons at every level in the school. Therefore, it is hoped that you will carefully consider the proposals for specific actions that are offered in the chapter, and that two recurring themes be especially noted:

1. Become directly involved yourself as much as possible.
2. Adapt the specific actions according to the special needs dictated by your particular situation.

5.1 A PRELIMINARY SURVEY: WHAT TO ASK AND HOW TO ASK IT

It is no great revelation that people are more likely to commit their hearts and energies to the successful implementation of a project if they have had an early opportunity to contribute significantly to its implementation. What may be less obvious is that teachers and other school personnel, most or all of whom may have little or no experience, skill or knowledge in the field of educational computing, may nonetheless be in a position to contribute significantly—and from the start—to the implementation of the school's computer project. The secret to making such productive, early involvement possible lies in knowing what to ask and how to ask it. Thus, a properly designed and executed preliminary survey to be

Computers are finding their way into schools across the nation. Our school is no exception. To help ensure that we make optimal use of the new technology, your responses on this questionnaire are important. Please feel free to attach additional sheets of paper for any more lengthy answers you may want to provide.

Name: Date:

1 . Have you ever used a computer yourself for non-educational purposes? If yes, please describe:

2. Have you ever used a computer yourself for educational purposes? If yes, please describe:

   If not, have you ever heard about, read about, or seen a computer being used for educational purposes? Please describe:

3. Would you like to learn more about how computers are being used as educational tools in the hands of teachers and students?

4. Would you like to learn more about how computers are being used in schools by administrators, secretaries and other non-teaching personnel?

5. If it ever became possible, do you think you might want to have computers available to you for the work you do in the school?

6. Do you know any computer languages? If yes, which?

7. Do you know anyone who has special exertise in computing and who might be willing to help the school in this area? If yes, please explain:

8. Do you have any concerns about the use of computers in our school? If yes, please explain:

9. Do you presently have any particular ideas of how computers might be best used in our school? If yes, please explain:

10. Do you presently have any ideas as to how you might personally want to be involved in using computers in our school? If yes, please explain:

11. Any other comments:

Figure 5-1. Computers in the School: A Preliminary Survey

carried out among school personnel is a key element in your overall plan to involve them.

The following criteria should prove useful in deciding upon and executing a survey with which you will be comfortable:

1. The formality with which you conduct the survey should reflect your overall style of interaction and be in direct proportion to the size of the school staff. With a total staff of twelve, for example, coupled with a non-directive style of interaction, the best way to conduct the survey may very well be through face-to-face individual or group contact. Given the uniqueness of computers for most school people, such an informal approach should work well in the appropriate setting.

In a large school, especially one in which a more formal atmosphere characterizes the interaction among the personnel, it would probably be more productive and efficient to circulate a printed survey. In such cases, rather than simply distributing it "out of the blue" through the mail boxes, it is advisable to hand it out at a regularly scheduled gathering of the staff, so that a few, brief introductory remarks can be made.

2. The detail of the survey, whether it is implemented by spoken or printed word, will depend on your assessment of the optimal balance between speed, ease and efficiency on the one hand, and the opportunity for more open-ended, creative input from the staff on the other. In this regard, the approach could range anywhere from asking people to respond to one question, "What is your reaction to the idea of having computers in the school?" to asking

them to respond to a very specific "yes-no" checklist, with no request for any narrative.

3. Timing is important. Since the survey will spark interest in at least a few, but more probably many of the staff members, there should be a preparedness on your part to implement follow-up steps on the basis of their responses. The excitement likely to be generated about a project as innovative as computer utilization is best capitalized upon at its peak. Strong as it may be at first, the daily distractions of school life will surely cause it to wane if no follow-up is provided.

Figure 5-1 provides you with sample content for a preliminary survey, which you can use and change as you see fit. On the whole, it is intended as a compromise in terms of detail so that more readers will find it more readily adaptable to their particular needs.

5.2 FOUR INNOVATIVE IDEAS FOR GENERATING A CLIMATE OF INQUIRY AND ANTICIPATION

Once you have conducted the preliminary survey, it is inevitable that some interest will be generated. The following four suggestions should go a long way in intensifying and solidifying that interest, to make sure that the right climate is created before you initiate the first encounter between people and machines.

1. In Chapter 4, it was recommended that one way to mobilize parental support was to arrange for visits to schools that were successfully implementing computers. Such visits should be arranged for key school personnel as well as for parents. While some saving in time and energy can be achieved by arranging for the two groups to go together, it might be better to keep the visits separate, since the focus of the groups is likely to be different, that is, parents would want an emphasis primarily on how much more the students are learning, whereas the school personnel would be equally interested in knowing how their daily work day can be made easier. (Of course, in certain circumstances it may be more desirable from a human relations point of view to have a joint trip.)

The selection of whom to invite from the school staff should be accomplished with care. Many factors will probably affect your decision, but don't overlook the feedback you have solicited through the survey. By making a special effort to include those who expressed the keenest interest, you demonstrate your sincerity regarding a commitment to take their contributions into account. Also, keep in mind that it is probably beneficial for you to attend as well.

It is a good idea to follow up your visits with a brief report by those who attended. Don't exclude comments that may be negative, because they help present a balanced, realistic view and can alert you and the other school personnel about the potential problem areas. These can then be addressed early, with your computer project benefiting in the long run.

2. Refer to Appendix A, and select two or three computer publications that are specific to educators. (While all those listed are good, two of them—*Classroom Computer Learning* and *Electronic Learning*—are especially appropriate at this point in your project, because of their quality and their focus on helping educators new to the field of computing.)

Depending on the size of the staff, order a few subscriptions of each publication. When they arrive, read through them first yourself, and then circulate them among the other people in the school. Based on the preliminary survey results, as well as what you know of the people otherwise, earmark particular articles for each person to read. Besides adding a nice personal touch, it re-emphasizes your real commitment to understand and respond to their needs in this new and sometimes intimidating field.

Articles of general interest or exceptional quality should be photocopied and distributed to everyone. If the suggestion for a certain article to be widely circulated comes from someone other than yourself, all the better. In fact, a small, informal group might be appointed specifically to decide which articles everyone should read.

3. An additional recommendation made in Chapter 4 with regard to parental support was to arrange for a presentation on computers at a PTA meeting. To help stimulate interest among the school personnel, a presentation at a regularly scheduled staff conference would also be appropriate. Again, you should consider that the perspectives of the two groups are probably somewhat divergent, so use your judgment in planning how to meet specific needs. In deciding what to include in a presentation to school people, the following advice should prove helpful:

• If you decide to use a commercially or more locally prepared filmstrip, film or videotape as the basis of the presentation, be sure to preview the content first. Those persons who contribute to the content are often technically oriented and may therefore fall into the trap of being somewhat pedantic in their approach. That sort of orientation is probably the least productive at this point in your plan to involve school personnel. One highly recommended, half-hour film with a strikingly non-technical orientation is entitled, "Don't Bother Me, I'm Learning." It is available through:

CRM/McGraw-Hill
110 Fifteenth Street
Del Mar, CA 92014

- If you decide on one or more guest speakers, it is usually better at this point to seek, not experts, per se, but rather other "ordinary" school people who have used computers themselves. They are more likely to avoid the use of jargon, to speak to the point on matters of direct concern, and, because of their unabashed and "innocent" enthusiasm, to generate excitement and inspiration at many levels. Such people can be found in neighboring schools, among your school's parents, or even lurking in the ranks of your school's staff.

4. Another source of inspiration, too often overlooked, lies in the testimonials of students in the school who have experienced the benefits and perhaps even the thrill of having learned something through interacting with a computer. Such students may have used computers at a different school or they may be part of a rapidly growing number of families who have a microcomputer with some educationally oriented programs right at home. Their testimonials have been known to include some remarkably insightful comments, such as the following, all from elementary school children:

- "If kids can learn while they are having fun, whatever they're learning will really sink in."

- "Computers should stay in school, but only to help teachers. Computers can't take the job that was meant for people."

- "Computers can't be as good as mankind because without mankind there would be no computers."

- "A computer tells you right away that you made a mistake and lets you try again. That's a lot better than getting your paper back all marked up in red pencil."

- "Most computers do good things, but that is not their intention. They only do what they are programmed to do."

5.3 TIPS ON WHO SHOULD BE INVOLVED AT THE BEGINNING

Brief mention was made in Section 5.2 of the possibility of having a small group of people in the school deciding on what journal or magazine articles should be photocopied for general distribution. Of course, such a group could be involved in any or all of the decisions regarding each phase of the computer project. To organize such a group or not, whether formal or informal, or to deal only on a one-to-one basis with a few persons is a decision that is best left entirely in your hands. However, it is clearly advisable to have at least some other people involved from the beginning. The following tips are intended to help you decide on who those people should be:

1. *Include everyone who displays some interest.* You will want to encourage as broad a base of interest, commitment and support as possible. Therefore, any person, from the custodian to the media specialist, from the teacher-aide to the vice-principal, can be included in some way. For example:

- The teacher-aide could be asked to be on the lookout for articles in the local press that are easy for the lay person to understand and that could then be circulated among her colleagues.
- The custodian could be asked to explore and briefly present to the rest of the staff how a microcomputer might be used to help reduce energy consumption in the school.
- The librarian or media specialist could be invited to make recommendations regarding what materials would be best for presentations to school staff and parents.
- The vice-principal could take part in shaping and analyzing the results of the preliminary survey.

2. *Do not include anyone who displays a lack of interest.* At this early stage, it is usually better to be extra cautious with those persons who seem cool or otherwise unreceptive to the idea of incorporating computers into the school's programs. Allow them their "space," on the basis of your awareness that the idea can seem foreign, unappealing and actually threatening. Many will come around on their own as time goes on, and most of the hold-outs will soften with gentle encouragement at a later date.

3. *Look especially for interest among "key" people.* You will know what "key" means in your special circumstances: those who are quietly influential, those who are the most vocal, those who formally represent one or another subgroup, those who are the hardest workers, those who might otherwise work against a new approach, etc.

Optimally, you will find a balance among those persons who are involved from the beginning, so you won't find yourself overloaded with "techniks" or only math teachers or those who tend to be considered in some way radical or off-beat. Toward this end, you may need to watch or listen more acutely than usual to pick up subtle signs of interest from the more reserved or conservative corners.

5.4 FOUR RESULT-ORIENTED SUGGESTIONS FOR IMPLEMENTING THAT CRUCIAL FIRST ENCOUNTER BETWEEN PEOPLE AND MACHINE

Once the suggestions presented in the first three sections of this chapter have helped you to create the right climate, where a sense of anticipation at least has been generated, you are ready to initiate that critical first exposure of the school's personnel to an actual computer. Keep in mind that you will be facing three categories of people:

1. Those who will be biting at the bit, eager to see what it is all about and all but convinced that they are about to share something significant.

2. Those who maintain a real or assumed air of "reserved judgment" and are waiting to be convinced.

3. Those who for one reason or another will not be moved by the angels themselves.

Of course, groups 1 and 3 will not be of primary concern to you in planning for the initial encounter. With group 1, whatever you do will probably pique their interest; you will only need to turn them loose. Group 3, hopefully few in number and perhaps non-existent, are so set in their ways or emotionally invested in strongly resisting this (and perhaps any other) potential change in their lives, that they need to be at least watched at this point and kept in check if unreasonably disruptive.

Your main objective is to offer group 2, which is no doubt by far the largest in number and probably the backbone of the school's staff, an experience that will enhance the probability of their seeing their working hours made not only easier, but more fulfilling as well. The power of the computer in front of them can help them do a better job with less effort. And the beauty of your presentation lies in the fact that there is no manipulation whatsoever in your approach. The truth is there to be revealed. If you proceed carefully, most people will be touched by it.

The following list of suggestions for implementing the first encounter will help you realize your primary goal:

1. *Be sure that you make most, if not all, of the presentation yourself.* Nothing you can say, no matter how well you say it, could take the place of your actually operating the equipment initially, and demonstrating a relative expertise gained after only a few hours of preparation. Your willingness to tackle this new technology will go a long way to inspire and comfort others.

2. *Try to have an "expert" available, mainly to help answer hard questions which may come up.* It is your show, but there is no contradiction in having someone with broader experience available to provide depth where needed. Furthermore, you demonstrate your sincere readiness to learn from others in a field of explosive technology. Your expert can be found in many places: on your school's staff, in a neighboring school, within a local business, on the salesforce of a computer company or a software publishing house, or in the student body of a local high school or a nearby college. (See Section 4.3.)

3. *Don't overdo it.* Though you are harnessing the power of a revolution, there is no reason why the introduction of it in your school cannot be evolutionary in nature. The impact can be overwhelming, but need not be if you present, on first exposure, only a select, representative sampling of hardware and software—just enough to show what is in store for those persons present. A gradually expanding awareness and mastery of the technology's impact can easily follow where necessary.

4. *Make your presentation to small groups.* Avoid a large group introduction for several reasons: (a) detailed information on the TV screen of a microcomputer can be difficult to see from far away, (b) each member of the group should be strongly encouraged to sit at and to some degree operate the computer, and (c) various subgroups need to be initially exposed to very different applications.

5.5 THREE SHORTCUTS FOR OVERCOMING RESISTANCE

Up to this point, we have been considering suggestions that apply equally to the different categories of personnel in your school. Now we tackle concerns specific to each of the three major subdivisions of labor in your building: administrative, teaching, and secretarial/clerical. Since you may expect at least a little resistance from most people, the following guidelines are presented as tested methods for anticipating and easily dealing with what seems to be for most of us a natural inertia or at least ambivalence when confronted with a request for change.

Shortcut 1: Overcoming Resistance Among Administrative Personnel

At some point in your initial presentation to a group of administrators, invite them to take turns complaining about one recordkeeping task they feel interferes with their more essential functions in the school. After each description, state flatly and with confidence that utilizing the computer would reduce the time and effort presently required for that recordkeeping duty by anywhere up to 25 percent!

Underscore the fact that the accurate and rapid manipulation of information is a computer's forte. Bring the point home by taking one of the complaints aired previously and sketching out how the data involved can be automatically accessed by the mere push of a button, according to whatever parameters are deemed important. (There are several excellent, general purpose programs commercially available for just such application, for example, Visi-Calc, Profile, Microfiles, etc. Your selected computer expert will know more about them.)

Shortcut 2: Overcoming Resistance Among Clerical Staff

As a rule, secretarial and other clerical personnel are less likely to be intimidated by the introduction of new technology than are other members of the staff. After all, the use of machines— including typewriters, photocopiers, adding machines, calculators, etc.—are already part of their daily lives. Their main concern will most likely be: "How much more work will it mean for me?" By the conclusion of their first encounter, they should walk away asking themselves instead: "Well, now I wonder just how much busywork it actually can save me!"

A good program to have this group of people experience on first exposure is a word processing program (see Chapter 9). It will demonstrate the effectiveness of a computer in alleviating some of a secretary's most annoying problems involved in the production of written matter.

Shortcut 3: Overcoming Resistance Among Teachers

If you are going to meet any significant resistance at all, it is most likely to come from teachers. Their hesitation can probably be traced to a fear that either they will not understand how to work the newfangled gadgets or they could be more or less replaced by them. Neither of these preoccupations has any actual basis in reality. Therefore, your presentation to this group will focus mainly on two points: (1) properly selected hardware is absolutely simple to operate, and (2) any software of value serves to enhance a teacher's efforts and frees him or her for those interactions for which the computer is unsuited.

The best way to ease the teachers into the world of computers is to let them see some of the school's students sitting at a machine, gaining some obviously valuable experience as a result. The sight of children they know, sitting entranced, deeply involved in learning, and able to operate the equipment after only a few minutes of instruction from you, will go a long way to dissolve their apprehensions regarding the computer's operation.

To deal with their other misgiving, make sure that the program their students are working with is one that clearly requires the teacher's active judgment in terms of selecting exactly what sort of exercises will be presented. Much of the currently available commercial software is of this type.

Once you have loaded an appropriate program into the computer, and before a student actually sits down, have one of the most respected teachers sit before the computer to respond to such messages as:

    HELLO TEACHER! I AM GEORGE, YOUR COMPUTER. I AM READY
    TO GIVE YOUR STUDENTS PRACTICE PROBLEMS IN DIVISION.
        FIRST, I NEED DIRECTION FROM YOU.

    IF YOU WANT WHOLE NUMBER PROBLEMS, PRESS THE LETTER
    "W."
    IF YOU WANT DECIMAL PROBLEMS, PRESS THE LETTER "D."

Teachers immediately realize that they can handle what is being asked of them and also that they are indispensable to the process. The machine does not know what Billy or Jane needs; it is the teacher who can best determine the sort of practice that would be appropriate.

The display on the screen might then continue with:

THANK YOU! NOW I NEED TO KNOW HOW MANY DIGITS LONG YOU WANT THE NUMBERS I GIVE FOR PRACTICE TO BE. PLEASE TYPE IN THE APPROPRIATE NUMBER (1, 2, 3 OR 4).

The message is now clear to the teachers. The machine needs professional guidance all along the way. The teachers will be further put at ease if the computer programs initially selected by you to show them are ones that tackle some of their more pressing teaching problems.

In summary, teachers must see that the machine is not a threat to them, but will actually be useful. They have to feel comfortable using it and want it to be a part of their routine. As with so many new things, the by-words are, "Go slowly." The machine and its instructional applications will sell themselves.

5.6 A CHECKLIST OF WHAT IS NEEDED FOR A SUCCESSFUL FIRST ENCOUNTER

In order to help you organize for the activities suggested in Section 5.5, the following checklist is provided for your convenience:

( ) A 40-minute block of time, at least, per subgroup

( ) At least one machine per 12-15 participants

( ) At least one appropriate example of easy-to-use software for each group

( ) A basic knowledge on your part of how to operate the machinery and the selected software

( ) An expert, if appropriate and possible, to help respond to more technical questions which may be raised

( ) At least one student for the teachers' first encounter

( ) Copies of one or two easy-to-read, yet inspirational articles, if not already distributed (optional)

( ) Copies of the "Workshop Feedback Forms" (see Section 5.8— may be distributed at a later time)

( ) A readiness on your part to expect the unexpected

5.7 ESSENTIAL COMPONENTS OF THE SECOND ENCOUNTER: A FUNDAMENTAL TRAINING WORKSHOP

As all seasoned educators know, the linchpin of any successful innovative school project is adequate and proper training for the relevant members of the staff. The importance of such training is directly proportional to the significance of the change being introduced. Given that the introduction of computer power into the fabric of your school's life represents a potentially enormous improvement at many levels, it follows that success or failure can easily hinge on how well the staff's needs for worthwhile fundamental training are met.

Therefore, the staff's second encounter with the computer should take the form of a two-session workshop. That workshop could, for the time being, conclude the actual formal training of many of the participants. The two sessions, lasting anywhere from 40 minutes to an hour each, will provide them with the essential fundamentals as well as with additional components that you will decide upon beforehand. It is possible to accommodate groups of four to five people per machine.

The people in the school must be able to do at least two things if they are to be in any way independent in their use of the computers:

1. They must know how to turn the equipment on and off.
2. They must know how to load and run programs, from a cassette tape, from a diskette or from a cartridge, depending on the equipment you have.

If the computer programs to be utilized are properly designed and/or if adequate accompanying documentation is provided, then the two basic skills just noted are the only absolute requirements.

In covering those basic skills, the following procedures are recommended:

1. Let the participants do everything.
2. Strongly encourage each person to try loading and running a program.
3. Start with the machine(s) turned off and even unplugged.
4. With a cassette-based machine, make sure that:
   (a) any critical setting or adjustment of the recorder/player has been preset and previously double checked
   (b) the programs are short, so that time for loading them into the computer is minimized

5. With a disk-based machine, make sure that:
    (a) the diskettes used are formatted in such a way that as soon
        as the machine is turned on with a diskette in the disk
        drive, a program on the diskette automatically loads and
        runs
    (b) the participants know which parts of the diskette may be
        handled and which may not
6. Try to make sure that the almost universal misgiving that
   people have at first—that they might create real problems or
   even hurt the equipment by pressing the wrong key—is immediately dispelled. Pressing down on the keyboard a few times
   with your whole hand while the machine is running should
   alleviate much of their apprehension. At worst, a program
   will have to be reloaded.
7. Have one knowledgeable person available at each machine to
   guide the uninitiated.
8. As the newly initiated learn what to do, let them start helping
   those who follow.

Select from the following list those topics or items that you feel
should be included as additional components of the two-session
fundamental training workshop, in order to round out the staff's
basic training:

1. an overall review on the uses of computers in schools
2. a short glossary of computer terminology
3. an overview of criteria for judging the value of software
4. a list of programs available in the school, along with brief
   descriptions of their uses
5. a question-and-answer period (strongly recommended, but be
   sure to allow for extra time)
6. a short, annotated list of valuable outside resources, including people, places, books, and magazines
7. a prepared list of "start up" and "shut down" procedures for
   the computers

5.8 A MODEL FEEDBACK FORM
FOR PLANNING FOLLOW-UP ACTIVITIES

As noted earlier, there will be personnel for whom further
formal training will be unnecessary, at least for some time to come.

Now that you have had at least a brief opportunity to come into contact with a computer in our school, your responses to the following questions will be utilized in mapping more long-range strategies for optimally phasing computer use into a variety of our school's programs. Use additional sheets as necessary.

Name: Date:

1. Do you see any applications to your work in this school? If yes, please explain:

2. Given a microcomputer, a little time and the right computer programs, would you at this point be able to start utilizing it in your work? Please explain:

3. Are you interested in receiving further training?

   right away _____   some time in the future _____

   not in the foreseeable future _____

   What topics or areas should be covered?

4. Would you like to learn how to program a computer? If yes, in which language(s)?

5. What are your ideas now as to how you might be more generally involved in the use of computers in our school?

6. What concerns, if any, do you now have regarding the use of computers in our school?

7. Would you like some additional information right away? If yes, please describe:

8. Summary statements and any other comments:

Figure 5-2. Workshop Feedback Form

Chapter 10 will provide a framework for making some hard decisions as to how much additional training should be provided for whom and when. Meanwhile, your presence when school personnel encountered the computers, both initially and during the double-session workshop, will have had the additional pay-off of providing you with the first-hand, raw data you will want for planning any follow-up activities. Now is the time to add to the myriad of reactions, impressions and comments to which you have been directly exposed (and which you should probably jot down somewhere) a more structured approach for gathering feedback on the activities engaged in thus far.

The feedback form provided in Figure 5-2 has been designed so that it will provide useful information in a wide variety of settings. However, it may be advisable for you to modify or otherwise custom tailor it to meet more pinpointedly the special demands of your situation.

6 | Exploring Instructional and Curricular Applications

6.1 SURVEYING COMPUTERS IN THE CURRICULUM

In Chapter 2, we surveyed four main uses for computers in education—the computer as teacher, tool, learner, and object of instruction. Most school computer projects include all of these, though some concentrate almost totally on teaching programming skills (the computer as learner), others concentrate on computer-assisted instruction (the computer as teacher), and many integrate much of their work on the computer as object of instruction into activities in the other three categories.

The teaching of programming is usually best handled through a separate curriculum component, either a course given in a computer lab by a computer specialist or a time block or learning station in an elementary school classroom. On the other hand, it is usually best to integrate into the existing curriculum most uses of the computer as a teacher or tool. For this reason, it may be helpful to look at educational uses for computers from a new viewpoint—how computers can be used in the various school curriculum areas.

Computers can be used in any curriculum area, primarily as a teacher or tool. The following survey describes how computers can be used in each area of the curriculum, both in narrative and tabular form. This information will provide an overview that can serve as a basis for planning your school computer project.

Using Computers in Language Arts

In the language arts, computers are often used to teach reading, spelling, or grammar through drills and tutorials. Computerized spelling activities usually flash words on the screen to help students

Category	Description
Computer as Instructor	Drills and tutorials on reading comprehension, vocabulary development, spelling (flashing words or dictation with speech synthesizers)
Computer as Learning Environment	Vocabulary development games (hangman, guess the word), story generation and completion activities
Word Processing	Creative writing (students can write, revise, and edit their compositions on the computer), spelling and grammar (with spelling and grammar checkers)
Testing	Determining reading level of written material, testing students' reading comprehension levels, diagnosing specific skill deficiencies
Computer-Managed Instruction	Test students, give assignments, and store progress records, usually combined with drill or tutorial courseware package
Instructional Materials Generation	Vocabulary activities (crossword puzzles, hidden word games)

Figure 6-1. Using Computers in Language Arts

form a mental picture of the words. With the increasing availability of speech synthesizers, computers can dictate spelling words orally as well.

Educational games such as hangman or "guess my word" are used for vocabulary development. In addition, some exploratory games have been developed to encourage students to write. One game for young children presents an array of words from which to create sentences. The computer displays each sentence and "acts it out" with graphics on the screen.

In writing classes, teachers have found that access to word processors encourages students to write longer compositions, to revise their compositions, and to edit them more carefully. Recently, spelling and grammar checkers have become available for micro-computer word processors. These devices pinpoint possible errors in spelling or grammar, but the computer is not intelligent enough to be certain it has found a real error, or how to fix errors it has found. For this reason, these spelling and grammar checkers are excellent educational tools because they pinpoint problems, but leave the solution of these problems up to the student.

Several computer programs to determine reading levels of text material have been developed. These can be used to check the difficulty of commercial or teacher-prepared material before it is given to students, or to test the reading level of students' compositions. The latter can provide motivational feedback to students about the level of sophistication of their writing. Figure 6-1 lists categories and descriptions of ways to use computers in teaching Language Arts.

Using Computers in Mathematics

Mathematics was one of the first curriculum areas to benefit from computer-assisted instruction, and "computer as instructor" materials continue to be the most widely used software in this area. Many packages include drill-and-practice or tutorial courseware spanning a wide range of computational skills, combined with testing and record-keeping functions.

Many mathematically-oriented games are available for computers. In grid-search games, an imaginary creature (sometimes called a "Hurkle") hides on a cartesian coordinate grid. Students try to find it by guessing coordinates. In the process of playing the game, they learn about cartesian coordinates and signed numbers.

Logic games require students to solve problems through deductive reasoning. A student may have to break a code or discover a number by making guesses and receiving clues based on these guesses. Many of these games are computerized versions of similar non-computer games such as "Mastermind," "Wiff 'n Proof," or "Attribute Blocks."

Microworlds place on the computer an environment for students to explore. A microworld in probability, for example, would use a random number generator to simulate probabilistic experiments. Students might explore questions such as how many throws of a die it takes to get all six different numbers at least once. The

Category	Description
Computer as Instructor	Drills and tutorial materials on computations, applications, story problems, algebra, other content areas
Computer as Learning Environment	Search games to teach coordinate systems, signed numbers; logic and attribute games; microworlds to explore geometry, trigonometry, elementary functions, calculus, probability and statistics
Computer as Tool for Problem Solving	Performing complex calculations to make real-world applications accessible; using utility programs that solve equations, invert matrices, plot graphs, etc.
Computer as Learner (Programming)	Solving mathematical problems through student-written computer programs
Generation of Instructional Materials	Printing out worksheets with randomly-generated problems from teacher-chosen categories
Testing	Diagnosing specific skill deficiencies
Computer Managed Instruction	Tests students, gives assignments, and stores progress records; usually combined with drill or tutorial courseware packages

Figure 6-2. Using Computers in Mathematics

results of the microworld experiments can be compared to the predictions of probability. On computers with high resolution graphics, microworlds in geometry, trigonometry, and calculus allow visual exploration of concepts that often seem abstract and difficult.

The computer can be an important tool for mathematical problem solving because it eliminates difficult or tedious calculations that otherwise provide a formidable obstacle. If a computer is available, complex, real-world applications problems can be given in place of simplified textbook examples. In addition, the students are free to concentrate on the problem-solving process rather than on the calculations per se. If the students know how to program, they can use this skill in problem solving; if not, a problem-solving course can be one entry into programming for students who are mathematically inclined.

Computers can also generate worksheets with problems randomly selected from teacher-specified categories. This facility can save teachers many hours of tedious work. Figure 6-2 lists several uses of computers in teaching mathematics.

Using Computers in Science and Social Studies

In these two areas of the curriculum, there are four major uses of computers—as an instructor, as a learning environment, as a tool for problem solving, and as a tool for information retrieval.

In both science and social studies, the computer is used to provide instruction through tutorials and through drill-and-practice programs. Most often this mode of computer use is employed when there are bodies of information to assimilate, such as the names of the states and their capitals, the bones of the body, etc. Graphics are used frequently to label objects or to illustrate concepts in programs of this type.

Computer simulations provide an appropriate learning environment for many aspects of science and social studies. In social studies, for example, computers can simulate historical events such as presidential elections or events leading up to a world war. Students can make the same decisions faced by the historical figures in these events, and then see the consequences of these decisions on the computer screen. In this way, real world events can be brought into the classroom, time is compressed, and students gain access to experiences that can help them achieve a richer understanding of the events they are studying than would be possible without a computer.

In science, computer simulations can perform experiments that would be too costly or dangerous to present "live" in the classroom, or experience environmental effects too extensive in time and space to observe in reality. For example, students can experiment with a computer simulation of an atomic reactor on the verge of going out of control, with no danger to themselves. They can observe a simulated lake or forest ecosystem, experimenting with the effects of pesticides or elimination of predators.

Computers can be problem-solving tools in science and social studies by helping to analyze data from experiments. In some

Category	Description
Computer as Instructor	Drills and tutorials on the subject matter of the various sciences
Computer as Learning Environment	Simulations of scientific experiments or natural phenomena which could not otherwise occur in a classroom
Computer as Tool for Problem Solving	Data analysis for experiments— data entered by students or computer monitoring experimental apparatus directly
Computer as Tool for Information Retrieval	Searching through a data base (electronic information file) to find information or to test hypotheses

Figure 6-3. Using Computers in Science

Category	Description
Computer as Instructor	Drills and tutorial materials on subject matter in the various social sciences
Computer as Learning Environment	Simulations of historical events, geographical exploration, business operation, social conflict resolution, psychological experiments, etc.
Computer as Tool for Problem Solving	Data analysis of experiments in the social sciences; model building in economics
Computer as Tool for Information Retrieval	Searching through a data base (electronic information file) to find information or to test hypotheses

Figure 6-4. Using Computers in Social Studies

science lab experiments, the computer can be linked directly to the experimental apparatus to actually collect the data as well as analyze it.

Research in science and social studies often involves searching for information, either to formulate hypotheses about a phenomenon, or to test an hypothesis already formulated. If appropriate information is stored in a data base (an electronic filing system), computers can expedite such searches. Most data base systems make it possible to find or compare items of information simply by pressing a few keys. For this reason, computers make this type of research much faster, easier, and more enjoyable.

Figures 6-3 and 6-4 list various uses for computers in teaching science and social studies.

Using Computers in Other Curriculum Areas

As mentioned above, computers can be used in all areas of the curriculum. In fact, some of the most exciting new uses of computers are in areas other than the four discussed above.

In foreign language instruction, the development of speech synthesizers is starting to have an impact. Programs that pronounce words and provide sound discrimination exercises are beginning to appear, along with electronic bilingual dictionaries in written and oral formats.

Word processors can also be used to advantage by second-language writing students, particularly if spelling and grammar checkers are available for the language the students are studying. Working with computers also provides a useful context for student-student and student-teacher communication in a second language.

The enhanced graphics capability of many microcomputers is starting to have an impact on art instruction. Programs designed to let students create graphic art on the computer are starting to appear, as are graphic design utility programs for computer-assisted graphics on the screen, or in written form via a printer or plotter.

Now that video disks containing tens of thousands of pictures can be linked to microcomputers, information retrieval systems have been designed allowing instant access to large art slide collections. Computer graphics also make an excellent focus for computer programming courses for students who are artistically inclined.

Computers that have sound-generation units can be used to work with music notation and aspects of music theory in a drill/ tutorial format or using a learning environment approach. There is a great deal of interest among professional composers in computer-generated and computer-enhanced music, which is becoming widely available via music synthesizers attached to microcomputers.

In health-oriented curriculum areas, computers can be used for many of the tool functions served by home computers. For example, computers can determine quantities of ingredients needed to prepare specific recipes for a given number of people, and even print out appropriate shopping lists. They can analyze the nutritional content of meals, manage household budgets, compute taxes, and perform many other time-saving functions.

Physical education teachers can use computers to prepare physical fitness reports and to plan training regimen. Coaches can use computers to analyze scouting reports to find patterns in the strategies of opposing teams.

In business education, computers can be used to teach operation of business machines and various procedures in areas such as accounting and inventory. Simulations of actual businesses in operation are quite valuable in providing real-world experience without financial jeopardy, and are used extensively in college-level business courses.

In addition, computers can be used as tools in all the ways businesses use them—word processing, data base management, financial planning, accounting, inventory control and others. These computer applications will be discussed in more detail in Chapter 9, as they apply to school administration.

In industrial arts, computers can be used for training on a variety of shop procedures, as they have been in industry for the last several years. Schools offering comprehensive industrial arts programs are also starting to follow the lead of industry in using computer-aided design (CAD) and computer-aided manufacturing (CAM) processes.

Since computer-related jobs skills are in great demand (and expected to remain so for the foreseeable future), vocational education programs are providing training in computer operation and repair. Some schools have obtained the cooperation of a microcomputer manufacturer in setting up an actual factory-approved microcomputer repair facility in the high school vocational education program.

Finally, microcomputers are beginning to have a major impact on special education. For mentally retarded and emotionally disturbed students, computer assisted instruction in basic skills has proven quite beneficial. Programming in Logo has helped the cognitive development of many types of handicapped students. Physically handicapped students are benefiting from a variety of computer-driven devices, such as voice synthesizers, wheelchairs that respond to computer-monitored voice commands, and computers that can scan printed pages and read them aloud.

As computers become less expensive and more widely available, educators will find more and more ways to integrate them into the school curriculum. The possibilities are many, and we have just begun our exploration. Figure 6-5 lists computer applications for various curricular areas.

Category	Computer Uses
Foreign Languages (including English as a second language)	Drills and tutorials on vocabulary and grammar. Pronunciation and oral discrimination with a speech synthesizer. Word processing (with grammar and spelling checkers) to assist in second-language writing activities. Electronic bilingual dictionaries. Computer use to elicit conversation in the second language.
Art	Computer learning environments which allow students to explore screen graphics. Programming activities using screen graphics and graphics on printers and plotters. Graphic design utility (tool) programs. Video disk information retrieval systems for art slide collections.
Music	Drills and tutorials on musical terminology and notation (with a sound generation unit). Computer learning environments which allow students to explore computer-generated music. Music synthesizers as tools for composers and music students.
Health, Home Economics, Physical Education	Utility (tool) programs to determine recipe ingredient quantities and shopping lists,

	analyze nutritional content of meals, plan diets, manage household budgets, compute taxes, etc. Utility programs to analyze scouting reports, predict athletic success, plan training programs.
Business Education	Drills and tutorials on typing, operation of business machines, using business procedures. Simulations of actual business operations and procedures. Business applications software including word processors, data base management systems, electronic spreadsheets, accounting and inventory packages.
Industrial Arts	Tutorials for training on machine operation, various procedures. Utility (tool) programs to determine materials specifications. Computer-aided design and computer-aided manufacturing.
Vocational Education	Computer operation. Computer installation and repair.
Special Education	Drills and tutorials on basic skills. Programming in Logo. Computer-driven prosthetic devices for the physically handicapped. Utility (tool) programs to prepare Individual Education Plans (IEPs).

**Figure 6-5. Using Computers in Other
Curriculum Areas**

6.2 GUIDELINES FOR USING
COMPUTER-ASSISTED INSTRUCTION

The computer can have a place in any curriculum area, at almost any instructional level. Many schools use computers to individualize instruction so that they are better able to serve those with special educational needs. Other schools use computers for general instruction in specific curriculum areas. A few schools even use computers as their primary means of instruction.

Meeting Individual Educational Needs

Because a teacher's available time for instruction is limited, it is often difficult to provide instruction at levels optimal for all the students in each class. Teachers tend to teach to the average student, in which case those needing extra help struggle to keep up and those who learn most quickly and easily are often bored. Computers can help alleviate this problem by providing individualized instructional material for these students while the teacher is working with the other members of the class.

For students needing remedial work, the immediate feedback provided by computer-assisted instruction can help a great deal. All learners make mistakes, but those with learning difficulties often do not notice their mistakes, so they go on making them again and again. When this problem occurs, the students practice their mistakes, making matters worse instead of better. Through immediate feedback, computer-assisted instruction forces students to notice their mistakes, helping to prevent misunderstandings from persisting.

Computer-assisted instruction also helps learners focus their attention on the matters at hand. When the computer poses problems and provides immediate feedback, the learner-computer dialogue is highly interactive. This interactivity helps keep learners' attention focused on what they are doing. The attention-drawing power of a television screen seems to help as well. Studies have shown that learners who have difficulty concentrating spend more time on task when working with a computer than in a conventional classroom environment.

Finally, computer-assisted instruction can help motivate slow learners to work harder and longer. All of us respond to challenges that are difficult enough to require us to mobilize our inner resources, but not so difficult that we are defeated all the time. By tailoring the difficulty level of the problems to the abilities of each learner, the computer can insure that each learner will receive a challenge appropriate to motivate him or her.

Having a sense of one's own progress is also motivational, and the computer provides this through immediate feedback and score-keeping. Each student can compete with him- or herself to do better each time, without having to compete with others whose far superior resources leave little doubt about the outcome.

As long as computers remain a relatively scarce resource in education, simply using a computer is motivational in itself. Even though this factor will not last, it should not be overlooked as an initial reason for using computer-assisted instruction for remediation. In one New Jersey school, the children who left the classroom for special help had been stigmatized by their classmates. After the computers arrived, every child in the school wanted to go for special help, and the children who do so are now envied for their time with the computers.

Computer-assisted instruction for remediation usually consists of drill and practice programs, tutorial programs, or educational games in the "computer as instructor" mode. The following points may help you set up a successful remediation project:

1. Make sure that the students needing remedial help have regular, individual access to a computer.

2. For each student, carefully select software that focuses on what he or she needs to learn.

3. Monitor each student's progress and make sure that help is available when it is needed.

The computer as learning environment can also be used to solve learning problems. This topic will be considered in Chapter 8.

Computers can be used to provide enrichment activities for those who master the regular curriculum more quickly than the other students. Computer-assisted instruction can help these students move at their own pace and explore topics beyond those in the standard curriculum. Tutorials, simulations, and microworlds are the types of software best suited to this purpose.

When the computer is used for enrichment, bear in mind the following points:

1. Assign two or three students to a computer because the interaction among the students will enhance their educational experience.

2. Choose software that allows a great deal of user control, so that the students can move as quickly as they can and choose topics according to their interests.

Chapter 7 includes further discussion of computer applications which can be used for enrichment.

Computer Literacy
Through Computer-Based Instruction

For many schools, computer-assisted instruction represents one facet of a computer literacy project, the primary goal of which is to provide appropriate experiences with computers for all the students in the school. Computer-assisted instruction provides students with an opportunity to learn about computers while they are learning mathematics or social studies or art. The educational attributes of computers can be used to enhance the current curriculum and, at the same time, a great deal of computer literacy can be taught without displacing other subjects in the already-crowded school day.

If computer literacy is the primary goal of your school computer project, the procedures outlined in Section 6.6 will help you get started with computer-assisted instruction. That section also provides a more detailed discussion of computer literacy in the schools.

6.3 HOW TO SELECT SOFTWARE FOR YOUR SCHOOL MICROCOMPUTER PROJECT

Until recently, there was very little educational software available for microcomputers, and the quality of the available software was generally poor. This situation has been changing rapidly, however. As microcomputers become more and more widespread in American schools, many individuals, organizations, and educational media producers are developing microcomputer software at a rapid pace. Today, a great deal of educational software is available for microcomputers, and the variety and quality appear to be improving as well.

Even so, remember that educational use of microcomputers is still in its infancy. A time will surely come when we will consider as primitive even the most innovative and sophisticated software currently available. Keep in mind these three points about the current software scene:

1. Computer software is machine specific. In other words, a software disk or cassette for one brand of microcomputer will not work on any other brand. This situation is unlikely to change, although some software producers are making versions of their software for several different microcomputers and several minor manufacturers (mainly Japanese) have recently announced an agreement for a standard disk format.

2. Even though a great deal of microcomputer software is now available, it is not evenly distributed by brand of microcomputer, subject area, or type of software. This situation is also unlikely to change, because the most popular brands and subject areas attract most of the software development activity. As more software is produced, however, it is likely that at least some good quality software will be produced in areas where now none is available.

3. Despite a number of efforts to develop a single, objective mechanism for software evaluation, it appears that criteria for judging good software vary according to the type of software and the specific use to which it will be put.

In software selection, then, it is best to proceed slowly and carefully, focusing initially on those areas for which quality software is available. If it is crucial to your project to have good quality software available of specific subject matter and type, you may need to select software before you buy your computers. Software evaluation should be done with specific applications in mind, preferably by those who will be using the software. In general, software should not be purchased from catalogs, sight unseen.

Identifying Software to Evaluate

Depending on the brand of microcomputer, subject matter, and type of software you want, you will most likely have one of the following initial problems:

1. So much software is available that it is impossible to look at all of it.

2. So little software is available that it is difficult to find anything to look at.

In either case, your first job will be to identify software to evaluate. The following sources may help.

1. *Journals.* Almost all of the journals dealing with microcomputers carry software reviews that can help you identify good software. Advertisements and new product announcements can also help you keep abreast of what is available. You may want to subscribe to a few of these journals and keep a card file of promising software. Appendices A and B contain lists of journals.

2. *Software Directories.* Several directories of educational software have been published. Most cover one particular computer manufacturer, and are indexed by subject area and, in some cases, by type of software as well. A list of software directories can be found in Appendix E.

3. *Catalogs.* Hundreds of microcomputer software manufacturers and distributors produce catalogs of their wares. Every piece of software listed in these catalogs is purported to be wonderful, of course, so use these catalogs mainly to identify software that seems to fit your needs, but preview it before you buy. In Appendix G, we have listed a few software producers whose work is currently popular and/or promising in our judgment.

4. *Recommendations.* Colleagues who are using computers in their schools are an excellent source of software information. You may even be able to preview the software by seeing it "in action." Computer dealers can often provide recommendations as well, since it is to their advantage to keep well informed about promising software for the machines they sell. Many dealers also sell software, and some are now beginning to set up preview centers where educators can come to look over software before they buy.

5. *On-Line Data Banks.* At least two on-line data banks currently provide information about microcomputer software: Lockheed Dialog and BRS. The former provides an on-line version of a comprehensive software directory (useful for obtaining a list of what is currently available in specific software categories); the latter contains RICE, an evaluation data base set-up by MicroSift, a large-scale software evaluation project funded by the National Science Foundation.

6. *Local or Regional Microcomputer Centers.* These centers often have journals, directories, catalogs, and personnel who can pinpoint resources and make recommendations. Centers sometimes have demonstration software collections and on-line search capabilities as well.

7. *Public Domain Software Exchanges.* Some microcomputer centers have collected public domain (not copyrighted) software from various sources and made it available for copying. This free (or very

inexpensive) software varies widely in quality, but some of it can be quite useful and the price is certainly right.

If you already have computers, focus your search on programs that will run on them. Besides the brand of computer and type of mass storage available (disk, cassette, or cartridge), you may need to consider the amount of memory available, computer language and version available, and disk operating system.

Arranging to Preview Software

Once you have identified software that seems to fit your needs, the next step is to arrange a preview session. As mentioned above, colleagues, dealers with preview centers, and microcomputer centers with demonstration software collections are good contacts in this regard.

Most software producers and distributors will not send you software to preview because they are concerned about illicit copying. From the producers' point of view, illicit copies of their software deprive them of revenue, forcing them to charge higher prices for the legitimate software they sell. Unfortunately, higher prices make it more attractive for people to copy rather than buy, and we have a vicious circle.

Many software producers have responded to the copying problem by developing "copy protection" schemes for their disks and cassettes. These schemes make it difficult to copy their software without advanced technical skills. Unfortunately, copy protecting adds still more to software cost, and prevents legitimate purchasers from being able to make backup copies (in case the original disk or cassette is accidentally damaged) or to modify the programs for their own purposes.

Some software users have suggested that lowering prices and removing copy protection is the most sensible answer to the copying problem. To understand their reasoning, consider this question: "Why were you not tempted to photocopy this book instead of buying it?" Pragmatically speaking, photocopying is either more expensive or so close to the book price that the extra work of copying would not be worthwhile.

One additional cause of software copying among educators is the need for multiple copies in a school or school system. When disks cost $150 or $200 apiece, many school users are tempted to buy one disk and copy the others. Perhaps the solution to this problem is a multiple-use agreement providing additional copies of software at reduced prices.

In the long run, illicit copying of software hurts everyone, because it forces up the price of software and discourages further software development. High software prices, copy protection, and high prices for backup and multiple-use copies also contribute to the problem. Educators can help most by:

1. not engaging in illicit copying of software
2. buying from software producers who cooperate by charging reasonable prices, not copy protecting their software, and offering multiple-copy use agreements for schools and school districts

Some software producers will let you preview their materials. Others provide demonstration diskettes or cassettes with selections from their materials. Others will arrange preview sessions through one of their marketing representatives or through a distributor. Some software distributors now offer a return policy—usually 10 to 30 days during which you can return for a refund or credit software that proved inadequate for your needs.

Do not buy software sight unseen unless there is a return policy. Look for producers and distributors who will let you preview software or return purchased software that does not meet your needs. If enough of us insist on these conditions as a prerequisite for our business, we can encourage software producers or distributors to adopt policies that will benefit both seller and buyer in the long run.

Evaluating Software

Once you have identified a piece of software you would like to preview, the following steps will help you determine if it will suit your needs.

Step 1

Look over the documentation (printed material) that comes with the program.

a. Check to make sure the software will run on your computer.
b. Find out the intentions of the software producer:
   What are the educational objectives?
   Who is the software intended to serve?
   What physical arrangements are suggested?
c. Find out how to operate the software.

The documentation should tell you what hardware is required to run the program. If the program is furnished on a disk or cassette, there will be a minimum memory requirement. A specific computer language, disk operating system, or peripherals may be needed as well.

Once you know your computer will run the software, look for a statement of objectives to use as a standard against which to judge the program. Evaluating against objectives will help insure that you are looking at software on its own terms rather than imposing your own preferences or biases on it.

Suppose, for example, that you are evaluating a program designed to teach touch typing skills. This particular program has an arcade game format, in which the user shoots down enemy rockets by typing letters or combinations of letters on the screen. The arcade game is so much fun that one might be tempted to evaluate the program highly. On the other hand, if one is opposed to arcade games, one might evaluate the program negatively for this reason. Nevertheless, both reviews would be missing the essential question—Does the program teach typing?

Actually, two questions must be asked about the objectives of any piece of software:

1. Does the software meet its objectives?

2. Are the educational objectives of the software worthwhile?

The answers to both questions involve judgments, but the second is especially dependent upon the circumstances in which the software will be used. When teachers are previewing software, they should evaluate the educational objectives in terms of their own students, and the suitability of the intended audience and physical arrangements in terms of their own teaching situations.

When software is being evaluated for a whole school or school district, however, these judgments become problematic. In this case, measure the stated objectives of the software against the school or district curriculum, and look for maximum flexibility in terms of software content, audience, and necessary physical arrangements.

If the objectives of the software pass inspection, read over the operating instructions. For many programs, these instructions will be quite simple, and it may even be possible to operate the program without reading them. For complex programs like word processors or computer-managed instruction packages, the operating instructions will be essential. In some cases, the instructions will be in the form of a tutorial, step-by-step printed instructions that you read as you begin working with the computer program.

Step 2

Run the program to get an overview. Note general strengths and weaknesses of the program, and features that you would like to explore further.

While you are working with the program, keep in mind the following three general questions:

1. *Is the software effective?* This question is impossible to answer definitively without actually trying out the software. When you are previewing, look at whether the software seems suitable for its intended purposes and whether it follows good educational practices.

2. *Does it make good use of the computer?* Computers make possible interactive learning through a dialogue between the student and the computer. Look at the quality of this dialogue, including the amount of interactivity and student control over the program, and the nature of the feedback the student receives from the computer. Also consider whether this program is doing something with the computer that is difficult to do without the computer (or cannot be done as well).

3. *Is it easy to use?* Consider whether the students will be able to understand and follow the directions, and interact with the computer successfully. How much guidance will students need from the teacher? Can the teacher change the program or the subject matter in the program? Does the program load into the computer and run without any problems?

Step 3

Run through the program again from each of the following perspectives:

a. responding as a typical student might respond
b. making as many mistakes as possible, pressing inappropriate keys, generally trying to disrupt the normal execution of the program
c. thoroughly exploring the content, following up on the features noted in Step 2

The first run-through will help you estimate the effectiveness of the software and the ease of use from a student's point of view. The second provides a useful approach for testing the reliability of the program. The third should be a complete inspection that may take more than one run-through. This time, check to see if all the content is correct, including spelling and grammar, if the sequence of activities is appropriate, if the presentation is pedagogically sound, etc.

If it is possible to observe some students working with the program, this observation will add another dimension to your preview.

Even though the three general questions listed above will serve for any software evaluation, each type of educational software should be examined on its own terms. For example, the feedback in a drill-and-practice program tells whether the student's answer is correct and provides some reinforcement. Feedback in a simulation, on the other hand, produces a consequence to an option that the student selected. One would not expect the computer to judge answers right or wrong in a simulation, but one would expect feedback to provide further information to help students understand the simulation model.

The software evaluation process involves many judgments, so differences of opinion can be expected. If a teacher is evaluating software for classroom use, the judgments can be made with particular students and particular circumstances in mind. If software is being evaluated for school or district purchase, however, it may help to have two or three people review it together and discuss their findings. In this manner, the differences of perspective found in any group can be used to help choose the most generally useful software.

6.4 TWO EXAMPLES OF USING COMPUTERS TO STIMULATE INSTRUCTIONAL INNOVATION

In this section, we will briefly describe two innovative approaches to computer-based instruction. The first is Logo, a computer language that is becoming well known in educational computing circles as a powerful way to introduce children to programming. The second is a lesser-known courseware package called Visible and Tangible Math, which takes a unique approach to mathematics instruction, in some ways bridging the gap between the computer as instructor and the computer as learning environment.

Logo

Logo began in 1966 as a deliberate attempt to invent a computer language that would be accessible even to very young children, yet sophisticated enough to handle complex programming problems.

Seymour Papert, the MIT professor who is the primary author of Logo, often describes this goal as, "no threshold and no ceiling." Through years of testing and refinement, Logo has become a philosophy of education through computers as well as a programming language. Perhaps the best introduction to this philosophy is Papert's book, *Mindstorms* (New York: Basic Books, 1980).

The most famous feature of Logo is the turtle, a small triangular shape that "lives" on the video display screens of computers running this language. This totally electronic turtle is actually the descendent of a mechanical robot model that first appeared in 1970, attached by wires to a time-sharing terminal in Cambridge, Massachusetts. In either form, the turtle can move forward or back, turn left or right any number of degrees, and trace its path as it goes, either on the display screen or on paper placed under the mechanical turtle on the floor.

Part of the Logo language consists of turtle commands, words and expressions that can be typed into the computer to make the turtle move and draw. Children and adults alike find "turtle graphics" inviting, because it enables them to create strikingly intriguing and beautiful graphics on the computer screen after only a short acquaintance with the language.

Programming in Logo means teaching the computer new words out of the words it already knows. For example, we can teach Logo the word SQUARE as follows:

```
TO SQUARE
REPEAT 4 [FORWARD 50 RIGHT 90]
END
```

Once these lines have been entered into the computer, it knows how to SQUARE—go FORWARD 50 turtle steps, turn RIGHT 90 degrees, and REPEAT this process 4 times (see Figure 6-6).

The lists of instructions created in teaching Logo new words are called *procedures*. Once a procedure has been created, the word defined by that procedure can be used just as any other Logo words, often to create new procedures. Complex procedures are created by using simpler procedures as building blocks or modules (see Figure 6-7).

Computer scientists generally believe that modular programming using procedures is the most efficient approach, and the one that should be taught to student programmers. Logo proponents feel strongly that this language encourages an understanding of programming that will provide an excellent foundation for any further work in computer programming.

The turtle graphics in Logo creates a "microworld," in which children can explore interesting questions in geometry. For exam-

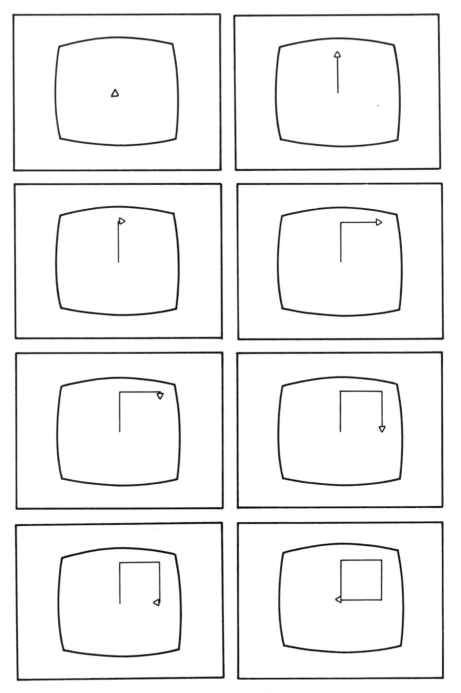

**Figure 6-6. The Logo Turtle Executing the
Procedure SQUARE**

ple, we can define a procedure called POLY that makes the turtle repeat indefinitely a set of two commands: first, move forward a certain distance and then turn a certain angle. If we say POLY 90, meaning that the turtle will turn 90 degrees to the right after each forward motion, the turtle will trace out a square. But suppose we substitute a different angle for 90? How many degrees must the turtle turn to trace out a triangle? a hexagon?

By exploring the POLY procedure, children can gain insights into the geometry of polygons. Similarly, many other turtle procedures can provide insights into geometrical topics—from those appropriate for young children to differential geometry and other college-level topics. See *Turtle Geometry* by Harold Abelson and Andy DiSessa (Cambridge, Mass: MIT Press, 1981) for further details.

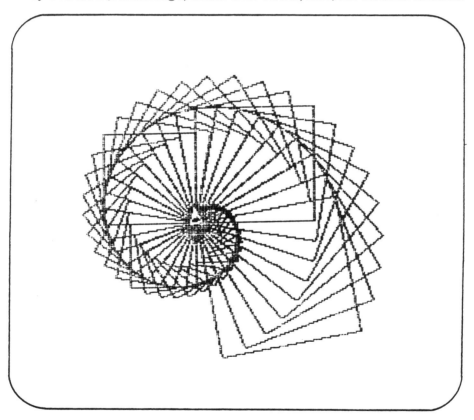

Figure 6-7. A Logo Procedure Called
SPINSQUARE

Many Logo microworlds can be created for children to explore many different subject areas. In fact, Papert believes that microworlds make possible a new freedom in the learning process that can help children work in the ways they find most natural.

Papert's work with Logo and microworlds raises two important issues for education:

1. As a computer language, Logo claims to provide children with a natural introduction to sophisticated programming concepts. Does Logo really make a difference in how quickly and well children learn the fundamentals of programming?

2. The concept of a microworld provides a new model for how the computer can serve education—by providing appropriate learning environments for children's self-education. Can this vision become a reality? What will be the role of teachers in this approach?

The definitive answers to these questions still remain to be found, though there is reason for optimism in the research conducted at MIT and the recent experience of teachers using Logo in schools. Efforts are now underway to conduct more systematic research on how Logo affects children's thinking, including plans for a school based on microworlds.

Teachers using Logo for the first time are usually surprised by the overwhelming, universal enthusiasm it inspires in children, and the care and sophistication with which they work. Teachers usually find an entry into a new way of teaching as well. Since the students interact mainly with the computer, teachers are free to observe more. When they do, they usually find that their students are much more capable and resourceful than they had imagined. They see that their observations can help them know precisely what to do for the students, and when it is best to leave the students to their own devices. Many teachers find that the approach they develop in working with Logo can carry over into other aspects of their teaching with good results.

These positive results come at a price, however. To use Logo effectively, teachers must be willing to spend the time and effort to learn to use Logo themselves, and to rethink some of their teaching strategies in light of what is happening to them and their students. Fortunately, most teachers find Logo almost addictive, and are convinced by their own learning experiences to re-examine their teaching practices.

As Logo becomes more popular, many turtle graphics programs are appearing on the market. Most do not have the same structure as Logo, however. If this structure is an essential part of learning what Logo has to offer, these programs will not do as well. If the turtle geometry microworld is most important, on the other hand, non-Logo turtle graphics languages will serve as well as the "real thing."

Based on the evidence now available, we would use a full implementation of Logo whenever possible. If you already have computers for which Logo is not available, however, another language featuring turtle graphics may provide a similar addition to your school computer project.

Visible and Tangible Math

Visible and Tangible Math is a somewhat different approach to using the computer as a learning environment. In this approach, a series of learning environments is presented, each one structured to focus on particular insights in elementary mathematics. In some ways, the series has the form of a tutorial with the spirit of an exploratory learning environment.

The content of Visible and Tangible Math is beginning arithmetic, from numeration through addition and subtraction. The materials consist of ten disks that run on the Apple II, Apple II Plus, and Apple IIe microcomputers. Each disk contains several modules that can be selected independently from a menu program. Each module starts with an exploratory activity and concludes with a test, with automatic branching to the next module on completion.

Since the series was designed primarily for young children, no reading or typing expertise is assumed. Children can interact with the computer via a light pen or joystick, and all instructions are given orally by means of a speech synthesizer.

To understand how Visible and Tangible Math works, let's briefly consider one of its topics—subtraction. Stop reading for a moment and do the following subtraction:

453 − 199 =

How did you find the answer? Surprisingly, the easiest way is not to do the problem given above, but rather to transform it into an easier problem. If you noticed that 199 is almost 200, then you can say, 453 − 200 = 253, so 453 − 199 must be one more, or 254. Alternatively, we can transform the given problem into an equivalent one by adding one to both the minuend and the subtrahend:

$$\begin{array}{r} 453 \\ -199 \end{array} \quad \begin{array}{r} +1 \\ +1 \end{array} \longrightarrow \begin{array}{r} 454 \\ -200 \end{array}$$

In much the same way, almost any subtraction problem can be made easier through transformations.

Figure 6-8 shows a sample screen from Disk 9 of Visible and Tangible Math. Down the right side of the screen is a menu—the

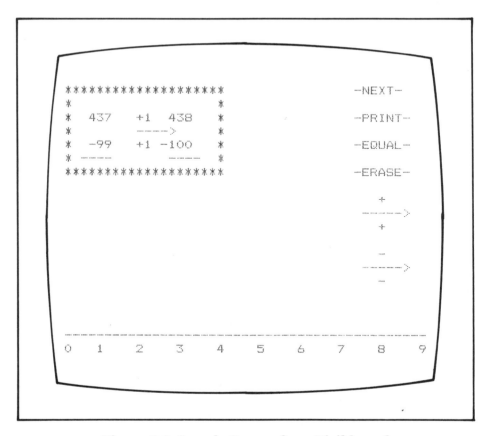

**Figure 6-8. Sample Screen from Visible and
Tangible Math**

equivalent of a set of keys that can be "pressed" with the light pen.
Similarly, the row of digits at the bottom of the screen functions as a
set of numeric keys. The box at the top of the screen is a
"scratchpad," where material can be placed and examined before
being entered permanently.

This setup allows students to explore transformations in subtraction in the following manner. The computer poses a problem,
either at random or from specified categories. Students can transform the problem by pressing one of the menu items marked with
transformation arrows, and then entering numerals to tell the
computer how much to add to or subtract from the minuend and
subtrahend of the original problem. When the PRINT key is
touched, the computer transforms the subtraction. The students can
use the transformation keys to change the given subtraction into any

number of equivalent ones. When the problem has been changed into an easy one, the answer can be entered with the EQUAL key.

In this way, a learning environment for exploring equivalent subtractions is created on the screen. This environment has been defined in such a way to focus on a particular insight in mathematics—using transformations to solve subtractions. Within this environment, there is a carefully determined sequence of activities designed to make what there is to learn striking to the learner. First, the computer suggests fruitful transformations and does much of the computational work; later, these jobs are transferred to the students, to make them independent of the computer.

In Visible and Tangible Math, the computer always responds to student input without comment. If the input is acceptable, the computer goes on with the next activity; if not, it simply waits for another input. This procedure is very different from the error correction, branching, and score-keeping functions usually found in tutorial programs. Not responding to errors preserves the nonjudgmental character of the computer, creating an environment that continually throws students back on their own resources.

How, then, will students find help when they need it? In this approach, the learning environments must be designed well enough to be self-supporting. That is, each environment must contain all the information necessary for children to master it.

How does the program insure that students master one activity before proceeding to the next? Because the computer ignores incorrect responses, the students must respond correctly to each challenge put to them before going on. There is no possibility of doing ten problems, getting three correct and seven wrong. When ten problems are finished, ten must be correctly done. Although it is sometimes possible to keep on guessing until the correct answers have been produced, children only do this if they are not intrigued with the activity and see no hope of figuring it out. By carefully designing the computer learning environments to provide the proper support, these possibilities have been minimized.

Visible and Tangible Math is based on the pioneering educational work of Caleb Gattegno, and represents a computer adaptation of his general educational approach, which he calls the subordination of teaching to learning. The courseware was developed and classroom-tested under the auspices of the National Science Foundation, but is not yet widespread in use. We believe that the underlying approach shows great promise, however, and hope to see both wider distribution of this courseware and development of other materials in the same spirit.

Further information about the computer programs and the general approach can be obtained from Educational Solutions, Inc., 95 University Place, New York, NY 10003.

6.5 TEACHING COMPUTER PROGRAMMING: WHICH LANGUAGE IS BEST?

Beginning programmers are often surprised to find that there are scores of computer languages, with more being invented all the time. It is very unlikely that any one language will supplant all the others because, like natural languages, each computer language has its own unique features that make it relatively easy to solve some kinds of problems and more difficult to solve others.

As we have gained experience in using computers for a variety of purposes, our understanding of the activity of programming has evolved. Modern programming practices are much more efficient and effective than those used with the first programming languages during the 1950s. The most important breakthrough in programming technique is generally known as structured programming.

Structured Programming

To understand structured programming, let's start with an analogy. Suppose you have to write an extensive report, say 30 or 40 pages in length. You could simply sit down at the typewriter (or word processor) and start writing, but you would be much more likely to create a concise, clearly-written report if you did some planning first—creating an outline to break the report into sections that could then be more easily written one at a time and assembled into the final report. On the other hand, if you are writing a note—say, two or three sentences—you would not be at all likely to find an outline helpful.

Roughly speaking, structured programming is like writing an outline before writing the program. In structured programming, you start with a statement of your overall goal or purpose, and then break down this goal into subgoals, continuing this process until the subgoals are small enough to be easily programmable. Each section in this outline becomes a module of the program, which is written in such a way to make the structure as clear as possible for whoever might happen to read it.

For relatively long, complex programming projects, structured programming has been shown to save a substantial amount of time and effort, and to facilitate a team approach. Business now uses structured programming almost exclusively, and computer scientists agree that structured programming concepts are fundamental for student programmers.

Although it is possible to program in a structured way using any computer language, some languages facilitate this process and others make it relatively difficult. For this reason, some educators advocate teaching only languages that facilitate structured programming; others minimize the importance of the choice of language. At this point, we will take a brief survey of the languages most often used for teaching programming, and then return to the language choice issue.

Educational Computer Languages

The first computer language to gain widespread use is called FORTRAN. This language is used mainly for scientific applications that were programmed in FORTRAN long ago and never substantially changed. Some schools with older, large computer equipment still teach FORTRAN, but interest in this language is declining. FORTRAN makes structured programming (and many other aspects of programming as well) relatively difficult.

BASIC is currently the most widely-used programming language in education and in the world of personal computers. It is also the language most widely available because it is suppled in the ROM memory of most microcomputers. BASIC is a relatively easy language to learn, but it is unstructured, and therefore relatively cumbersome to use for large or complex programming projects.

Pascal is the language most in favor among computer scientists and educators at the college and graduate school levels. Its organization is highly structured, very precise, and elegant. For this reason, it is useful to give student programmers experience with the fundamental principles of programming. Since Pascal is the language used on the College Board Advanced Placement Examination starting in 1984, it will certainly be offered by an increasing number of high schools.

Various versions of Pascal are available for most microcomputers, but complete implementations are just now beginning to be widespread. Any complete version of Pascal will need 48K to 64K of memory. Microcomputers with high resolution graphics generally will implement UCSD Pascal, a complete version with enhancements, including turtle graphics.

Logo is a structured language designed to be both easy for beginners to learn, yet sophisticated enough for experienced programmers. It has been described in more detail in Section 6.4. Logo will soon be available on most microcomputers that support high resolution graphics and sufficient memory expansion (48K to 64K).

PILOT is a very simple computer language, initially designed to make it easy for teachers to develop CAI materials. Recently, PILOT has also been used as a first programming language for children, most notably by Atari® PILOT, which also includes turtle graphics. The various versions of PILOT are quite different from each other; at present, only the Atari® version has been primarily designed for children, although many of the turtle graphics languages now available are very similar to PILOT in structure. PILOT's structure is somewhat similar to that of BASIC, and is just as cumbersome for relatively long, complex programming projects.

Choosing a Computer Language

The vast majority of programming courses for students up through high school are now given in BASIC. Most people who have learned BASIC have not learned it in a structured way; as a result, they have bad programming habits and often find it difficult to transfer to structured-programming environments. This negative experience with BASIC is what motivates some educators to advocate eliminating it from the curriculum.

It is possible, however, to teach BASIC in a structured way. If this is done, transferring from BASIC to Pascal or other structured languages is straightforward. We believe that the case against BASIC has been overstated, but it is very important to teach BASIC in a structured way, if it is taught at all. If those who will be teaching programming are relatively inexperienced, it is unlikely that this will happen. For this reason, particularly at the elementary school level, Logo should be strongly considered.

6.6 DEVELOPING A MASTER PLAN FOR COMPUTER LITERACY

Computer literacy has become a catchall term, used to describe many different approaches to computer education. For this reason, it is very easy to agree that we want to teach computer literacy in our schools, but somewhat more difficult to decide just what computer literacy is and how best to bring it about.

Some people distinguish between computer awareness and computer literacy. In this viewpoint, computer awareness refers to knowledge about computers and their impact on society, whereas literacy refers to computer-related skills. Most people seem to include both of these components under the general label "computer literacy," however, and we will also follow this practice.

Not everyone has jumped on the computer literacy bandwagon. The question has been asked: Instead of making people computer literate, why not make computers people literate? This question is not entirely facetious. Strides have been made towards making computers more able to interact with people in "human" terms, and the computers of the future will be undoubtedly much more "user friendly" than those now in existence. Computer literacy must prepare people for the computers of the future even more than for those of today.

There is good reason to believe that computers will become easier and easier to use. Most new technologies are especially difficult at first, both because of general public unfamiliarity with them and because the technology is in a primitive state. The first automobile owners, for example, had to develop many forms of expertise (like cranking engines) not required of modern-day motorists. Even though we may not be able to entirely avoid teaching some material that will become obsolete, we will be most likely to prepare students to meet the computers of the future if we emphasize skills and understanding rather than knowledge.

Programming is often included in computer literacy courses, and some educators even equate programming with computer literacy. One argument for teaching programming is that those who know how to program have the most control over the computer—they are most able to make the computer do what they want it to do. On the other hand, many uses of computers do not require programming experience, and as computers become more and more "people literate," fewer and fewer people will need to know how to program. Maybe programming should be considered a specialized vocational skill for computer scientists only.

If we consider programming as a process rather than a product, its educational value is much more general. The process of programming requires students to use and develop a whole range of cognitive skills that will be useful to them no matter what they do in life. These skills, which fall under the general label of "procedural thinking," definitely belong in every computer literacy project.

Components of a Computer Literacy Curriculum

The following five components of computer literacy can be identified:

1. Basic Concepts—what computers are and how they work
2. Applications—how computers are used in business, industry, government, and other areas
3. Computers and Society—the impact of computers on society, and ethical issues such as invasion of privacy through computer records
4. Operation—using computers for a variety of purposes
5. Programming—teaching the computer to do what you want it to do.

Those who differentiate computer awareness from computer literacy would consider items 1 through 3 in the first category, and items 4 and 5 in the second.

Teaching Computer Literacy

There have been two main approaches to teaching computer literacy in the schools: creating a special computer literacy course, or integrating computer literacy into the existing curriculum. The main reason for creating a special course is to minimize staffing and equipment needs. One computer specialist, working out of a single computer lab, may be able to serve a whole school.

There are some important disadvantages to the special course approach, however. Foremost is the need to find additional time in the already crowded curriculum for yet another course of study. Moreover, many aspects of computer literacy fit in very well with the existing curriculum, so that the special course may fragment knowledge and repeat content much more than an integrated approach.

For these reasons, we believe that an integrated approach is best for teaching the first four computer literacy components outlined above. Programming, on the other hand, does not fit neatly into the existing curriculum, and should probably be handled separately.

Integrating Computers into the Curriculum

If you are planning to use the computer as a teacher and tool in your school, you can accomplish most of the computer literacy objectives listed above quite easily. When students use microcomputer software to help them learn mathematics, for example, they will certainly learn how to operate the computer, and something about what computers are and how they work as well. If you use the computer as a tool—word processing or data base searching, for example—the students will be able to understand how these same tools are used in the world of work. Discussing the impact of microcomputers on the classroom and the school can also provide a basis for discussion of their impact on society as a whole.

The following procedures may help you formulate your school computer literacy master plan:

1. Form a committee including people responsible for curriculum as well as people responsible for computer education.

2. Identify areas of the curriculum that can be taught using computers and revise it accordingly; try to find at least one curriculum unit that can be "computerized" at each grade level and in each subject area.

3. Identify places in the curriculum where basic computer concepts and the impact of computers on society can be discussed.

4. Plan how to introduce these changes gradually, taking into account needs for in-service staff development and availability of equipment.

Bear in mind that each aspect of computer literacy need not be taught at every grade level. There is no need to develop an elaborate scope and sequence chart breaking down every computer literacy component into thirteen parts, one for each grade level from kindergarten through high school. In fact, this fragmented, knowledge-oriented approach is far less likely to prepare students for the unknown future than the one outlined above.

Procedural thinking is one aspect of computer literacy that should be included even though it is interdisciplinary in nature. If computers are available, procedural thinking can be part of a programming course. If not, computer-independent activities and computer toys such as Big Trak can be substituted. An excellent reference on this topic is *My Students Use Computers: A Guide for Computer Literacy in the K-8 Curriculum* (Reston, VA: Reston Books, 1983).

7 | A Closer Look at Unique Instructional Applications

Having computers in a school opens avenues of study and exploration that can significantly enhance the education of students in areas that transcend traditional academic pursuits. From art for the visually talented to improved communication with the visually impaired, from the development of sophisticated computer programs by five-year-olds to the simulated experience of operating a complex nuclear plant, the computer can provide students with unique learning opportunities that would simply not exist otherwise. This chapter will introduce you to an array of tantalizing possibilities, each of which is already an actuality in a number of schools across the country.

7.1 TWO WAYS COMPUTERS HELP IMPROVE THINKING PROCESSES

We engage in many activities that force us to think through problems carefully and devise solutions that require a disciplined use of our mental resources. Most board games, including chess or checkers, Monopoly or Scrabble go far beyond the element of chance, and decidedly tax the thinking processes of the persons playing, some to a greater extent and others to a lesser extent. Even old favorites like hangman or anagrams present challenges that in many cases are best met through careful planning and a disciplined carrying through of strategy. Alert and creative teachers have always found ways to translate experiences of students engaged in such activities into more generalized approaches to dealing with a wide range of questions and problems that need to be faced both in and out of school. Computers are the perfect ally of educators who consider such overall improvement of thinking processes to be part of their mission.

There are two uses to which you can immediately put computers in your school that will directly benefit your students' capacity to analyze and synthesize components of puzzling situations, and thereby strengthen those skills that separate people from all the other creatures who cohabit our planet.

Computer Programming

To program a computer is to teach it to do something you want it to do. The word "teach" is used here in a very broad sense; a computer cannot actually learn anything in the same way that people learn. This limitation of the equipment is the very quality that makes programming the computer an activity so rich in opportunities to improve one's thinking processes.

As pointed out in Chapter 1, a computer is strictly literal in its interpretation of input. The simple fact that it is restricted by design to reduce and process all information in the form of "open" or "closed" electronic "gates" leaves it incapable of deciding more than whether a minute pulse of energy is or is not passing through one of its circuits. Of course, it can make such decisions at a speed which is, for most practical purposes, nearly instantaneous and it can make large numbers of them simultaneously. But the fact remains that it is pitifully simple-minded. How, then, can it be so remarkably flexible and powerful in its applications?

Computers derive their power directly from the power of the minds of the people who program them. Since computers are essentially so limited, it takes both discipline and creativity to transform them into useful instruments. The process of translating a specific idea about how a computer can be used into a specific code (that is, a computer "language") that the computer can actually execute to make it perform according to that original idea is one that places a number of educationally beneficial demands on the programmer:

1. She must clarify with great precision what her idea really is. A vague intuition or thought about how the computer could be used for something is only a starting point. The notion must be honed into an exact scenario of how the machine will perform.

2. She must reduce what is in her mind as precise mental images into a series of steps, often interrelated in a complex fashion and following a definite sequence.

3. She must select from a highly restricted "vocabulary" those words that are part of the computer language she is using. Even the highest-level and easiest-to-use computer languages are extremely

limited in the number of words they make available to the programmer. The more educationally useful languages pay heed to this fact by allowing the programmer to, in essence, create her own words that are then added to the vocabulary of the language. In such cases, the absolute dependence of the computer on the power of the mind of the programmer is crystal clear. In any event, the limited vocabulary available in any particular computer language must suffice the programmer in her efforts to translate the precise steps derived from her original idea into code to which the computer can respond. That translation is a distinctly demanding and creative process. Every step is a puzzle whose secret is unlocked only if the programmer recognizes that it is similar to another puzzle previously tackled or else reaches an insight into a certain internal logic of the situation that is compatible with the limitations of the machine with which she is working.

4. The code that results is almost never free of error. The programmer must "debug" the program, that is, remove the errors in the code she has written. While a number of procedures are available to programmers to help them track down their errors, the process is often unavoidably frustrating, at least to some extent. Two things become critical: disciplined searching and the capacity to free oneself from a mind set into which one has become locked.

The four steps outlined above clearly involve the programmer in uses of her mind that will enhance her thinking processes. The act of programming forces one more deliberately:

- to examine through careful analysis the contents of one's mind
- to chisel an idea into a detailed plan
- to transform specific procedures that exist in one's mind into logical operations which interrelate in a very restricted number of ways
- to translate the operations and relationships among the various steps into a very restricted code that is terribly intolerant of errors
- to make oneself focus one's attention with great intensity in order to uncover one's mistakes
- to "step aside" within one's mind in order to view a problem one has been working on, perhaps for a long time, from a different angle and to come up with a fresh approach even though it may not be at all obvious or even comfortable at first

Such mental gymnastics assure that involving students in computer programming will provide them with enormous opportunities to improve in how they use their mental resources.

Logic/Reasoning Games

Games that tap and stretch our capacities to solve problems through careful reasoning and the application of logic have existed from antiquity. With the computer come renewed and expanded opportunities to engage people in internal dialogues that lead to more refined and conscious uses of those skills. There currently exists a large number of commercially available computer programs that involve the user in games which can improve his thinking processes.

One example of a game that enhances logic and reasoning skills is called "Psycho-Logic." To play up to a very advanced level, one needs only to understand how a letter can represent a variable so that simple equations such as $A + 2 = 5$, can be solved. For anyone who knows how to solve such equations, "Psycho-Logic" becomes an exciting arena for testing and strengthening reasoning skills. The game, at a relatively simple skill level, is played as follows:

Nine groups of .'s and *'s appear on the screen.
For example,

```
. . *           * . *           * . .

***             . . *           . . *

. * .           . . .           . . *
```

Each group has a value which simply equals the number of *'s in the group; for example, the value of the group at the upper left is 1, whereas the value of the group in the middle column on the bottom row is equal to zero.

The computer has selected a formula, say $A + B$, from several possibilities for the skill level, that is, $A + B$, $A - B$ or $A + B + C$. The computer has also selected one of the nine positions of the group and named it "A," a second of the nine positions and named it "B," and a third out of the nine positions of the groups and named it "C." The player of the game does not know which group position has been assigned which letter, nor does he know which of the three possible formulas has been selected. Both of these unknowns must be deduced in as few guesses as possible, given only the solution to the equation, which changes as the game progresses and the value of each group keeps changing. To illustrate, look back at the groupings shown above and imagine that the computer has assigned letter names to the positions as follows:

(B)   * . *   * . .

***   . . *   . . *

. * .   (A)   (C)

What the computer would do is to display the groupings,

. . *   * . *   * . .

***   . . *   . . *

. * .   . . .   . . *

along with the statement, "The answer is 1." At this point, the only useful deduction the game player can reach is that the formula being used cannot be $A + B + C$, since the minimal sum possible of any combination of any three groups must be two. If the formula the computer has selected happens to be $A - B$ and if the computer has assigned the middle group on the left (***) the letter name, "A," then the middle group on the top (*.*) must be "B." However, if the computer has assigned the letter name "B" to the middle group on the bottom, then "A" could be assigned to any of the six groups that have a value of 1. And what if the formula preselected by the computer is $A + B$? Then what possibilities are there for assigning "A" and "B" to the various groups? Obviously there are many. The game player must make a guess out of the many good possibilities at this beginning point in the game and test his hypothesis on the next display of groupings that appears on the screen. That display might be:

. **   . . .   . * .

* . *   . * .   . . .

. . *   ***   * . .

Accompanying the display would be the question, "What is the answer?" Now, the game player cannot offer an answer without having made assumptions as to which equation is being used and which group locations have been assigned which letter names. For the sake of argument, let's say the game player has assumed that the equation is A + B and that the lower left group is "A" and the lower middle group is "B." Such an assumption is compatible with the evidence from the first display. Operating on that assumption, the game player simply adds the values of the groups in the second display which hold the assumed "A" and "B" positions. He responds to "What is the answer?" by typing in the number 4. Lo and behold, the computer responds with the statement, "No, the answer is 5." Immediately after this admonition, the computer kindly presents a third display and again patiently awaits the player's guess to the answer for the equation it has preselected. (If you don't remember, it was A + B.) Okay, now what?

Well, looking back at the first two displays, which fortunately remain on the screen, the solution becomes obvious. If the third display looks like this:

```
 . . .              ** .            . . *

*   *              ***             **  .
  .                                   .

  . *  .            . . .             . **
```

then the answer for the third display must be 0!

When the player is correct, a new display is given and another answer is required until six correct responses are given in a row. That way, the computer can be sure that the player has not just made one, two or three lucky guesses. To make six right answers in a row for six separate and differing displays really requires that the player has correctly deduced both the formula that has been pre-selected as well as the assignment of the letter names.

Many, many games like "Psycho-Logic" are available, most of them less complicated, but any of which, if worth their salt, similarly tax the mental prowess of the player.

7.2 HOW TO VASTLY EXTEND LEARNING OPPORTUNITIES THROUGH SIMULATIONS

Imagine the sensational possibilities for learning that would be made available through a machine that could instantly transport students through time and space, leaving them anywhere in the known universe and at any point in history. Dream further that even though they would be actively participating in the events of the time and place in which they found themselves, they would be incapable of actually adversely affecting the events or of being harmed themselves. The educational applications would be endless and astounding:

- An eighth-grade class in American History could sit with General Grant in his tent and plan strategies. They could spend the day with the troops in the trenches, sharing first hand their hunger, fear, and commitment.

- A high school class in Consumer Economics could become part of the executive committee of a corporation. They would make choices about how best to allocate company resources in order to increase sales and overall profit.

- Members of a fourth-grade class working on a unit in Social Studies could assume the role of a health official in a large city who must come up with a plan to eliminate or at least control the growing danger of rat infestation in certain corners of the metropolis.

- Second graders could directly observe, study and evaluate the effects of various approaches to caring for the health and welfare of a giant python.

The list could go on indefinitely, but there are two problems: first, we are indulging in unabashed fantasy and second, the variables in such situations are liable to be so numerous and complexly interrelated that they would unproductively confuse and confound the students.

Computer programs that simulate such educationally relevant experiences solve both problems: they exist and are commercially available to schools; also, they incorporate only a selected number of the variables that are part of the real life situation being simulated. The latter point is occasionally used as a criticism of computer simulations, that is, the situations are simplified to the point where any educational value is seriously jeopardized. It should be noted that simulations are by nature only models of the real world and that carefully designed models are of enormous benefit in trying to make sense out of natural phenomena, whether those models are computerized or not. The point, emphasized at the end of this section, is that the model must be properly designed and presented. Given that care of preparation, computer simulations effectively focus the learner's attention on a selected number of critical variables and their relationships.

One simulation, called "Lemonade Stand," has already become something of a classic. We offer it as an example partly for that reason, but mainly because it demonstrates that simplicity can be a virtue. The computer program "Lemonade Stand" causes the computer to display on its screen a representation of a lemonade stand that some children might set up in front of their house. The graphics are effective because they encourage the students to become part of the little make-believe world created and they help focus attention on matters of importance. The computer informs the student about three critical variables: the cost to make a glass of lemonade, the cost of advertising (making a sign), and the day's weather forecast. Other significant events, such as reduced traffic due to construction, may also be reported. The student must decide on values for three variables under her control: how many glasses of lemonade to prepare, how much to charge for each glass, and how many signs to make. The computer analyzes all of the data according to a model determined by the person(s) who wrote the computer program. In a flash, the student is informed as to: how many glasses were sold, total preparation and advertising costs and, as a function of all that, what the net profits were. As the simulation continues, the computer varies the values under its control (for example, the cost to prepare a glass of lemonade drastically increases because mother is no longer providing sugar for free) and the student must adjust those under her control, all the while trying to maximize profits.

A small sampling of other available simulations include those that involve students in making decisions about:

- population control, including variables relating to sex distribution, age distribution, and number of births
- disease control, where students must make decisions that coordinate the smooth integration of such resources as number of field hospitals, types of pesticides used and medication administered
- water pollution, which students can help reduce by making the right decisions on the treatment of waste once they have properly integrated information on the rate of dumping of waste, the temperature, and the type of body of water being contaminated
- volcanoes, especially how best to allocate resources available to study them, including the type of volcanoes in the area, the cost to investigate them, and the past history of the volcanoes
- civil war battles, whose outcomes depend on the student's judgment on how to distribute limited funds for ammunition, food, and salaries

• explorations or pioneering, particularly across continents or oceans, thereby reliving the need to make hard decisions about how best to use available means

In selecting simulations for use with students in your school, keep the following criteria in mind:

1. Where appropriate, graphics should support the lesson. The closer the student can reasonably come to "seeing" the results of her decisions, the better. Thus, graphics that demonstrate the explosion of a volcano or the internal operation of a nuclear reactor or the growth of a plant are generally more effective than lines of text on the screen to describe such events. Other effective uses of graphics which are often built into simulations are actual graphs used to highlight the relationships of variables being manipulated.

2. Avoid using a simulation simply because it is attractive or otherwise motivating to the teacher and the students. Be clear as to how using it enhances the opportunities for students to develop in areas that are clearly appropriate.

3. Ascertain through documentation provided with the simulation or, where possible, through direct examination of a listing of the actual computer program, what formulas have been used by the programmer to determine outcomes once the values of variables are entered. Make sure that the bases of those formulas are sound, both educationally and with regard to the slice of reality being modeled.

Furthermore, in using simulations with students, it is important that time and effort be spent both in preparing the students for the experience and in "debriefing" them afterwards. It is all too tempting to set up one or more students with a simulation and to leave to chance that their enjoyment in using it will be sustained and will lead to significant learning. The value of the experience is often maximized only through introductory and follow-up activities that lend a proper perspective to what the students go through. For example, with "Lemonade Stand," students could be asked subsequent to their time at the computer, "What other things could affect how much money you make?" Students are likely to think of many factors not included in the computer program, such as the place where the stand is set up, the chance that someone will accidently spill the pitcher of lemonade, whether it is a weekday or a holiday, and so forth. By exploring such questions, the simulation is properly used as a springboard for exploring the real world at large.

7.3 TESTED APPROACHES TO ENHANCE WRITING, MUSICAL, AND ARTISTIC TALENT WITH COMPUTERS

Skepticism is not an uncommon response to the claim that computers can significantly contribute to students' growth as artists. Nonetheless, the machines are proving to be an extraordinarily valuable tool in enhancing writing, musical, and artistic talent. Upon reflection, an initial reaction of skepticism gives way to the realization that it is the concept of the "computer as a tool" that opens the door to some very exciting possibilities. As we shall see below, computers commonly used in schools today are easily transformed into tools for aspiring artists to more easily explore, refine and otherwise develop a wide range of techniques in the verbal, visual and musical fields. The key in each case is the extent to which the computer can manage literally to put at the user's fingertips the means to transmute easily the contents of his or her mind into an objectified form that can be freely examined and manipulated.

A suitably programmed computer releases a person's energy from the more restraining, time consuming and sometimes expensive mechanical aspects of techniques needed to convert thoughts and ideas into products that can be seen, touched or heard. Thus, the emerging musician or graphic artist, for example, can postpone, until a suitable time, having to learn fingering techniques or how to sweep a brush to yield a certain effect, and instead concentrate at an early stage on techniques traditionally considered more advanced, such as how to combine colors or notes in unique ways. The experience of employing sophisticated techniques early in one's development as an artist can be intensely satisfying and propelling. Talent that might lie indefinitely dormant without that early experience is thereby more likely to be realized by the individual. Such realization can be expected to increase the chances that the discipline and practice required to train one's hands or fingers will be accepted and that, as a result, a far greater number of learners will experience themselves as gifted in areas generally considered the domain of relatively few people.

Writing with a Word Processing Program

Word processing computer programs have the following features and benefits as tools to enhance writing talent (see Chapter 9 for a further, more thorough discussion of how computers can function as word processors):

1. The computer becomes a supremely efficient typewriter, inviting very fast entry of information and incorporating the simplest methods for immediately correcting errors as they are keyed in. The writer is thus encouraged to write more and is less likely to experience the waste of energy that can accompany frustration caused by slips of the pen or fingers.

2. Rewriting is immensely facilitated through editing functions that permit the overtyping, insertion, deletion or movement of text which appears on the video screen of the computer. Cutting and pasting, extensive retyping of material, difficult to read or follow handwritten revisions are all avoided. As a result, the writer is encouraged to concentrate far more attention on the critical stage of rewriting and polishing her work, particularly in response to the suggestions or corrections of others.

3. Spelling errors and a certain number of common grammatical mistakes can be automatically monitored by computer programs that are companion to the word processors. Consequently, aspects of writing that inhibit and intimidate a substantial number of people can become immediately far less threatening.

4. Letter-perfect final product is generated automatically by a printer that is connected by a cable to the computer. Once all editing and proofreading is completed and all revisions made while the text is stored in the computer, the simple pressing of one or more keys triggers the printer into action, producing final copy which conforms to the writer's wishes regarding format. Because she has such easy control over how many characters are printed on a line, how many lines are printed on a page, what words get underlined or typed out in boldface, whether the right margin is justified or not, etc., the author can experiment with subtleties that enhance the overall visual impact of her work. Neatness also is assured, thereby increasing confidence in the presentability of her writing.

Composing with a Music Synthesizer

The following features of Music Synthesizers enhance the development of musical talent:

1. No manual dexterity, special breathing or other physical skills are needed to produce musical products of high quality. A person is able to compose music without having to manipulate the keys on a piano or sustain a note on a saxophone or play any musical instrument whatsoever. Anyone is free to explore at any early stage

in the development of her musical talents how sounds have a variety of components (attack time, delay time, sustain time, and release time) that can be manipulated in interesting and creative ways.

2. Musical notes are reproduced by the computer according to scales that correspond to standard notation, so that what is learned on the computer applies directly to work with actual instruments and vice-versa. The computer will print out a representation of the familiar musical staff with all appropriate notation, thereby avoiding the tedious chore of producing and editing it manually.

3. Depending on the sophistication of the synthesizer used, the computer can replicate up to sixteen distinct voices (or instruments), which can be combined and played together or listened to separately. The learner gains total control over a very complex process by being able to program in one voice at a time, to get immediate feedback and to hear the voices in varying combinations. She is thereby freed to explore at her own pace how chords are constructed and manipulated. Furthermore, she finds a small orchestra at her beck and call, summoned by the mere touch of a few buttons on the computer keyboard.

Drawing and Painting with a Graphics Program

Talent in the visual arts is brought forth by the following typical qualities of graphics programs:

1. A marker of some sort appears on the screen and is under the complete control of the person operating the computer. Its movements are controlled by certain keys, a joystick, or game paddles. As the learner moves the marker, usually called a "cursor," from place to place on the screen, she determines whether or not a line is drawn behind it. Any shape imaginable can thus be drawn, with no need whatsoever for manual dexterity. The emerging artist is again entirely free to produce externally whatever is in her mind, long before skills formerly considered prerequisite are acquired. Indeed, she need not even be able to hold a pencil or a paintbrush, yet she can create permanent products of great beauty and sophistication if the computer is connected to the right printer or graphics plotter.

2. Many graphics programs permit their users to manipulate created shapes in a variety of ways: automatically increasing or decreasing size, rotating, changing locations, or even viewing from different angles, thereby simulating a three-dimensional represen-

tation. Placing such total control in the hands of virtually everyone bypasses the need for years of prior training and assures the neophyte unprecedented control over the visual medium.

3. Colors can be automatically added or deleted, depending, of course, on the capabilities of the system. Experimentation with the use and combination of colors is thereby stimulated, often leading to remarkable efforts from people who would otherwise be unprepared to take bold initiative.

7.4 HOW TO MAKE COMPUTERS WORK FOR STUDENTS WITH VISUAL, HEARING, AND PHYSICAL HANDICAPS

Among the growing number of uses of computers for handicapped people, for example, robotics or other forms of environmental control, clearly the most significant applications for their education lie in the twin areas of communication and access to information. Microcomputers commonly used in schools today, either on their own or in combination with reasonably priced companion equipment, are well suited to enhance the effectiveness and ease of both expressive and receptive language and to vastly extend easy access to information for persons with visual, hearing, and physical handicaps.

Uses for Your Basic System

An obvious, yet sometimes overlooked fact is that any fundamental microcomputer system is ideally suited for work with persons who have a hearing impairment. The computer is basically a silent and deaf device. Hearing impaired students, therefore, are not at a disadvantage because of their handicap, *per se,* when it comes to using the vast majority of educational computer programs. So long as they can read and write at a level appropriate to the difficulty of the material presented, they find that the microcomputer creates a learning environment in which they can function entirely on par with their normally hearing peers. For hearing impaired students, particularly those educated in the mainstream, the experience can be profoundly moving.

Physically disabled students who cannot hold a pen and who therefore have been limited to standard typewriters find the basic microcomputer system to be a very valuable aid. The process of expressing themselves in writing is often hampered by numerous errors due to their inability to touch type or sometimes a need to use special devices, such as mouthsticks or headsticks. The video screen and easy text editing features of micros virtually eliminate the time consuming and frustrating aspects of error correction and rewriting. For such persons, generating language on a computer can be a freeing experience indeed!

Specialized Software Packages

The addition of special software packages to a basic computer system opens other doors:

- Letters can appear on the screen in a much larger size than normal, greatly facilitating the chore of reading for those who have visual limitations.
- There are commercially available programs that help teach sign language and which, through the use of animated cartoon figures, assist hearing impaired persons and others with delayed or otherwise inadequate language to develop critical insight into how nouns and verbs combine to create meaningful units of expression.
- Severely physically disabled persons can select input of any keyboard character with the pressing of only one preselected key or the button on a game paddle or joystick through the use of a program that transforms the computer into a scanning communications aid. A pointer on the screen moves consecutively from one letter to another on an array displayed on the screen, and the user merely presses the key or button at the right moment to indicate the input desired.

Speech Synthesizers

Mechanical devices that provide microcomputers with the gift of speech are now available at a low cost—approximately $100 to $400. These peripherals, some of which require special software and some which do not, connect to the computer with a simple cable and, for the most part, require no specialized training before they can be utilized easily and effectively. For people with handicaps, the most dramatic benefit is afforded to those whose visual disability is so severe that they are unable to read even greatly enlarged text and who previously have been dependent on braille or expensive special readers for any independent access to the world's vast store of printed information. Now, any textual information that can be stored in a microcomputer can be read out loud to a blind person by the computer.

The burgeoning world of speech synthesis is exciting and complex, and it would take us too far afield to examine it in any detail. For our purposes, it is enough to note that for a minimal investment, what sounds quite acceptably close to normal speech is readily available through the combination of a speech synthesizer and a microcomputer. As text is typed into a computer or as it is brought up onto the screen from a storage device or the computer's internal memory, a voice can be saying the words with sufficient clarity and accuracy for a person to fully understand the meanings the text is intended to convey. Some synthesizers even include the possibility of having punctuation marks read aloud, if the listener/reader so desires.

Voice Input Devices

We still appear to be a long way off from the time when we will be able to sit down before a microphone, say whatever is on our minds and watch as our words and phrases are miraculously transformed into print. As astounding as computers are today, they cannot handle the enormous complexity of standard human speech. As with speech synthesis, speech recognition is a fascinating, yet highly technical and complicated field. It is adequate to our purposes to note that computers have a particularly devilish time dealing with three aspects of spontaneous, normal spoken language:

- They cannot easily determine where one word ends and another begins.
- They cannot easily adjust to different people's voices.
- They cannot easily use context to determine the particular meaning or even, at times, the relevant grammatical category of a vast number of words.

Add to these problems widely varying dialects within any given language as well as the fact that few persons speak all that distinctly, and you can sense the immensity of the challenges involved in creating true speech recognition devices. They simply do not exist at the present time.

What do exist, however, are systems commonly referred to as voice command devices. As with speech synthesizers, but somewhat more expensively, they attach easily to common microcomputers. However, instead of providing the machine with a voice, they provide it with ears. Their limitations lie in the facts that they provide the computer with an understanding of a rather limited number of words or phrases and that they pretty much need to be programmed to "understand" the voice of any particular user. Currently, that programming is rather easily accomplished, but still requires the equipment to be specially "trained" for each individual human user.

In spite of their limitations, as compared to the capabilities that would be characteristic of a true speech recognition system, voice command systems can literally change the educational life of the most severely physically disabled people. For those who are unable to move at all, but who can utter at least some words, voice command devices convert a microcomputer into a powerful interface for communicating with the world. In combination with scanning communication aids, as described above, a voice command device allows such persons to say anything they want, merely by using words like: pointer up, pointer left, pointer right, print, etc. They can even write their own computer programs if the limited, pre-selected voice command vocabulary includes the essential words of a particular computer language. Reportedly, computer programs have already been written in BASIC with a voice command device and without the keyboard's having been touched.

7.5 HOW NETWORKING OPENS WHOLE NEW VISTAS OF EXPERIENCE AND KNOWLEDGE

Generally, networking means linking together two or more computers so that information can be passed back and forth between them. In educational settings, it specifically refers to either:

1. giving several computers in one room or building access to a centralized mass storage device
2. utilizing any one of the several popular brands of microcomputers to become part of large networking systems that give immediate access to literally thousands of computers throughout the country, many of which are connected to enormous stockpiles of information on a plethora of subjects

Before turning our attention to the second category, which is clearly the more exciting, a few words to clarify the first seem in order.

Networking, in the first, narrower sense, is often called disk sharing. A typical disk-sharing system would be set up, for example, in a math lab, where a number of non-disk based microcomputers are hooked up through cables and a special linking device to one disk-based machine. The primary advantage to such an arrangement is that virtually all of the power of the one disk-based "master" machine is lent to each of the far less expensive "slave" computers linked with it. As a result, a large number of more powerful computer programs can be run on each machine for a fraction of the cost of providing each work station with its own disk-based machine.

Several other advantages to disk sharing include:

a. centralizing control in the teacher's hands
b. eliminating the need to make back-up copies of a multitude of individual student disks
c. avoiding having to pass disks among a large group of people, thereby preventing needless accidental or deliberate abuse of materials

More likely to kindle the imagination of educators is the application of networking which transforms the school's computers into cost effective devices for instantaneously tapping tremendously valuable sources of information. Through the use of a "modem" (*mo*dulator-*dem*odulator), a microcomputer can communicate with other small or much larger computers through a standard telephone, and hence provides access to expanded opportunities to gain experience and knowledge. Here is a list of some of the direct benefits to students who use microcomputers hooked up to formal, large networking systems or to another, single computer at a remote site.

- A computer program written by a student in one school can be easily and quickly shared with other students in the district for them to examine, use or work on.

- Students can utilize programs that provide the most up-to-date preparation available for college entrance examinations.

- New instructional software can be immediately accessed in areas such as: computer programming, foreign languages, engineering, mathematics, etc.

- Encyclopedias are now available in electronic form. They provide students with constantly updated information on just about any subject they need to research.

- There are opportunities to evaluate the depth of one's skill or knowledge through tests in a variety of areas, including geography, movie trivia, sports, reading, vocabulary, and spelling.

- Late-breaking news is always at students' fingertips. "Old news" is kept on line and is as easily retrieved.

- Locating desired information maintained in large data bases forces students to sharpen their organizational skills and their capacity to think through a problem in a disciplined, logical manner.
- Guidance and counseling is available in the form of up-to-the-minute information on the job market and on drug and alcohol abuse.
- Current information can be readily obtained in such critical areas as money management, nutrition, food preparation, and personal health.
- Library networks yield vastly extended information on where and how to locate hard-to-find periodicals and books, both in print and in electronic form.
- Students can access directly the power of mainframe computers and experiment with a wide variety of computer languages.

In addition to the direct benefits to students, teachers and administrators find in networking systems, specifically designed for educators, other features that help them fulfill their professional responsibilities are:

- Current information on educationally relevant and timely topics is at hand, for example, funding, the economy, conservation, legislation.
- "Electronic bulletin boards" allow for a sharing of information among teachers or administrators who may be thousands of miles apart and who would otherwise never be in a position to easily share suggestions, ideas, concerns and solutions to common problems.
- Updated reports on recent educational research are easily obtained.

8 | How Computers Are Used to Help Solve Specific Learning Problems

Of the various productive uses for a computer in an educational setting, perhaps the most dramatic is solving specific learning problems. There is little doubt, even at this relatively early stage in its implementation in a wide variety of school settings, that a computer can be significantly helpful in this area. At the same time, however, applying computer power to aid in the solution of learning problems is a relatively delicate matter, and success in such applications is more dependent than ever on the sensitivity and careful judgment of those who are in control of the computer project. Therefore, before launching directly into the body of this important chapter, a few preliminary remarks will hopefully help put the matter into perspective, thereby paving the way for what follows.

To make the computer function in ways that really do help to solve problems in learning, the machine is best conceived of as a piece of clay to be molded through a computer program into a highly refined instrument for learning. As we discovered in Chapter 1, a computer is actually just a plastic and metal device, consisting of many interrelated parts all connected together with wires. Even granting that the incorporation of a television or a television-type of unit for the display of information will be inherently motivating for most students, at least for awhile, nevertheless, a box of plastic and metal pieces, in and of itself, is of little value as an instrument for learning. A critical fact, perhaps in danger of being taken too lightly because of its obviousness, is that the success with which the computer is used to help solve learning problems is wholly dependent on the appropriateness of the conception and design of the computer programs used for that purpose. Of course, the same is true for a computer's application in any area; however, it is somehow more poignantly felt in the area of present concern, simply because the end results of our efforts—improved learning for those who have experienced notable and probably repeated failure—are more precious.

At the same time, we are faced with a situation in education where competing theories, philosophies, approaches, methods, and materials abound. Perhaps the one most widely accepted notion is that no generally accepted "science of education" yet exists. This issue cannot be avoided in considering how a computer can be used to help solve learning problems simply because the conception and design of relevant computer programs are, at least to some extent, unavoidably dependent on the programmer's ideas about:

1. how people learn

2. how a particular subject area should be handled

No matter who the programmer is—whether it is you or a co-worker or a well-respected authority in education—that person's notions about how best to help people learn and how best to deal with the skills or knowledge contained in a subject area will certainly influence the shape of the final product. The "piece of clay" will be molded by one or more individuals' ideas in those two critical areas.

Again, the situation we are confronted with is not unique to the use of computers to help solve learning problems. Using them to educate in more generalized ways, as with computer-assisted instruction (see Chapter 6) or with regard to a number of unique instructional applications (see Chapter 7), raises similar issues. What we experience again, however, is a quickened awareness of the situation, this time because most students will most of the time essentially teach themselves most of what is presented to the satisfaction of most adults, regardless of the techniques used or the philosophy underlying the techniques. Where we find learning problems emerging are in those circumstances where "most" no longer holds true, and "special" approaches seem to become necessary. Whereas educating with a computer in other areas will succeed, more or less independent of the biases of the programmer, we are more likely to find legitimate cause to be dissatisfied with the specific shape a computer program is given when it is applied to the solving of a learning problem.

We are therefore faced with the following two factors when we consider how best to utilize computers to assist us in solving a specific learning problem:

1. The computer is molded into an instrument for learning by the programmer.

2. The particular biases of the programmer with regard to critical educational issues will produce a relatively acceptable or unacceptable product.

Yet, we need some common ground of understanding before we can proceed productively in this exciting, but delicate area. Therefore, on the basis of what hopefully is one universally accepted impression—that no one can ever learn anything for anyone else—let us simply refine ever so cautiously the idea of the computer as an instrument for learning by thinking of it as an instrument used by the student for his or her own learning. On that basis, a number of very specific suggestions can be offered that should have productive applications in the wide variety of settings where help is sought for solving specific learning problems.

8.1 DETERMINING WHERE THE COMPUTER CAN HELP

The two senses through which we do most of our learning are seeing and hearing. This condition is especially true of the learning that transpires in schools, where auditory and visual presentations predominate. It is no surprise, then, that most learning problems that develop somehow revolve around the students' difficulties in dealing, in an expected manner, with information that is perceived through their eyes or ears. Modern microcomputers are ideally suited to help solve such problems.

We have already seen how readily the popular brands of microcomputers lend themselves to the visual display of information and how the video units, coupled with the computer's internal capabilities, not only permit but encourage sophisticated graphic presentations of information. Users have in their hands machinery that goes far beyond the mere display of numerical data and printed words in pleasing or functional ways. Rather, they have a visual medium that approaches in flexibility the mental imagery that is part of the human mind.

As an example, try the following exercise. Picture in your mind eight circles, all the same size lined up in a row, side by side. Imagine that two of them are removed and examine how many remain. Return to your "mental screen" the two that had been removed. Regroup the eight circles into subsets of two. How many subsets are there? Combine each subset of two with another subset of two. Now how many subsets are there? How many circles are there in each subset?

All of the imagery just generated by you in your mind can be easily displayed on the video screen of a microcomputer. Variables such as size, location, order of presentation, speed of movement, rotation, and even three- versus two-dimensional presentation of objects are all controllable by the programmer and, if desired by the programmer, then by the learner as well.

Auditory imagery is also within the capability of the microcomputer. Any frequency of sound audible to the human ear can be produced and controlled. Thus any sound imaginable to us in our mind can be duplicated by a computer connected to the right sound producing device. Voice synthesizers are now available at low cost, so that something that very closely resembles the human voice is being generated in classrooms across the country by machinery not much bigger than this book. It is now possible to present students with any speech sounds in isolation or blended with one another in any possible way.

Add the following items to the computer's capacity to match the mind's auditory and visual functions: its affinity for interactive operation, where the ultimate user-learner can input responses and get immediate feedback; its infinite patience; its ability to deal with complex matters; its ease at handling large amounts of information at great speed. What we end up with is a device that can help solve many of the most stubborn learning problems which now or in the future may manifest themselves in your school.

Use the following checklist to develop a sense of where the computer can specifically help.

If the student can:

- in one way or another depress the keys on the computer's keyboard
- maintain attention on a task for short periods of time
- see well enough to read a book with normally sized print
- hear well enough to comprehend speech

then the same computers now commonly used in schools can help solve learning problems, such as the following.

Problems in Reading and Writing

- The student continually misreads common words.
- The student constantly misspells many words.
- The student does not comprehend what he reads, though there is oral fluency.
- The student may decode well, but reads word-by-word or otherwise without sufficient fluency.

- The student guesses wildly at how to pronounce the middle or end of multisyllable words.
- The student does not sufficiently utilize syntactic or semantic clues.
- The student has difficulty distinguishing speech sounds.
- The student reads too slowly.
- The student reverses letters or whole words in her writing.
- The student omits words in writing or oral reading.
- The student's written expression is seriously disorganized.
- The student chronically omits necessary punctuation.
- The student's written grammatical errors are significantly greater than oral errors.
- The student proofreads or edits poorly or not at all.

Problems in Mathematics

- The student misreads numerals, especially those larger than 999.
- The student confuses visually similar numerals.
- The student incorrectly writes numerals.
- The student constantly misreads or ignores signs ($+$, $-$, etc.).
- The student must always count to answer, "How many?"
- The student has difficulty naming numerals in sequence.
- The student seems unable to master the steps of common algorithms, carrying out some in the wrong sequence or omitting others altogether.
- The student cannot solve word problems.
- The student chronically makes "silly" mistakes.
- The student cannot seem to learn the multiplication tables.
- The student seems unable to retain simple addition or subtraction facts.
- The student often transposes numerals, either in reading or writing.
- The student appears not to "think through" the solution to a problem, overly relying on "rote" memorization.
- The student continues to rely heavily on finger or mark counting to carry through simple calculations long after his peers solve the problems "in their heads."
- The student constantly misplaces commas and/or decimal points.

- The student is stymied by the concept of fractions as operators.
- The student cannot tell time.
- The student cannot count change.
- The student puts down answers that are obviously well off the mark, with seemingly no effort or skill at estimating answers.
- The student has no grasp of coordinate systems.

The above lists are by no means intended to be exhaustive. Rather, it is hoped that you are left strongly with the impression that the computer is an instrument suitable to helping solve a very wide array of specific problems.

8.2 SUGGESTIONS FOR UNLOCKING MENTAL RESOURCES WITH COMPUTERS

By thinking of the computer as an instrument we can put in students' hands for them to use for their own learning, we create the possibility of:

1. unlocking mental resources that are not as readily accessible to some students as they are to others
2. tapping those resources, once they are available to the students, for use in solving particular learning problems they may be facing

We are, of course, making an assumption, namely that the mental resources needed to learn are actually accessible to students, even if they have not spontaneously shown themselves to be available to meet specific challenges in one or another area of study presented in school. Assuming such accessibility, we now turn to examine what suggestions will be most likely to produce the results we want.

Suggestion 1:

Select those computer programs that, as much as possible, permit the student to explore possibilities at her own pace with opportunities for her own initiatives.

The computer is unique, as an instrument for learning, in its capacity to react appropriately to a wide spectrum of initiatives on the part of the user. A programmer can provide it with a repertoire of responses that is large enough to handle the actions of the many unknown people who will be using the particular learning instrument into which it is shaped by the programmer, if two conditions are met:

1. The "world" created by the computer program must be sufficiently rich in terms of the possibilities offered the student. (The notion of "world," as used here, simply refers to a situation in which things happen within certain boundaries or limits and where particular actions can be found by the student to have predictable and consistent results.)

2. The imagination and/or experience of the programmer must be sufficiently unrestricted so as to anticipate what different people in very different circumstances are likely to do.

While these two demands, in and of themselves, may not actually be too difficult to meet, incorporating a third element into the mix is decidedly challenging:

Construct a world such that, as the student explores what can be done with it, he is required to call upon mental resources that (a) are needed by him to proceed in ways he wishes to proceed, and (b) are relevant to learning something that has shown itself to be problematic for him.

Computer programs that accomplish all this do not, as yet, abound. However, some do exist and increasingly larger numbers are likely to be available. Several examples are offered in subsequent sections of this chapter.

Suggestion 2:

While students are interacting with the computer, and probably before and after, as well, it is generally best not to intervene any more than is absolutely necessary with regard to their performance at the computer.

Having selected an appropriate computer program, it is best to rely, as much as possible, on its ability to mold the computer into an instrument used by the student for his own learning. Intervention of any sort should be kept to a minimum. However, that advice does not preclude any intervention whatsoever, which at times is not only appropriate, but required. The critical point is that the staff members who are directly involved in using the computers for solving specific problems should be encouraged to show restraint. They should intervene when needed, but only when needed.

An associated and perhaps more controversial issue relates to the dispensing of praise. Those computer programs that are more successful in unlocking mental resources tend not to utilize built-in praise or specially designed reinforcers (for example, smiling faces, explosions, music, brief words of praise). The intrinsic motivation that accompanies the conquering of challenges through the use of one's wits obviates the need for such "external motivators." Even more importantly, they can actually interfere in some cases by distracting the learner from the relevant matters that precede or follow their occurrence. Those educators implementing computer programs that support learning without employing such devices might be wise to follow the programmer's lead and allow the experience of inner growth to propel the student. Of course, there is no suggestion here to abandon sincere expressions of wonder or delight with the achievements of one's students and to share those expressions, particularly with the students; however, the unique dialogue that gets established between a human mind, even one which has experienced problems in learning, and a properly pro-grammed computer, can become profound enough to earn our deep respect and admiration. In such a context, praise manufactured for the purpose of positive reinforcement clearly has no place.

Suggestion 3:

Use carefully designed materials/techniques to ensure that skills developed with the computer will display themselves in a more tradi-tional guise.

The unlocking of mental resources with a computer for the solving of specific learning problems is best accompanied by some precise effort to translate the mastery that is achieved into a more standard form. So long as learning is generally demonstrated through some printed or oral means of expression, whether formal or informal, there seems to be no reason to feel that improvement through computer utilization should not be similarly demonstrated. As always, a sensitive teacher's careful planning and readiness to adapt to a student's changing needs is central to the process.

The judicious use of the computer as an instrument for learning implies its use as an instrument for teaching. As such, it becomes part of a wider set of instructional devices that teachers and other instructional personnel will implement as appropriate. We there-fore face a situation in which such persons are having to constantly make decisions about how to most advantageously have the student apply unlocked, relevant mental resources in such a way that any previous "symptom" of a learning problem gets dissolved or at least substantially ameliorated. While the transfer of learning should not present a problem, the techniques for ensuring the transfer may not always be obvious. To illustrate, a detailed example is offered in the following section.

8.3 SAMPLE TECHNIQUES FOR SOLVING
A PERSISTENT WRITING PROBLEM

A prime example of a computer program that turns the machine into an instrument students use for their own learning is "Turtle Geometry." This program, often referred to as turtle graphics, is available in several versions, appropriate for almost all of the more popular brands of microcomputers. Turtle Geometry transforms a microcomputer into an instrument for exploring how one's mental resources for generating images in one's own mind can be used to generate similar images on the screen of a monitor or TV set attached to the computer. Originally and most notably a primary domain within a computer language called Logo (see Chapter 6), turtle graphics have now been incorporated with a reasonable degree of success into at least two entirely different computer languages: PILOT and BASIC.

Interestingly, the researchers who spent several years developing Logo under the direction of Dr. Seymour Papert at the Massachusetts Institute of Technology had a far broader aim in mind than the solving of specific learning problems. Their goal, now realized, was to develop a general purpose computer language whose structure lent itself to direct manipulation by virtually everyone, including young children. Through such manipulation, which is manifested in the Turtle Geometry mode in a visual display that provides immediate feedback to the person operating the computer, the learner, without special effort, develops deeply significant mathematical concepts and other uses of his mind—including models for thinking about thinking—which otherwise might lay dormant for years, perhaps never to be realized.

Since Logo is dealt with in greater detail in Chapter 6, we had best turn our attention immediately to an example of how Turtle Geometry can be applied to solving a specific learning problem. For the purpose of illustration, we select a fairly common problem—the tendency of some persons to confuse in their reading and writing the lower case letters "b" and "d." For some persons, particularly of elementary school age, the confusion is very persistent and is usually accompanied by a host of similar or related problems. Once transformed by Turtle Geometry into an instrument for a student to help himself learn, the computer can help solve this specific learning problem. The following steps would be relevant to that process.

Step 1:   Allow the student to explore the world of Turtle Geometry at his own pace.

Purpose: A large number of mental resources and insights are called upon as students explore possibilities in

Turtle Geometry. The ones we are specifically concerned with unlocking here are: visualizing shapes; rotating them on an axis; recognizing orientation in space as a distinguishing characteristic; noting that in moving from a vertical to a horizontal plane, there are two distinct choices, each producing a result which is the opposite of the other; realizing that the command, "RIGHT," will have opposite effects depending on which way one is facing ("up" or "down") on the vertical plane and that the same holds true for the command, "LEFT"; accepting that the command words themselves are arbitrary, but that the results, taking into consideration one's orientation in space at any given moment, are consistent and predictable.

Step 2:   Have the student create, on the screen, the following shapes: b , d ,db. Allow him to examine different procedures for creating them in various sizes and in differing locations. Have him transform the b's into d's and vice versa.

Purpose: The same mental resources that had been called spontaneously into use by the student for his prior, self-directed projects should now be available for meeting this new challenge. In this way, the previous open-ended learning can be easily transformed into what we know is an academic exercise with important implications for the student.

Step 3:   Have the student divide the screen in half with a vertical line. On the left half of the screen, he is to create d's and on the right, b's—as many as he likes and of whatever size suits him. Agree that the shapes on the left side will be called "dee's" and those on the right, "bee's." Have him add or delete bee's and dee's at your say so.

Purpose: To provide practice, derive feedback regarding mastery, and crystallize the awarenesses that a pair of distinct "objects" exist, with only their left-right orientation to distinguish them, and that each has its own particular name.

Step 4:   Replace the computer screen with a sheet of paper and a pencil. Engage the student in activities similar to those in Step 3.

Purpose: To ensure that the learning on the computer is transferred.

To summarize what has been accomplished in our illustration, we can see that a carefully selected computer program has turned the computer into an instrument that the student has used for his learning. The mental resources deliberately unlocked in that learning process were turned to solving a specific learning problem faced by the student through the intervention of a teacher who presented a series of exercises that produced the targeted knowledge.

8.4 THREE WAYS COMPUTERS HELP STUDENTS WHO HAVE BAD HABITS

One of the most common and troublesome aspects of a serious learning problem is its persistence. Often, such tenacity, frequently in the face of both long range and intensive attempts at remediation, can be traced, at least in part, to poor learning habits. Fortunately, computers can help students who have the following bad habits:

- giving up easily
- forever seeking attention or praise, even for the smallest accomplishments
- feeling a chronic and debilitating fear of being wrong
- constantly looking to the teacher for feedback regarding the correctness of responses
- not looking or listening with sufficient attention
- careless monitoring of one's efforts

The following three characteristics of computers are easily recognized as vital components of the work that needs to be done with students who have such habits.

Computers Are Infinitely Patient

"Infinite" is only a slight overstatement. In fact, so long as electric current remains to power it, and its circuits are not worn out, the computer will wait through indefinite periods of a student's failure to respond correctly or at all, for that matter. Certainly the length of time it can remain ready to go on would outlast the most demanding student.

The computer's neutrality is another aspect of its patience. No amount of inappropriate student responses, even if deliberate, can make a computer lose its composure. It never needlessly misplaces its energy into anger or temper or despair, no matter how dull-witted or immovable a student may at times appear. It is forever prepared to repeat itself or a segment of a lesson endlessly and calmly, when required.

Computers Can Provide Immediate Feedback

For students with learning problems, one of the sad facts of life in most school situations is that their bad habits may be perpetuated, at least to some degree, simply because it is not normally possible to provide them quickly and consistently enough with direct and clear feedback during their attempts at learning. Computers are ideally suited to provide them with absolutely consistent and instantaneous feedback. As a result, rather than carelessly responding to questions posed in a worksheet or workbook format, questions that will not be corrected for minutes, hours, days, or perhaps, ever, students find out at once how well they are meeting each step of a challenge put to them. That situation keeps them more alert and attentive to what they are doing.

An additional benefit to the swiftness of a computer's feedback is that students can be more easily weened from an overwhelming dependence on the teacher as the only perceived source of truth and knowledge readily available. Suddenly the computer is recognized as a resource for checking the adequacy of one's responses. While care must be taken that overdependence is not simply shifted from the teacher to the machine, an important first step is made when the student recognizes that there is an alternate, easy way of getting reliable feedback.

A Computer Provides Individual Attention

Associated with its ability to furnish instant feedback is the computer's more general capacity to satisfy some students' need to feel attended to. The computer actually interacts with the users; hence, they know at all times that what they are putting into it is being processed and considered. What they do matters, since it is being taken into account.

In fact, the computer functions so remarkably well as a provider of attention that a word of caution can help you avoid a possible trap in using computers with students who display learning problems.

The computer can easily be relegated to the unproductive role of "babysitter." Students can feel so well attended to that they may sit for hours on end without complaint, even when they may be learning little or nothing of real value. While better learners are far more likely to complain about such a situation, those with whom we are presently concerned might feel rather used to not learning much. As long as they are receiving an adequate amount of attention, even if it's only from a machine, it may be enough to keep them going.

While few educators would deliberately engage in abusing the computer's "holding power," it can be terribly tempting to a teacher, even one who is highly dedicated and skilled, to let the computer solve a potential behavior problem or alleviate an otherwise frustrating encounter simply through permitting one student to remain at the computer working on a relatively unproductive task. The best protection is awareness of the potential problem, which can lead to self-discipline on the part of those implementing the computer project.

8.5 HOW TEACHER-PROGRAMMERS MAY PROVIDE THE ULTIMATE ANSWER: FOUR EXAMPLES WITH AN ACTUAL, READY-TO-RUN COMPUTER PROGRAM

Teachers who learn how to program a microcomputer find themselves in a singular position. Given access to a machine, they can turn it into a remarkably powerful instrument for learning, limited only by their imagination and insight into the particular needs of the students they serve. For teachers of students who exhibit learning problems, the contribution of a teacher-programmed microcomputer can be especially dramatic. There follows an example of one such teacher, who found he could use microcomputers to help solve the learning problems of children he worked with daily in a Resource Room setting.

In his work on reading and spelling with twenty to twenty-four elementary school youngsters, formally diagnosed as learning and/or emotionally disabled and placed in a special education environment in small groups for one or two hours a day, he was confronted with the barrage of persistent symptoms typically displayed by learning disabled children, the most pernicious of which were: misreading and misspelling common words, poor recall of reading and spelling words, inadequate fluency and lack of comprehension. When he found himself with the opportunity to adopt two TRS-80 Model I's, he had an intuition that the power and flexibility of the equipment would provide a particularly effective instrument for helping to attack the symptoms. He spent nearly three weeks during his summer vacation with a borrowed microcomputer and a self-teaching programming manual for BASIC. He returned to school in September with barely adequate programming skills and the two TRS-80's at his disposal.

Even more importantly, he returned armed with a vision and a great deal of inspiration. Within three months, he prepared four computer programs to help in his assault on the four most difficult problems his students were facing in language arts. On the whole, he was guided by three assumptions:

1. The microcomputers should, as much as possible, be transformed into instruments the students could use to help them solve their learning problems.

2. The students, in spite of consistent previous failure, had the mental resources necessary for solving their problems.

3. The focus should be primarily on triggering in students functional uses of their mental resources, and secondarily on specific subject matter.

The first computer program capitalized on the students' capacity to form, in their minds, visual images of objects in the environment. The ability to close their eyes and visualize an apple or a pencil or anything else was applied to written words. The computer screen displayed portions of each of the letters of a word and the students' job was to type in the word that was only partially represented. The students controlled the situation to the extent that they could elicit additional clues from the computer until such time as they felt they knew the word. As in all the programs, the teacher could easily change the words that would appear on the screen.

The second program tapped the students' ability to take a few components and construct from them a wide variety of products, simply by combining them in different ways. This ability was applied to letters representing sounds: the five "short vowel" sounds and several consonants. The computer displayed the letters, a, u, i, e, and o, across the top of the screen and the letters, p, t, s, m, and n across the bottom. A box appeared in the middle of the screen with a "gap word" that was missing one or more letters, for example, pa_. The students had to choose, from the limited selection of sounds represented at the top and bottom of the screen, those which would fill the gap and thereby yield an English word. Letters chosen by pressing the appropriate key would become animated, leave their spot on the screen and "march" to the box in the middle. The letter would "knock" on the side of the box and be admitted if it correctly completed the "gap word" in the box. The children controlled whether they would have the opportunity to try additional solutions or move on to another "gap word."

The third program, utilizing the students' skills at uttering properly sounding English sentences, presented a set of words, any one of which would selectively blink on and off several times. Reading the blinking words in the order in which they flashed produced an English sentence, thereby inviting a transformation of the printed language into spoken language. After the last word of each sentence finished blinking, the student was prompted to type in the whole sentence, one word at a time. Both the length of the sentences and the speed of their blinking were under the control of the teacher and/or student.

The fourth program provided students with sets of six sentences that could be reordered into coherent stories. Thus, students were being asked to transfer their capacity to comprehend spoken language in order to deal with its written form. Students merely punched in the numbers of the sentences in the order they preferred and then judged for themselves the adequacy of their response once the results were displayed on the screen in the form of a full paragraph. They had the choice to rearrange the sentences as many times as they needed to satisfy themselves. There was no one right answer, so students were directed to record their products on paper for later review with their teacher.

Figure 8-1 provides an actual listing of the fourth computer program, which can be typed in as-is and run on a TRS-80 Model I, III, or 4.

```
10 REM *** HOUSEKEEPING ***
20 CLS
30 CLEAR 2000
40 RANDOM
50 REM *** INTRODUCTION & INSTRUCTIONS ***
60 PRINT "1.    A"
70 PRINT "2.    MAKE"
80 PRINT "3.    STORY"
90 FOR TT=1 TO 600: NEXT TT
100 PRINT @474, "MAKE-";: PRINT @64,"              ";: FOR TT=1 TO 300: NEXT TT
110 PRINT @479,"A-";: PRINT @0,"         ";:FOR TT=1 TO 300: NEXT TT
120 PRINT @481,"STORY": PRINT@128,"            ";: FOR TT=1 TO 300: NEXT TT
130 CLS
140 PRINT:PRINT:PRINT "              INSTRUCTIONS":
150 PRINT @256,"   TO PLAY THE GAME, 'MAKE-A-STORY,' ALL YOU HAVE TO DO IS READ
    A SET OF SENTENCES THAT APPEARS ON THE SCREEN, AND THEN PRESS";
160 PRINT @384,"   NUMBER KEYS ON THE COMPUTER KEYBOARD TO TELL THE COMPUTER
    THE ORDER IN WHICH YOU THINK THE SENTENCES SHOULD BE ARRANGED   TO MAKE THE B
EST SOUNDING STORY."
170 PRINT @640,"   SEVERAL GOOD POSSIBILITIES EXIST FOR CERTAIN SETS OF
    SENTENCES.  DON'T TRY TO FIND THE 'RIGHT' ANSWER, BUT DO        CHOOSE AN ARR
ANGEMENT OF THE SENTENCES THAT MAKES SENSE";
180 PRINT @832,"   TO YOU AND THAT YOU CAN EXPLAIN TO SOMEONE ELSE."
190 PRINT @970,"WHEN YOU ARE READY TO BEGIN, PRESS THE SPACEBAR"
200 DD$ = INKEY$
210 IF DD$=" " GOTO 230
220 GOTO 200
230 REM *** READ DATA ***
```

```
240 FOR X=1 TO 8
250   FOR Y=1 TO 6
260    READ A$(X,Y)
270   NEXT Y
280 NEXT X
290 REM *** PICK RANDOM # & REPICK IF NECESSARY ***
300 R=RND(8)
310 IF R = R1 GOTO 300
320 R1 = R
330 CLS
340 REM *** DISPLAY SENTENCES ***
350 FOR P=1 TO 6
360 PRINT"(";P;")   ";
370 Y=8
380   FOR X = 1 TO LEN(A$(R,P))
390    Y = Y+1
400     IF Y>55 AND MID$(A$(R,P),X,1)=" " THEN PRINT:PRINT"       ";:Y=8
410     PRINT MID$(A$(R,P),X,1);
420   NEXT X
430 PRINT"."
440 NEXT P
450 REM *** GET STUDENT'S CHOICES ***
460 AA$ = STRING$(58,128)
470 PRINT@767," ";
480 PRINT "WHICH SENTENCE DO YOU WANT FIRST IN YOUR STORY? "
490 S$(1) = INKEY$
500 S(1)=VAL(S$(1))
510 IF S(1) <1 OR S(1) >6 THEN 490
520 PRINT@896,S(1)
530 PRINT@768,AA$;
540 PRINT@767," ";
550 PRINT "WHICH SENTENCE DO YOU WANT SECOND IN YOUR STORY?   "
560 S$(2) = INKEY$
570 S(2) = VAL(S$(2))
580 IF S(2) <1 OR S(2) >6 THEN 560
590 IF S(2) = S(1) THEN 560
600 PRINT @900,S(2)
610 PRINT@768,AA$;
620 PRINT@767," ";
630 PRINT "WHICH SENTENCE DO YOU WANT THIRD IN YOUR STORY?   "
640 S$(3) = INKEY$
650 S(3) = VAL(S$(3))
660 IF S(3) <1 OR S(3) >6 THEN 640
670 IF S(3) = S(2) OR S(3) = S(1) THEN 640
680 PRINT @904,S(3)
690 PRINT@768,AA$;
700 PRINT@767," ";
710 PRINT "WHICH SENTENCE DO YOU WANT FOURTH IN YOUR STORY?   "
720 S$(4) = INKEY$
730 S(4) = VAL(S$(4))
740 IF S(4) <1 OR S(4) >6 THEN 720
750 IF S(4) = S(3) OR S(4) = S(2) OR S(4) = S(1) THEN 720
760 PRINT@908,S(4)
770 PRINT@768,AA$;
780 PRINT@767," ";
790 PRINT "WHICH SENTENCE DO YOU WANT FIFTH IN YOUR STORY?   "
800 S$(5) = INKEY$
810 S(5) = VAL(S$(5))
820 IF S(5) <1 OR S(5) >6 THEN 800
830 IF S(5) = S(4) OR S(5) = S(3) OR S(5) = S(2) OR S(5) = S(1) THEN 800
840 PRINT@912,S(5)
850 PRINT@768,AA$;
860 PRINT@767," ";
870 PRINT "WHICH SENTENCE DO YOU WANT SIXTH IN YOUR STORY?   "
880 S$(6) = INKEY$
890 S(6) = VAL(S$(6))
900 IF S(6) <1 OR S(6) >6 THEN 880
910 IF S(6) = S(5) OR S(6) = S(4) OR S(6) = S(3) OR S(6) = S(2) OR S(6) = S(1) T
HEN 880
920 PRINT@916,S(6)
930 REM *** DISPLAY STORY ***
940 CLS
950 PRINT "                    HERE IS YOUR STORY"
960 PRINT "****************************************************************
";
970 Y=6
980 FOR Q = 1 TO 6
990   FOR X=1 TO LEN(A$(R,S(Q)))
```

```
1000    Y=Y+1
1010    IF Y>50 AND MID$(A$(R,S(Q)),X,1)=" " THEN PRINT:PRINT CHR$(8);:Y=0
1020    PRINTMID$(A$(R,S(Q)),X,1);
1030    NEXT X
1040 PRINT ". ";
1050 NEXT Q
1060 PRINT CHR$(13);
1070 PRINT "*******************************************************************"
1080 REM *** FINALE ***
1090 PRINT"IF YOU LIKE THE WAY THIS STORY CAME OUT, COPY IT                    O
NTO A CLEAN SHEET OF PAPER, THEN PRESS 'Y'."
1100 PRINT "IF YOU WANT TO CHANGE THE STORY AROUND, PRESS 'N'."
1110 CC$ = INKEY$
1120 IF CC$ = "N" THEN 330
1130 IF CC$ = "Y" THEN 1150
1140 GOTO 1110
1150 CLS
1160 PRINT:PRINT:PRINT:PRINT:PRINT:PRINT
1170 PRINT "                 IF YOU WANT TO PLAY AGAIN, PRESS 'Y'."
1180 PRINT "                 IF YOU WANT TO STOP, PRESS 'N'."
1190 CC$ = INKEY$
1200 IF CC$ = "Y" THEN 300
1210 IF CC$ = "N" THEN 1230
1220 GOTO 1190
1230 CLS
1240 PRINT:PRINT:PRINT:PRINT:PRINT "             THANK YOU.  GOOD BYE."
1250 GOTO 1250
2000 DATA "THEIR MOTHERS HAD GONE SHOPPING AND TOLD THEM TO WATCH THEIR PETS", "
AMY AND AMANDA WOULD NEVER LEARN THEIR LESSON","IT WAS TOO LATE TO DO ANYTHING N
OW"
2002 DATA "THE DOGS TORE UP THE FLOWERS, MESSED UP THE KITCHEN AND BIT THE MAILM
AN","TWO YOUNG GIRLS AND TWO YOUNG PUPPIES CAN CAUSE A HEAP OF TROUBLE","A CAR W
AS PULLING INTO THE DRIVEWAY"
2004 DATA "THE DOOR OPENED AND SHE STOOD IN THE SOFT LIGHT, SMILING AND BEAUTIFU
L","HIS ANXIETY WAS SO GREAT THAT HE COULD HARDLY MOVE","THE EVENING WAS PERFECT
 AND SO WAS SHE"
2006 DATA "HE FELT THAT HE MIGHT NOT BE ABLE TO SPEAK","IT WAS KENNY'S VERY FIRS
T REAL DATE","BUT NOW HE HAD TO ACT"
2008 DATA "THEY FELL- ONE, TWO, THREE- BEFORE HIS RAPIDLY MOVING HANDS AND FEET"
,"WALTER KNEW HE WAS BRAVE, BUT THAT MIGHT NOT BE ENOUGH","HE APPROACHED CAUTIOU
SLY, HOPING NOT TO BE SEEN UNTIL THE LAST MOMENT"
2010 DATA "WHEN HE SAW THREE BULLIES PICKING ON HIS PAL, CHRIS, HE HAD TO HELP",
"WHEN THE TIME WAS RIGHT, HE MADE HIS MOVE","WALTER WALKED WITH HIS HEAD HIGH, F
EELING THAT THE YEARS OF TRAINING HAD MADE HIM READY FOR ANYTHING"
2012 DATA "BRIAN WONDERED IF HE WOULD BE CAPABLE OF DOING WHAT HAD TO BE DONE","
THERE WERE TWO OUTS AS THE NEXT, AND MAYBE LAST BATTER STEPPED UP TO THE PLATE",
"THE WHOLE CHAMPIONSHIP DEPENDED ON WHAT WOULD HAPPEN NEXT"
2014 DATA "THE GAME WAS TIED IN THE BOTTOM OF THE NINTH INNING","THE PITCHER STR
AIGHTENED HIS CAP AND LOOKED HIM IN THE EYE","A TRUE BATTLE WAS ABOUT TO TAKE PL
ACE - BETWEEN THE PITCHER AND THE BATTER"
2016 DATA "HALF-AWAKE, HALF-SLEEPING, THE BLOND HAIRED GIRL STARED AT THE FLAMES
, AS IF IN A DAZE","WINTER VACATION HAD JUST BEGUN","HER BABY BROTHER'S CRIES BR
OKE THE TRANCE"
2018 DATA "SHE WISHED THAT TIMES LIKE THESE COULD LAST FOREVER","PERHAPS EVEN SC
HOOL WAS BETTER THAN BABYSITTING","JILL SAT NEAR THE FIRE DADDY HAD STARTED IN T
HE FIREPLACE"
2020 DATA "THEY LOOKED AT ONE ANOTHER AND WITHOUT SAYING A WORD EACH KNEW THAT T
HE OTHER WAS READY TO TRY IT","INSIDE, IT WAS AS EMPTY AS THE OLD STORIES WHICH
HAD ONCE SEEMED FULL OF TERROR","THEY NO LONGER BELIEVED IN DRAGONS"
2022 DATA "MARK WAS FIFTEEN AND MICHELLE WAS JUST ONE YEAR YOUNGER","STANDING ON
CE AGAIN AT THE BOTTOM OF DRAGON MOUNTAIN, THEY LAUGHED AT THEIR OLD FEARS","ON
THEIR CLIMB UP THE MOUNTAIN, THEY NOTICED THE OPENING TO A LARGE, DARK CAVE"
2024 DATA "THE STRONG SUMMER SUN BROUGHT INSTANT WARMTH TO THE LAND","PETALS FEL
L TO THE WATER AND SWAYED WITH THE RHYTHM","THE CLOUDS OVERHEAD MOVED SWIFTLY, B
RINGING A RAPID CHANGE IN THE WEATHER"
2026 DATA "DROPS OF RAIN FELL SOFTLY ONTO THE GENTLY RIPPLING SURFACE OF THE PON
D","FROM BEHIND THE DARK GREEN BUSHES, A BULLFROG BELLOWED HIS DEEP SONG","STREA
KS OF SILVER LIGHT SHOWED WHERE FISH FLASHED THROUGH THE WATER"
2028 DATA "SUDDENLY, ALL WAS QUIET AND STILL ONCE AGAIN","A BROWN DOG WITH FIERC
E RED EYES JUMPED OUT, BARKING LOUDLY","FROM INSIDE, HE COULD SEE A TALL MAN SLO
WLY WALKING HIS WAY"
2030 DATA "A LARGE, RED TRUCK WAS PARKED ACROSS THE STREET, NEAR THE BIG ELM TRE
E","IT WAS A DARK, COLD NIGHT","THEN, WITHOUT WARNING, THERE WAS A FRIGHTENING B
ANGING SOUND ON HIS DOOR"
```

Figure 8-1.

Besides the virtually effortless learning that took place when the students worked through the programs, there was an unanticipated payoff. The teacher found himself having to be concerned with efficient use of a limited video display area and machine memory. Such rigors of programming forced the teacher to focus with a previously unimagined intensity on a number of instructional issues that otherwise were perhaps passing without his adequate attention:

1. Precisely how much knowledge actually needs to be passed on and how much can instead be formulated by the students through the activities in which they are engaged?

2. What exactly is the difference between feedback and reinforcement?

3. How can a student's actions and perceptions be made to force his awareness of uses of his mental resources in activities for which it may not be obvious that such uses are appropriate?

4. How can pacing, levels of difficulty, and dynamic visual presentations all be interwoven into a smoothly functioning system that promotes an optimal combination of delight, anticipation, and profound experience of inner growth and learning?

Having been forced into an intimate dialogue with such issues, the teacher-programmer finds himself in an increasingly enhanced position to transform instructional time into substantial learning, not only with the computer as a resource, but at all other times, as well. Programming for the teacher thus becomes a doubly beneficial endeavor: the computer becomes an extension and thereby a multiplier of his skills and capacities while the act of programming forces a refinement of those same abilities.

8.6 HOW TO READ BETWEEN THE LINES WHEN READING SOFTWARE REVIEWS

This section could have appeared elsewhere in the book. What makes it most appropriate for a chapter on learning problems is a fact alluded to in the preliminary remarks of this chapter: whereas most educational programs will perform reasonably well with students who do not experience learning problems in the area covered by the program, far fewer will be satisfactory when used with students who do have problems in the targeted area. For most readers, it is simply impossible to devote the time that would be required to carefully screen programs for use with students with learning problems. In fact, given the plethora of educational programs that are now on the market, many of which promise to help solve learning problems, there is no practical way to thoroughly prescreen more than a small percentage of what is available, even if one or more members of the staff are assigned that duty.

A practice that can go a long way to alleviate this problem is to read software reviews in appropriate journals (see Appendices A and B). In so doing, one can earmark those programs that seem most promising and then concentrate one's efforts in a more focused manner. However, one must know how to deal with the following situation in order to get the most out of the reviews, so that a significant amount of time and money can actually be saved.

1. Rather than any commonly accepted science of education, there prevails a wide discrepancy of opinion with regard to what learning is and how one should teach to best enhance it.

2. The criteria that guide a reviewer in his or her judgment are often far from explicit, due to a lack of sufficient clarity in the reviewer's own thinking, or to editorial policy, or deliberate evasiveness, or to some other equally effective interference.

The only reasonable way of dealing with this dual dilemma is to develop a facility for quickly identifying a reviewer's biases and weighing those against one's own beliefs. One is thereby in a position to "read between the lines," as necessary, and consequently keep the comments in perspective. As a result, the reader is able to avoid the trap of thinking that a reviewer, in suggesting a strong or weak point, is somehow referring to something even vaguely resembling a universally accepted set of standards. That way of reading a review of educational software will yield information and insights about the program that far more closely resemble the impression the reader would be left with if he or she examined the program directly.

As an exercise, read the following sample review, which evaluates a computer program called "Space Waste Race." As you read the review, try to keep in mind the following two questions:

1. What are the reviewer's ideas about learning and how best to enhance it?

2. What specifically are the reviewer's criteria for judging the value of educational software?

Sample Program Review

(This review, written by T. Swartz, first appeared in the September/October 1982 edition of *Classroom Computer News*.)

A program like "Space Waste Race" presents a unique dilemma and also a unique opportunity to a reviewer of educational software. On the one hand, it falls decidedly short of the claims made for it in its accompanying documentation and, in that vein, represents some of what is least promising in the field; on the other hand, the program, in tapping some of the inherent power of the computer to turn experience into effortless learning, manages here and there to generate some real opportunities for self-directed learning. The dilemma is in trying to work through the apparent paradox; the opportunity stems from being forced, as a result, to be very precise about a number of critical issues with profound and far-reaching implications.

Features

"Space Waste Race" is actually a collection of three distinct programs united by a sharing of some graphic displays, but otherwise separate in design and intent. The first program is entitled "Storybook" and consists essentially of a nine-line poem with a graphic display to accompany each line. Once "Storybook" is selected from the main menu, the user has a new menu and a second choice to make. One option is to view the full story, which turns out to be a presentation of one line of the poem at a time, with its accompanying graphics. A second option is to look selectively at any one of the nine "pages." A third option is to hear a short tune playing while the "title page" of the story occupies the screen. Additionally, a choice is given that leads to the full poem's being displayed all at once on the screen, with no accompanying graphics.

The second and third programs are derivatives of the first, and certainly impressed this reviewer as afterthoughts that might cleverly transform the story/poem presentation into a more salable item. Borrowing graphics from the first program, the author has managed to generate a series of activities that could be described as more or less educational in nature. The second program, called "Look, Nod and Shake," consists of a screen showing three faces, each under the control of the user through the pressing of certain keys. The third program is named "Funtime." It contains six segments, the first five of which are purported to be educational games, with the final one serving as a score reporting device.

Educational Value

It is probably a blessing to all of us adults, who in one way or another fancy ourselves educators, that young children—say, up to about six or seven years of age—can do an excellent job of teaching themselves in spite of what we do to help. It is certainly a blessing to the author of this program and to anyone who chooses to use it with young children. As we shall see, young children can learn things while engaged in the activities that the program generates; but the emergence of that learning is far more a tribute to the fertile imagination and insight of children than it is to the expression of those qualities in the unfolding of the activities themselves.

The "story" that is told is described by the author as a poem. It is reproduced here, so that the reader may judge for her- or himself:

Imagine collecting the garbage from all the homes
  around
And building a giant rocket ship to lift it off the ground.
We could make a second moon and park it out in space
To make our first moon jealous and start a silly race.
Then round and round they'd go: rags, paper, cans, and
  glass.
And we would watch the whole thing, lying in the grass.
But what if they'd collide, right in the middle of June?
Would it dirty the face of the human race?
Or that of the Man in the Moon?

Now, this reviewer does not pretend to be a literary critic, nor do I maintain that four-year-olds need to be exposed to Shakespeare; but for heaven's sake, managing to produce some rhymes on the ends of adjacent lines does not a poem make. One cannot help feeling that it was quite fortuitous for the author that there was one month that rhymed with "Moon"! While many youngsters may very well find the "story" entertaining, we could only attribute such a phenomenon to their delightful innocence of mind and spirit. Anything outlandish can be fun. However, the presence of that strength in children is hardly justification for using a tool as powerful as a microcomputer as a page turner for such mediocrity.

Graphics scenes accompany the presentation of each line of the "story." The graphics for several of the "pages" are outstanding and prove the author to be a far better artist than poet. In particular, the scene of a man lying on his back "in the grass" is an excellent example of what a talented graphics programmer can do with the little rectangular boxes to which a Model I or III programmer is restricted. Such pictures undeniably enhance the verbal presentation. Whether or not their combination can truly "encourage good old-fashioned parental storytelling," as the author suggests, is, well, another story. The author also claims that, compared to what he has produced, "Mother Goose never flew so high." As a parent of a two- and a five-year-old, I'll stick with Mother Goose, even without the animated graphics, thank you.

The "Look, Shake and Nod" segment presents the best opportunity for learning on the entire diskette, simply because the child is allowed to play within a little "world" at his own pace and in his own way. The four arrow keys and the "greater than"/"less than" keys control three faces, which are actually "moons" borrowed from the story graphics. A face in the middle of the screen will look left, right, up or down, depending on which arrow key is pressed. The moon to the upper left of the screen will repeatedly nod as the "greater than" key is pressed; the one to the upper right will shake its head as the "less than" key is depressed. While these three faces do not exactly present the richest "world" for an inquisitive and creative young mind to explore, they do exemplify, in a small way, how the computer can function as an instrument for self-learning, since it permits a child to find out things about orientation in space, sequencing, simultaneity and, as the author aptly points out, how people control machines. In fact, the author does seem to recognize that this segment is the strongest, commenting that "Look, Shake and Nod is limited only by their imagination!"

UNIVAC only knows, then, why the collection of "learning activities" which follows segment two was ever included on the disk at all, except perhaps for padding and/or marketing purposes. Whereas the exploratory games just described could, at least to some degree, prompt a fertile young mind to use its powers of perception and imagery, four of the five games in the "Funtime" section are pedantic, petty and thoroughly uninspiring. At the risk of offending any readers who might consider it educationally sound practice to teach the "spatial concepts" of "over-above" or "under-below," one subprogram that purports to do so is taken as an example of how inappropriately the computer is sometimes used as an educational tool.

The activity Moon Pass consists of a display of two moons (our old friends again from the "Space Waste Race" story). One of the moons remains stationary on the screen while the second moon crosses the screen horizontally, passing either above or, you guessed it, below the first. The child's task is to press the "up" arrow if the moving moon goes above the other or the "down" arrow if it goes below the other. An incorrect response is countered with an arrow drawn on the screen pointing in the correct direction, along with the appropriate word ("above" or "below").

What make this activity such a good example of what is not good in the field of educational computing are that:

1. It tries to teach something that probably does not need to be taught at all, and certainly not with a microcomputer.

2. It attempts to condition the child through controlling him or her with a right/wrong answer format.

3. It treats what is actually an awareness as a tiny parcel of knowledge to be drilled and repeated until it is memorized.

4. It is really a test disguised as a learning activity, and poses no challenge whatsoever once the child realizes which key gets pressed.

Along with "Moon Pass," three other activities in the "Funtime" segment, namely, "Moon Drops," "Moon Looks," and "Hole in the Moon," are mostly arid, so far as opportunities for any significant learning are concerned. Respectively, they are designed to teach: counting up to 36; the concepts of direction; and numerical and alphabetical order. A fifth activity, called "Fall Out," is somewhat more productive. The expressed purpose of the game—to teach letter and number identification—is really secondary to a more far-reaching pay-off: as lines of "distractors" (", #, ÷, %, &) work their way rapidly down the screen, one's concentration and attention can be sharpened as one attempts to recognize a letter or number flashing very quickly on and off in varying positions on the line.

Design Quality

As mentioned previously, the animated graphics include some segments that are outstanding. The best use of the graphics is to illustrate the text in the "Storybook" segment. The incorporation of some of the designs into the games yields less dramatic, yet adequate results. One can always tell which direction the moons are facing and some expressiveness on their faces is achieved.

Some of the text displays are in a double-sized character mode, which would tend to be helpful for a young child. The large arrows all look pretty much like arrows, and it is easy to see in which direction they point. The organization of material on the screen during the games is functional and generally useful for the learner in trying to figure out what is expected.

The music is pleasant, requiring nothing more than a cassette cable and the inexpensive Radio Shack Mini Amplifier-Speaker. That set-up also produces sound effects throughout the programs, which help liven up the presentation.

Written Materials

The documentation is well written, clear, and thorough. Detailed descriptions of each of the segments are given along with rationales for their inclusion. By reproducing each of the several menus that appear as one works through the disk, the author has provided the first-time user with an annotated analysis of what to expect. Furthermore, loading and running instructions are detailed and accurate, at least for the Model III disk version. Be sure to heed the author's directions with regard to the version of TRSDOS that is needed to run the programs. They will most definitely not run on version 1.2; version 1.3 is required.

This reviewer would take exception to a number of the statements that appear in the documentation with regard to the educational value of the material. In particular, the repeated emphasis on what the author refers to as "in-context learning" is misleading, in that it only means that some of the graphics that serve so well in the "Storybook" section are adapted for use in the other segments. How that might truly serve in any significant way to enhance learning is beyond my ken.

Ease of Use

Each of the segments of "Space Waste Race" is designed for use by young children. Care has certainly been taken to make it as easy to use as possible. Examples are plentiful, but one or two should suffice in demonstrating how someone who has obviously watched children working at computers has solved some problems connected with the facts that youngsters are unpredictable and not usually eager to have to deal with typing in a series of commands before things happen.

With each menu, a pointing finger moves down along the left side of the listed choices. It remains alongside each selection for a five-second interval, affording the user the opportunity to press ENTER, which will trigger the running of the desired segment. If the pointer reaches the bottom of the list before a choice is made, it simply recycles back to the top. Pressing the SPACE BAR puts the moving finger under the user's deliberate control.

Another nice touch is the control the user is given to quit a game program and return to the "Funtime" activities menu. The child need only press the "s" key after any answer. Of course, the BREAK key is automatically disabled and error trapping is effective. Even pre-school children, after experimenting for awhile or being shown by an adult or older child what each of the selections will produce, should have no difficulty whatsoever in using the programs.

Summary

The author of "Space Waste Race" obviously possesses a number of skills critical to the development of successful educational software: he writes well, he programs well, he produces admirable graphic displays on a machine with decidedly limited graphics capabilities, and he knows how to make programs easy for youngsters to use. Should he develop within himself more stringent criteria for turning the children's time into more profound and enriching learning experiences, we might expect some very exciting things in the future.

You have just finished reading the review on "Space Waste Race." The likelihood of your making effective use of the review is dependent on how much you can recognize the following characteristics of the reviewer:

1. He considers young children to be model learners.

2. He trusts that, given the proper environment, children can manage to take charge of their own learning and make efficient use of their time.

3. He believes that children have significant mental powers that can transform enjoyable experiences into profound learning.

4. He maintains that an adult's role in the learning process is essentially to provide environments and experiences that lead to spontaneous and virtually effortless learning.

5. He would argue that a computer program is truly of educational value when:

   a. it helps students master something of enough depth and scope to warrant the use of such powerful and relatively expensive technology.

   b. it puts the computer under the control of the learner and, in place of an emphasis on eliciting simply *the* right answer, it provides a forum for her or him to develop criteria for arriving at a correct response.

   c. it attempts to force awareness in a student of some relevant matter that might otherwise escape his or her notice, and then provides sufficient and varied practice so that facility will lead to mastery and, where appropriate, retention.

   d. it invites the student to produce, through the activities, his or her own knowledge, thereby encouraging self-monitoring and testing on matters that are increasingly challenging.

Whether or not you share all the reviewer's convictions is certainly relevant to how valuable the particular review will be to you personally; however, it is not relevant to the exercise suggested above. All that matters for the exercise is your being able to infer, with sufficient clarity, what his convictions are, since your ability to reach such inferences is likely to impact significantly on how much you can benefit from the many reviews you will read in the future. And that ability is of course wholly dependent on how clear you are about your own specific assumptions and criteria, which may or may not be shared by most educational software producers and reviewers.

9 | How Computers Can Enhance the Overall Functioning of a School

Computers can serve a school and its students in many ways outside the classroom or computer lab. Nearly everyone who works in a school can use a computer to enhance their productivity.

Administrators can use computers to automate many of the repetitive and time-consuming activities they must undertake. For example, word processing can be used to minimize the time necessary to prepare reports, and to avoid having to completely retype bulletins that must be changed slightly and reissued periodically. Administrators can also use computers for data base management—storing student and personnel files in a kind of electronic filing cabinet, financial planning, student scheduling, grade reporting, and attendance records.

Guidance counselors can use computers to keep track of student records, and for information about careers and college placement. Computer-based aptitude tests are also available to aid in the counseling process.

Computers can be used in the library as an electronic card catalog, a data file containing borrowing records, or an information retrieval system connected by telephone lines to a large computer-based data bank.

The school nurse can use computers to store student health records, store emergency information, and to monitor students with extended absences due to illness. Cafeteria workers can use computers to monitor the nutritional content of school meals, to plan menus, order supplies, and keep track of inventory. School custodians can use computers to inventory school supplies and equipment, and to monitor school energy use. The list is seemingly endless. Figure 9-1 lists examples of how the computer can be used in non-instructional settings in schools.

Fortunately, nearly all of these time-saving computer applications use the same three basic types of programs. In this chapter, we

User	Uses
Librarian or Media Specialist	Information retrieval, card catalog, borrowing records, equipment inventory
Administrative Staff	Word processing, student and staff records, attendance records, grade reports, budgeting, scheduling
Guidance Counselors	Scheduling, career and college information, aptitude testing
School Nurse	Student health records, absence monitoring
Cafeteria Manager	Nutritional analysis, inventory, menu planning, preparing food orders
Custodian	Inventory, energy-use monitoring

**Figure 9-1. Non-Instructional Uses for
Computers in Schools**

will focus on the school administrator, exploring in detail the relevant computer applications.

9.1 HOW COMPUTERS CAN HELP SCHOOL ADMINISTRATORS

Most school administrators consider leadership to be their most important responsibility. In fact, studies have shown that administrators who spend most of their time out of the office—supervising classrooms, interacting with students, working with staff members— can significantly improve the quality of education in their schools.

Unfortunately, school administrators often find themselves so bogged down with paperwork that they cannot get out of the office as much as they would like. Even a computer at the school district office does not seem to help much; in fact, often the coding forms and delays in getting needed information contribute to the problem.

Using microcomputers to help with the administrative paperwork can help alleviate this problem. Microcomputers can:

1. save up to 25% of the time needed for administrative paperwork without the computer

2. increase the efficiency of the school in managing information such as student records

3. provide greater flexibility in performing administrative tasks

4. provide greater control over the information affecting important decisions in the school

The following sections will show you how to use microcomputers to gain these advantages for your school.

Kinds of Available Software

The software available for school administrative purposes can be thought of under two headings: general purpose software and specific software. Most of the administrative jobs needed by schools can be accomplished with three basic types of general purpose software:

1. word processors, which use the computer to simplify the preparation of documents, such as notices, letters, and reports

2. data base management systems, which use the computer as an electronic filing cabinet

3. electronic spreadsheets, which use the computer to store and update tables needed for budgets and projections

General purpose software has the advantage of flexibility—the computer programs are designed to make it easy for users to customize them for specific applications. For example, you can use the same data base program to create an electronic personnel file and to create a school equipment inventory file. Nevertheless, some administrative applications—scheduling, for example—do not fit into these three categories. For these applications, specific software must be used.

In the following sections, we will first consider the three main types of general purpose administrative software and the ways they can be used in schools. Then, administrative packages for specific purposes will be discussed.

9.2 USING WORD PROCESSING TO CUT DOWN ON PAPERWORK

When most people think of word processors, they think of the specialized machines often seen in modern offices or in television and print advertising. These machines consist of a typewriter keyboard, a display screen, and a cassette recorder or disk drive, usually in a single unit, and a printer that looks like a typewriter without the keyboard.

Actually, these office word processors are specialized computers. Inside the memory of each machine, a program that contains word processing instructions is permanently stored. Since this program cannot be erased, the machine is a "dedicated" word processor, which cannot be used for anything else.

A microcomputer can become a word processor simply by loading a word processing program into its memory. Using a microcomputer as a word processor has two main advantages:

1. Microcomputers and word processing programs are generally much less expensive than dedicated word processors.

2. Microcomputers are flexible. They can be word processors when needed, and still be available for other purposes at other times.

For these reasons, most schools considering word processing will want to use a microcomputer.

What Does a Word Processor Do?

Word processors assist with four main functions associated with document production: writing, editing, storing, and printing. After loading the word processing program into the computer, documents can be written at the keyboard simply by typing. The text appears on the display screen as it is typed, and is stored temporarily in the memory of the computer. Typographical errors can be fixed simply by backspacing and overtyping. You can throw away your correction fluid and lift-off paper!

Word processors contain a variety of editing features to help you revise a document once it has been written (or as you are writing):

1. Text can be inserted anywhere in the document simply by finding the appropriate place, pressing a key or combination of keys, and then typing the insertion. The text that follows the insertion will be moved automatically.

2. Text can be deleted from the document by finding the material to be deleted and pressing appropriate keys. Most word processors allow text to be deleted by the letter, word, sentence, or paragraph. The computer will automatically reformat the text to close up the space left by the deletion.

3. Blocks of text can be moved from one part of the text to another, inserted or deleted. This feature is useful for changing the order of sentences or paragraphs in the text, and for repeating sections of the text without having to type them more than once.

4. Many word processors can search through the text and find particular words or combinations of characters. This feature can be very useful when revising documents. Some word processors can also automatically replace the material found in the text.

5. Spelling checkers are available for almost any word processor. These programs compare the text to a large dictionary. When a word in the text does not match any word in the dictionary, the computer asks the user if the spelling is correct. Similar grammar checkers are starting to become available as well.

These editing features allow documents to be revised quickly and easily, saving much time and effort.

Once a document has been written and edited, the word processor can store it for future reference on a cassette or diskette, and print it out on paper. If you have a daisy wheel printer, the quality of the print will be similar to that on a good office typewriter with a film ribbon. If you have a dot matrix printer, the print quality will be more like that of a portable typewriter with a cloth ribbon.

Most word processors have a variety of print features, including automatically justifying both margins, choice of margin size and print spacing, automatic page numbering and labeling, footnote insertion, underlining and boldface, and many more. Almost any kind of print format can be designed by pressing a few keys. Most word processors can also read name and address lists stored on cassettes or diskettes and print out mail labels and sets of personalized form letters.

Using a Word Processor in the School Office

Word processors are most useful for documents that will need a lot of editing and for documents that can be used more than once with slight modifications. A simple example will illustrate how word processing can save time in the school office.

Suppose it is almost time for parents' visiting night. Chances are, your school has a notice that is sent home with the children as a reminder. The notice stays almost the same from year to year—most often, only a date or two is changed. With a word processor, preparing a new notice is simple: retrieve from a disk or cassette last year's parents' night notice, edit the date on the screen, and print out the new notice.

In addition to notices, typical school word processing applications include:

1. form letters
2. customized documents with a standard form, such as Individual Educational Plans (IEP's)
3. reports

If you look at the number of these types of documents you process in your school office every day, you will be able to see how much time and energy a word processor can save.

There is one small catch, however. Learning to use a word processor will take some time— a few hours for a simple version to a few days for a more complex and powerful one—and not much time will be saved on notices and customized documents until one version of each is available on disk or cassette. To get started with a word processor, one must be willing to trade some start-up time and inconvenience for the efficiency that will come later. Plan for people to start using the word processor during a relatively slack time for office work, so there will not be undue pressure for the new system to produce results faster than it can.

Who Should Use the Word Processor?

When a word processor is used to produce slightly modified versions of "boiler plate" text, like notices or form letters, a school secretary is probably the best person to use the word processor. When reports are produced on a word processor, the greatest efficiency is achieved when the report is actually written at the keyboard. If a draft is composed on paper and then typed into the computer, little time is saved unless the report subsequently needs extensive editing.

Learning to compose at a word processor, instead of with pencil in hand, takes some practice. At first, you will probably write less efficiently than without the word processor. After awhile, however, most people find that composing at a word processor is actually a freeing experience. It is so easy to make changes in the text that there is no need to feel at all inhibited about expressing thoughts just as they come to mind. This freedom to write is one reason why word processing has so much potential as a tool for teaching writing.

9.3 DATA BASE MANAGEMENT SYSTEMS: ELECTRONIC FILING CABINETS

A data base management system (DBMS) turns your computer into an electronic filing cabinet. Any information that can be stored in a set of file folders or record cards can be stored in a data base system. Data base management systems can create and maintain electronic files, search for information in these files, and prepare reports using this information. Computerized filing systems can save time for administrators because computers can search through information much more quickly and accurately than people can.

Setting Up a Data Base

The best way to understand how a data base management system works is to go through the process of setting up a typical file. Let's use a mailing list as an example.

Before we begin, imagine how the mailing list might look without a computer, perhaps on a set of index cards. We might have one index card for each person on the list. On each card would be similar information about that person: name, address, telephone number. In data base terminology, the entire mailing list is called a file. Each index card is a record in that file. The items of information on each record—name, address, phone number—are called fields.

The first step in setting up a data base is to specify the fields that will be in each record. In our example, we might make the following list of fields: Last Name, First Name, Street Address, City, State, Zip Code, and Phone Number. Next, we design a form with the field labels and space to fill in the needed information for each person on the mailing list.

So far, we have not used the computer at all. It is very important to plan carefully before entering any information into the computer. A few minutes making sure the form is well designed, for example, no fields have been left out, enough space has been allowed to enter information, can save hours of work later on.

Now we load the data base management system into the computer. There will probably be a number of options offered, one of which will be to create a new file. (See Figure 9-2.) We choose this option, and the computer will begin asking questions about our file, the fields we have chosen, and how we want to set up our form. After answering the questions, the computer will display the form we have designed on the screen and store it on a disk.

```
(1) DISPLAY/EDIT/DELETE  RECORDS
(2) ADD  RECORDS
(3) LIST  RECORDS  TO  PRINTER
(4) SET  UP  OR  PRINT  REPORT
(5) LOAD  OR  CREATE  NEW  FILE
(6) CLOSE  FILES  AND  EXIT
```

**Figure 9-2. Main Menu of a Typical Data Base
Management System**

Now the data base is available for use. The computer will display the menu once again. This time, we choose to enter data into our new data base. The computer will display our form on the screen, and store each record—the information about each person on our mailing list—as we type it in.

As we type in new records, the computer stores them temporarily in its memory. Before we turn off the computer, these records must be transferred to the disk created for our file. For this reason, data base systems have "file closing" procedures. Always use the file closing procedure when you stop using a data base system, or some of the information in your file may be lost.

Now we can use the other items on the data base menu to search through the records or to generate a report. For example, we can ask the computer to find the record of Mr. and Mrs. James King. If these people are in our organization (and we have entered their names and address into the field), the computer will display our form on the screen, filled in with the Kings' name, address and telephone number.

Well, so far this is not very impressive. It would be just as easy to look up the Kings' address in an alphabetized set of index cards. But suppose we want to know all the members of the organization who live on Ridgewood Avenue. With a set of index cards, someone would have to look through all the cards and either copy out the information or destroy the alphabetical order of the set of cards. But with our data base system, we simply ask the computer to find all the records with Ridgewood Avenue in the Street Address field, and display them on the screen or type the list on the printer.

Suppose we want to have a list of names and phone numbers, or a list of names and addresses printed in order of street address, or a set of mailing labels for everyone in the organization. Our data base program can do all of these by generating and printing reports. In response to questions from the computer, we design forms appropriate for each report, and then direct the computer to type each report on the printer. The computer can store report formats that will be needed more than once, such as our mailing labels format.

Using Electronic Files in the School

Using the procedures outlined in our example above, you can design an electronic file to replace any file needed for school administration. The possibilities are almost limitless, but student records, staff records, and inventory are probably good places to start.

Electronic files will be most useful for bodies of information that must be searched or ordered in more than one way, and for information from which reports must be developed. If you have a name and telephone number list that you only search by name, an alphabetical rolodex file will be easier to use than a computer data file, and much less trouble to set up. Student information files, on the other hand, are frequently needed by grade level, by class, and sometimes by ethnicity, home address, or date of birth as well. One electronic file will be much easier to set up and maintain than several manual versions.

The following advice may help you in getting started with data base management systems.

1. Plan carefully before you set up any data base file. Try out your record form manually before you set it up on the computer. Try out searches and report formats with a small number of sample records before entering all the records into the computer.

2. Phase in the electronic file gradually. Enter all new records into the computer, and enter old records as you have time. Continue to use the manual filing system until the electronic one is complete and has been found reliable.

3. Always make extra copies of electronic file disks, and store them in a different physical location from the originals. Disks cost a few dollars, but the information in a data base file can be worth hundreds or thousands of dollars in labor costs alone.

4. Do not computerize all your records. Files that are always used in a straightforward manner will be easier to use in physical form.

9.4 USING ELECTRONIC SPREADSHEETS

The third kind of general administrative software is the planning spreadsheet, a specialized program that facilitates work with two-dimensional tables. Just as microcomputer data base management programs permit users to custom design electronic data record forms, spreadsheets help users custom design electronic tables that can be used for budgeting and planning.

Spreadsheets are powerful tools mainly because the cells of the tables can be interrelated, so that changing the contents of one cell affects the contents of all the related cells. By making hypothetical entries into some of the cells of the table, users can see the effects of these entries on the table as a whole. In this way, spreadsheets can model complex processes, serving as simulators in many respects.

Unlike word processing and data base management, spreadsheets were invented specifically for microcomputers. The original spreadsheet, called VisiCalc, came out in 1978, and quickly became the most popular microcomputer business program in the world. It is now available for almost all of the microcomputers commonly used in education.

A Sample Spreadsheet Application

In order to understand how electronic spreadsheets can help school administrators, we will work out a useful application, projecting the professional salary budget for a school or school district. In this example, we will assume that there are ten salary steps and only one scale regardless of educational background. The program would work just as well with a more realistic salary scale structure, but the process of entering the model into the computer would be more difficult to describe.

When we load the spreadsheet program into the computer, we see on the screen a blank table, with rows numbered down the left side of the screen, and columns denoted by letters across the top. We will use column A to label the rows of our table, and rows 1 and 2 to label the columns, as shown in Figure 9-3.

In Column B, we would enter the district salary scale for the steps shown in Column A; in Column C, the number of teachers who will be on that step next year; in Column D, the number of teachers on sabbatical on each step. In Column E, we enter a formula that tells the computer to multiply the salary for each step by the number of teachers on that step, and then add the product of the number of teachers on sabbatical by the proportion of salary they

	A	B	C	D	E
1	STEP	SALARY	NUMBER	SABBAT	TOTALS
2					
3	1				
4	2				
5	3				
6	4				
7	5				
8	6				
9	7				
10	8				
11	9				
12	10				
13					
14	TOTALS				

Figure 9-3.

would receive. On Row 14, we tell the computer to add down the columns in Rows C, D, and E, but leave Row B blank (adding all the salary levels together does not make any sense). When we get finished, the screen might look like Figure 9-4.

	A	B	C	D	E
1	STEP	SALARY	NUMBER	SABBAT	TOTALS
2					
3	1	10000	6	O	60000
4	2	11000	4	O	44000
5	3	12000	1	O	12000
6	4	13000	3	O	39000
7	5	14000	2	1	35000
8	6	15000	1	O	15000
9	7	16000	3	1	48000
10	8	17000	3	O	51000
11	9	18000	4	O	72000
12	10	19000	10	2	190000
13					
14	TOTALS		37	4	566000

Figure 9-4.

Now that the table has been entered into the computer, we can use it to make some "what if" projections. For example, suppose two teachers on Step 9 requested sabbatical leave. Assuming that they would be replaced with teachers on Step 1, what would be the impact on the total expenditure for salaries? To answer this question, we need only change the 6 in Cell C3 to 4, the 4 in Cell C11 to 2, and the 0 in Cell D11 to 2. Since the entries in the cells of Column E are linked with the other cells through formulas, the computer will automatically adjust the figures and display the new total in Cell E14.

This type of table could prove helpful in other "what if" situations. Suppose, for example, that the school can afford a maximum of $500,000 for teachers' salaries next year. You may have to lay off enough teachers to cover the deficit, but perhaps some teachers would be willing to postpone their sabbaticals or to retire a year early. By changing the numbers in a few of the cells, you can quickly determine the effects of various options.

Using Electronic Spreadsheets in the School

The example above shows one use of the electronic spreadsheets in making projections. These programs can also help with other types of budget projections, and enrollment projections as well. Some schools use electronic spreadsheets to keep track of budgets and inventories of school equipment. These programs are also used in salary contract negotiations, often by both sides.

Spreadsheet programs can store the tables you develop on diskettes, and print them out as well. They can also generate printed reports based on the information in your tables, or pass this information to some word processing and data base management programs.

Educators have just begun to explore the uses of electronic spreadsheets. Based on their widespread and growing use in business, it can be predicted that they will be used more and more in the future.

9.5 USING SPECIFIC-PURPOSE SOFTWARE IN SCHOOL ADMINISTRATION

The three types of general purpose software discussed in the preceding sections can serve school administrators in many ways.

A few applications, however, either do not fit within the capabilities of these programs or are too complex for general purpose programs to be practical. In this section, we will consider the most common of these applications for which microcomputer software is available: attendance, scheduling, grade reporting, and financial packages.

Specific-purpose programs are generally easier to use than general-purpose ones. Unlike data base programs that require you to set up a form before you can enter data in an electronic file, specific-programs come with files already set up. Data can be entered right away, in response to prompts provided by the program.

The price of this ease of use is inflexibility. Since the form of the file is already on the disk when you buy it, you must use the program substantially as is. When buying a specific-purpose program, then, it is very important to make sure that the information stored by the program, the screen formats, and the report-generating capabilities are just what you need. If a specific-purpose program does not do exactly what you want it to do, chances are that it will not save you a substantial amount of administrative time, and, therefore, will not be a worthwhile investment.

Attendance Programs

Attendance programs can save a significant amount of administrative work in schools that keep track period by period. In these situations, it is not unusual for a clerical worker to devote full time to preparing and distributing period-by-period lists and updating records. Computer-based attendance systems can eliminate the need for much of this work.

The most efficient attendance systems use a card reader to input information. Card readers use optical scanners to read pencil marks from cards that look something like standardized test answer sheets. Instead of filling out period absence forms, teachers mark on the cards circles that correspond to the students who are absent. The cards are collected and fed into the computer via the card reader. The computer uses the information on the cards to update disk-based student attendance records and to print out absence sheets for distribution.

Scheduling Programs

The most efficient scheduling programs take information about the courses that are offered and each student's course selections and actually output printed student schedules. The larger the school and the more complex the scheduling process, the more time scheduling programs can save.

Before purchasing a scheduling program, it is crucial to check whether the program can manage the specific type of scheduling you need at your school. All scheduling programs can handle only a certain number of periods per day or courses per student. Some cannot work out schedules for classes that meet double periods or every other day. Unless the program can do exactly what you want, it is very unlikely to save you any time in the long run.

Grade Reporting Programs

Like scheduling programs, the most efficient grade reporting programs are those that are most fully automatic. A good grade reporting program should actually print out student report cards, sorted by class (or however they can be distributed most easily). Make sure that the program can store grades using your marking system, and that it can generate report cards in an acceptable format.

Efficiency of data entry is an important consideration in evaluating grade reporting programs. If a clerk or teacher must enter all the grades by hand, the program probably will not save much time over a non-computerized system. Grade reporting programs that accept information from card readers are probably most efficient.

Grade reporting programs are often part of a package, including attendance reporting, scheduling, or both. Integrated packages make optimal use of expensive equipment such as card readers, and permit some of the student information entered into the computer to be used for more than one application. For this reason, integrated packages probably represent the best choice in specific-application software, as long as the package will do exactly what you need.

Financial Packages

Financial management packages generally consist of three types of programs: accounts payable, payroll, and general ledger. With a suitable package, it is possible to use microcomputers to manage even fairly large school districts, with budgets up to 10 or 12 million dollars per year. Once again, it is vitally important that the software be reliable and easy to use, and that it conform closely to the management procedures you are using. Do not buy a financial management package without having the business manager of your district work with it and talk with people who are using it in comparable situations.

9.6 SELECTING HARDWARE AND SOFTWARE FOR ADMINISTRATIVE APPLICATIONS

Hardware requirements for microcomputers used for administrative purposes include at least 48K of RAM, two disk drives, and a printer. If the computer will be used for word processing, a daisy wheel printer should be considered. This type of printer will produce documents similar in quality to those produced on a good office typewriter with a film ribbon.

If the computer will be used for attendance records and grade reporting, a card reader is recommended. Even though card readers are still rather expensive, they save so much time in entering data into the computer that they will pay for themselves.

For administrative applications that set up electronic files on disks, the number of records to be entered is an important hardware consideration. A floppy disk drive system will handle roughly 1200 to 1500 records without requiring an inordinate amount of disk swapping. Beyond that point, however, a hard disk system is strongly recommended. Besides enlarged storage capacity, hard disk drives offer quicker and more reliable access to data.

Administrative software is so expensive, both monitarily and in terms of the time spent using it, that extreme caution in selection is recommended. Carefully consider each of the following points before buying any administrative software package:

1. *Ease of use.* The package should be easy to use. Instructions and prompts that appear on the screen should be clear. Data entry should not be cumbersome—remember that the package will not save time if it is hard to put information into the computer.

2. *Error trapping.* The program should check data entry, in terms of both form and logic. For example, the computer should not accept dates like February 31 or numbers that do not make sense in context.

3. *Reliabilty.* The program should function reliably. Incorrect data entry or improper feature selection should not cause it to stop working or lose data.

4. *Documentation.* The documentation should be clearly written, correct, and complete.

5. *Capacity.* The program should have sufficient storage and processing capacity to handle the school's needs with some room to spare. The program should work quickly enough so that it is not cumbersome to use.

6. *Track record.* Look for programs that have been on the market for some time and are being used successfully in situations similar to yours. All complex programs have bugs, but new programs have undiscovered bugs, some of which may be quite serious.

7. *Dealer and/or manufacturer support.* One or the other is crucial. Does the manufacturer support the software by updating it periodically and providing information about known bugs? Does it have a technical assistance hotline staffed by people who know the program? Does the dealer know this software well enough to provide competent technical assistance?

8. *Licensing and backup policies.* Does the manufacturer furnish an inexpensive backup copy of the program? If you have more than one computer that will be used for administrative purposes, is a multiple-copy licensing agreement available?

Our last bit of advice is to move slowly. Start out with one of the general purpose software packages and see whether you can use it to ease some administrative burdens. Once your initial applications are proceeding smoothly, try another. Expect some mistakes and frustrations at first; as you become more familiar with computers and administrative applications, you will be able to move more surely and quickly.

10 How to Maintain and Expand Upon Initial Success

10.1 A CURRICULUM OUTLINE FOR AN ON-GOING TEACHER TRAINING PROJECT

Once they have their feet wet, teachers need a continuous training project to reinforce their skills and understandings. Also, because of the many new techniques and materials emerging almost daily, an on-going project is needed.

Because the development of inexpensive computer systems has placed the cost of a computer within the reach of every school, many teachers who have avoided any contact with "machines" now find themselves surrounded by pupils and some colleagues who speak another language. Within any one school, there is likely to be a wide variety of knowledge and skills. Any curriculum that aims to meet the needs of teachers with disparate backgrounds and comfort levels in computers should emphasize the following themes:

1. appreciation of the major historical developments of computers
2. understanding the impact the computer can have on the teaching process
3. awareness of the difference between "teaching with computers" and "teaching about computers"
4. understanding how to use computers effectively as an aid to instruction and comprehending their advantages and disadvantages
5. insight into the major problems involved in the integration of computers into education

Some of the major topics that should be addressed are: software selection, hardware selection, programming in BASIC and other languages. In outline form, such a curriculum would include:

I.   Software Selection
     A. Identification of major types
     B. Evaluation of software
     C. Problems in production of software
     D. Identifying sources of quality software
II. Hardware Selection
     A. Knowledge of basic system components
     B. Advantages and appropriateness of various systems
     C. Ability to assess the contribution of various peripherals
III. Programming in BASIC and other languages
     A. Understanding and using simple BASIC program
        commands
     B. Understanding and using fundamental system
        commands
     C. Entering several example BASIC programs
     D. Modifying several example BASIC programs
     E. Writing simple programs in BASIC
     F. Becoming acquainted with specific educational lan-
        guages, especially Logo and PILOT, with opportunities
        for in-depth study by those interested

Software Selection

Available software can range from $6 for a cassette tape to a
package of floppy disks for $600. Publishers are spending large sums
on its development, and audio-visual producers now include software in their catalogs. Some of it is excellent, but some of it is
nothing more than an electronic workbook.

It is our responsibility to train teachers to view the array of
available software from many different angles. The author, programmer, distributor, evaluator, and student all see the software from
different viewpoints. Teachers should also be able to review different types of software: drill-and-practice, tutorial, simulation,
game, etc. Criteria should be mutually arrived at. Other important
questions to be addressed are: Who wrote the program? How can I
review software in my subject area? What is the cost effectiveness of
such software?

Hardware Selection

Before educators can contribute effectively to the evolution of
their school's computer project, they need a clear definition of

objectives or planned usage. For example, a system well suited for computer-assisted instruction in reading may not be as well suited for teaching computer programming. Ideally, all those who use the computers will take part in the refining of the project's implementation.

After the major objectives have been agreed upon, then the critical features in meeting these objectives must be determined. For example, the money available, the necessity of color or graphics, the availability of commerical software, all must be considered.

After the teachers have learned how to draw up appropriate objectives, they must be able to evaluate competing computer systems. The training program should provide information on evaluating the appropriateness of various peripherals such as fancy monitors, voice synthesizers, disk drives, printers, etc. Knowing what is new and available as well as cost effective should be part of the training. Since systems are upgraded and sometimes replaced, continuous awareness is necessary.

Programming in BASIC and Other Languages

Any curriculum for teacher-training should include the writing of programs, albeit simple ones. Your purpose here is not to make computer programmers out of all the teachers in the school, but rather to give them an appreciation of the capabilities and limitations of the computer by entering and modifying simple programs. The beginner's language most often used—and generally thought to be easy to learn—is BASIC. Other languages, most notably Logo and PILOT, have been developed specifically for use by educators and their students. Familiarity with them through special workshops will most likely breed intense interest and an in-depth study by at least a few of the teachers.

Teachers should become adept in the five major steps needed for computer programming that are appropriate for any computer language:

1. an understanding of the problem

2. a design of the solution

3. the writing of the program

4. the testing and correcting of the program

5. the documentation of the program

The most important part of this aspect of the training program is that the computer is a problem-solving tool and should be considered to be a means to an end, not the end itself.

Completing the Training

Upon completion of the in-service teacher training, there are certain objectives that the teachers should have met. These include, but are not limited to:

1. loading programs from a disk and/or a tape into a computer, accomplished during the initial phases (see Chapter 5)
2. evaluating software in different fields
3. discussing the merits of various systems
4. articulating the functions and advantages of various peripherals
5. entering and executing programs in BASIC and, perhaps, PILOT and Logo
6. gaining overall confidence in operating a computer

10.2 STRATEGIES FOR ORGANIZING THE TRAINING OF TEACHERS

Teaching teachers about computers can be very challenging. Yet certain strategies and techniques have worked in other communities and we want to share them with you.

After your initial success in getting teachers exposed to the computers, you must be prepared to follow up decisively and quickly to expand upon the basic skills they have acquired. To be effective, your training project must assess the level of competency the teachers have reached. You do not want to assume that they know more (or less) than they actually do. Such miscalculation will just make your training project frustrating and counterproductive.

Perhaps the most valuable source of data on the level of teacher's skills and understanding is through direct observation of the teachers' performance in the classroom. Too many teachers show understanding of computers in an after-school course, but freeze-up and avoid doing any computer work in their classroom. This kind of direct observation can serve to identify teacher strengths and weaknesses, providing the basis for planning specific types of in-service programs. Also, as a dividend, it identifies those successful computer techniques and methods that one teacher can share with colleagues on a buddy or peer level.

The organizing of the training of teachers remains the responsibility of the head of the school or department. However, the following activities involve all staff members and can be tried in your school:

1. Conduct individual conferences, both formal and informal, with teachers to discuss their comfort level with computers, the problem areas that concern them, and their aspirations for their pupils.

2. Have faculty conferences to explore problems of mutual concern. Teachers get a great deal of support when they hear of other teachers facing similar problems. This activity is also an excellent forum for sharing grass-roots solutions.

3. Organize intervisitations among classrooms or schools. Such an experience enables teachers to observe master teachers in action in their own school or elsewhere in the district.

4. Encourage teachers to carry on a program of advanced study in computers at a community college or university.

In organizing the training of teachers, it is important to select teacher-trainers who have human relation skills in addition to their relatively high skills in computing. This most important aspect of training involves a special constellation of attributes on the part of the trainers. Whereas the tendency in many situations is to emphasize only the technical knowledge of the computer trainer, our experience has shown the following traits to be as critical for trainers:

• recognizing the importance of variety in teaching styles
• willingness to communicate
• knowledge of how adults learn
• ability to stimulate attitude and behavior changes
• ability to serve as a catalyst in creating team spirit

Staff feedback is another important strategy to implement. It is vital that the teachers receiving the training have an opportunity on an on-going basis to tell their trainers what they think of the training. In some schools this takes the form of a "response sheet" at the end of each in-service course. Other schools rely on a rap session prior to the start of each session to guide the instructor on what has been learned and what needs still exist.

10.3 FOUR TESTED TECHNIQUES FOR OPTIMALLY MAINTAINING THE INVOLVEMENT OF ADMINISTRATIVE PERSONNEL

Teachers alone do not make up a successful school staff. Even small schools have administrative staff members who are part of a team approach. In the area of computer use, it is natural to find solutions to administrative problems through the effective use of available hardware and software packages.

As described in detail in Chapter 9, administrative uses of the computer will take different forms in different schools. The guidance department in a Los Angeles high school analyzed grades and Scholastic Aptitude Test scores during the preceding ten years. As a result, they were able to compare their school's grading and testing patterns to national norms.

Under the direction of an assistant principal, school secretaries in Denver, Colorado used the computer in a large junior high school to check the dates of pupil absences. When patterns were noted for certain pupils, the attendance officer was able to follow up and prevent further truancy.

An after-school center coordinator in Louisville, Kentucky used the computer to establish several extracurricular clubs. He matched pupil interest lists with available teacher strengths to form the clubs.

But how can you optimally involve administrative personnel? These four proven techniques have worked well for others:

1. *Involve them in planning for change.* Try to anticipate objections. Changes that upset routine, require new knowledge or skills, or inconvenience people are bound to meet with some objection or resistance. Looking at change from the staff's point of view will usually be enough to help determine what their objections are likely to be. Knowing the objections, we can, with a little creative thought, turn them into advantages.

2. *Continue to emphasize benefits.* People are naturally concerned with such questions as, "What's in it for me?" They want to know whether the changes being implemented will mean more satisfying work, greater security, opportunity to show that they can solve problems, more responsibility, higher pay, less fatigue, less confusion, and greater independence. The benefits used to motivate people to cooperate should be put on as personal a level as possible. It would be dishonest not to point out some of the disadvantages as well.

3. *Listen in depth.* Staff members have a right to be heard. Their questions may be their way of demonstrating interest in their jobs—a means of making suggestions that would facilitate change. Do not take their questions as a threat to the continued success of the computer project. If the administrative staff members are treated with respect, they will respond in kind. They will feel better, also, if they know their concerns have been considered.

4. *Follow up.* Just convincing the staff of the benefits of a computer in their lives is not enough. You must expand upon your initial success by following up. Did any problems come up that were not anticipated? Are adjustments necessary to realize the full benefit of the change? A sincere interest in how the change has affected the pupils and staff, together with a willingness to make refinements, help build the climate in which future changes will be initiated.

10.4 DESIGNING A TRAINING PROGRAM FOR NON-PROFESSIONAL STAFF

In recent years many paraprofessionals, parent aides, reading volunteers, and other non-professionals have come into the schools to perform a variety of tasks. These people have freed fully-trained teachers from some non-teaching and time-consuming duties. Others have helped individualize instruction or perform specialized duties.

It may be your responsibility to design and implement a training program for these workers. Begin by establishing a clear picture of paraprofessional (term to represent all non-professional staff members) capabilities. Make sure that the best person is assigned to carry out each activity or program required to meet the school's computer project objectives.

To make the necessary match-ups of talents and needs, prepare a chart listing each position and the functions involved and, to the extent possible, assign people to each position whose skills appear to tally most closely with the job requirement.

Like teachers, these non-professional staff members have skills beyond those indicated by their job title, skills that should be utilized. An attendance worker may have had key punch operator experience. A custodial worker may have had experience repairing complicated business machines. Design a training program that capitalizes on the interests, skills, and abilities of these workers.

Give them credit for life experience as well as any formal training they may have had.

For many school people, the training of non-professionals turns out to be a difficult and frustrating experience. What are some of the most common reasons so many have difficulty in this sensitive area? We have broken down the problems into the following areas:

1. *Saying too much or too little.* If you go into unnecessary details on the use of the keyboard with a paraprofessional who is an accurate typist, she will get bored and stop listening. She might miss an important point entirely or feel that you are treating her like a beginner and be uncooperative. On the other hand, if you don't tell a beginner enough, she spends a lot of time stumbling around, making very little headway.

2. *Not asking questions.* One way to ascertain that a beginner at the computer understands is to ask him to repeat a procedure in his own words. Many times he may be able to repeat your words without really knowing what he is actually supposed to do. If you suspect this to be true, ask questions that will test his understanding.

3. *Giving vague or incomplete instruction.* So often we assume that because we know something, everyone else possesses the same knowledge or that it is easy or obvious. Computer experts frequently talk a language that resembles English but to a novice, words like "run," "enter" and "load" do not carry the same meanings. Be sure your instructions are specific and detailed.

4. *Using pedagogical terms.* When you have been teaching for a number of years or have been dealing with teachers for a period of time, certain terms and phrases become part of your everyday vocabulary. Non-professional people are aware of their lack of formal training in education and may be particularly sensitive to that lack. Your training should be in lay language, but on an adult level.

10.5 FIVE TIPS FOR TURNING DISSENTERS INTO SUPPORTERS

In virtually every organization where there are three or more workers, it is inevitable that not everyone will support every project or idea. Schools are no exception. The advent of computers has, in some cases, exacerbated the tensions in schools. In some places there are actual schisms between those committed to computers and those dissenters who, at best, pay only lip service to the benefits of the new technology. Their dissentions lead to clashes, complaints and cliques—the three c's of disharmony where supporters and dissenters of computers in education exist in the same building. Here are five tips to help you deal with this common situation.

Handling Complaints

Dissenters will complain about the amount of instructional money being spent on hardware and software, and the impersonalization of computer-assisted instruction, etc. The way in which you handle these complaints—both legitimate and unfounded—affects the performance and morale of the entire school. One way to reduce the friction between the administration and the complainer is first to find out who's doing the complaining. Once determined, you need to consider what type of teacher or other staff member is doing the griping. If he's a high performer, you have to consider the fact that he feels a greater stake in his job than most workers. With this type of person, you should make a sincere effort to investigate the condition being complained about and correct it if you possibly can.

The low-performer usually gripes about things that concern his personal comfort or other nonproductive matters. He is usually just looking for some sort of recognition. Naturally you want him to be as happy as possible, so you correct the conditions that you can. But, more often than not, you can reduce his complaining by patting him on the back when he does a good job and generally letting him feel that he is needed and appreciated. In spite of what you think of the importance of another person's complaint, it is never insignificant to the person making it.

Reducing Clashes

When teachers or other staff members feel strongly about the place of computers, or anything else, emotional outbursts result. The best way to reduce these clashes is to keep them from going beyond the point of no return, where reconciliation becomes impossible. You cannot help by exchanging verbal blows in a clash of tempers. The best thing you can do in the event of another person's emotional outburst is to let him talk—and keep him talking. While he is talking, it is your job to listen. Try not to take offense at what an angry colleague or subordinate says, at least for the time being. Don't argue, interrupt or contradict. Instead, give him a free rein to say whatever he feels like saying. Give him a chance to blow off some steam. When two or more staff people are involved in a clash, it is imperative that you remain completely neutral. Do not succumb to the temptation of giving one combatant the idea that you are really with him while giving his adversary the same impression. Otherwise, it will be used against you at some future time.

Dealing with Cliques

Dissenters and supporters of a school's computer program will, quite naturally, band together. These groups cannot have considerable influence over the behavior and job attitudes of other individuals—especially teachers new to computing. Whether a clique is disruptive or cooperative depends a great deal on how it is handled.

In every group, there is someone who is the most popular and who is the acknowledged leader. There is a strong psychological factor in this leadership because it hinges on the group members' desire for authority that is not imposed on anyone else—they decide for themselves that one of their number deserves their loyalty. In most cases, the problem of dealing with cliques becomes a question of recognizing the popular leader and finding a way to enlist her cooperation.

Give and Take

You can both win over a dissenter and give encouragement to your computer project supporters through the use of an appraisal interview. This technique is applied on a regular basis to all staff members. Where it is used, the "anti-everything" teachers feel part of the team and turn "pro." Follow these simple steps:

a. Prepare carefully for the appraisal interview.

b. Begin with a positive statement.

c. Assure the staff member that the interview will be kept strictly confidential.

d. Ask the person's ideas for solving any computer project-related problem.

e. Take notes of his or her suggestions and follow up on them by referring to your written notes later on.

f. Keep an open mind and be willing to accept good ideas, no matter what the source.

Inter-Department Cooperation

It is essential that the computer department maintains good relationships with other departments within the school. Many a misguided computer coordinator thinks that hoarding a good idea or system will make his department stand out so that everyone thinks he's doing a bang-up job. But this attitude actually reduces the efficiency of the entire school by creating petty jealousies and factions. Help such persons to realize that the way to make themselves and their program look good is to let everybody in on a good thing. If they share their good ideas with others, they will be reciprocated and everybody wins.

10.6 A SAMPLE EVALUATION SURVEY YOU CAN PUT TO IMMEDIATE USE

In evaluating the effectiveness of your school's computer project, there is no better source of feedback than the teaching staff. The following survey has proven very useful in obtaining a wide range of valuable information from them. Adapt and modify it to meet your particular needs.

Computer Project Questionnaire

Student Performance

I. Please rate each of the following statements according to how strongly you agree or disagree with it.

1. Having the computers seems to have increased student skills in computer literacy.

(1)	(2)	(3)	(4)	(5)
strongly agree	agree	uncertain	disagree	strongly disagree

2. The computers seem to encourage students to work independently.

(1)	(2)	(3)	(4)	(5)
strongly agree	agree	uncertain	disagree	strongly disagree

3. The computers seem to motivate reluctant learners to master specific performance objectives.

(1)	(2)	(3)	(4)	(5)
strongly agree	agree	uncertain	disagree	strongly disagree

4. The computers seem to increase the speed at which students master specific performance objectives.

(1)	(2)	(3)	(4)	(5)
strongly agree	agree	uncertain	disagree	strongly disagree

5. The computers seem to increase the depth of mastery of specific performance objectives.

(1)	(2)	(3)	(4)	(5)
strongly agree	agree	uncertain	disagree	strongly disagree

II. Estimate the average percent of student time on task that is realized when students work with the computers, as compared to when they work without it (for example, +20%, -20%, etc.): _____

III. Estimate the percent of increase of the total number of specific objectives that are mastered in the academic curriculum as a result of using the computers:_____

IV. Estimate the percent of increase of the total number of specific performance objectives that are mastered in the behavioral curriculum as a result of using the computers:_____

Staff Reaction

V. For each of the following questions, please check the *one* answer that most nearly applies to you.

1. Which category best describes your instructional use of the computer?

   a._____ to augment instruction
   b._____ to provide new instruction
   c._____ to replace traditional instruction

2. What is your own interest in continued involvement with computers?

   a._____ very interested
   b._____ interested
   c._____ ambivalent

d._____ not interested
e._____ very unenthusiastic

3. To what extent does having computers free you as a teacher to do more actual teaching?

a._____ it frees me greatly
b._____ it frees me somewhat
c._____ it doesn't seem to matter
d._____ it only gives me an extra burden

4. What is your overall feeling about the computer project?

a._____ very satisfied
b._____ satisfied
c._____ ambivalent
d._____ dissatisfied
e._____ very dissatisfied

5. How important is it to have additional computers available?

a._____ very important
b._____ important
c._____ minimally important
d._____ unimportant

6. How important is it to have additional software available?

a._____ very important
b._____ important
c._____ minimally important
d._____ unimportant

VI. Please use additional sheets for any general comments and/or anecedotal reports you want to make.

10.7 HOW TO MAINTAIN PARENTAL SUPPORT

"From donuts to dollars" could be the public relations motto for a computer project to Southlake, Texas. The educators there were not content merely to get initial funding for their computer program, so they are successfully searching for the broader support and commitment that comes from continuously maintained parent involvement.

On the first Friday morning of each month, the Computer Lab in one of the schools in the district holds "Donuts for Dollars" where it hosts fathers from 7:30 to 8:30 in the morning before they go to work. A tour of the computer lab and the latest pupil-made programs are regular features. Over coffee and donuts, the project, its goals and needs are discussed. While originally planned for working fathers who could not make afternoon meetings, it has now been expanded to include all working parents.

In a similar vein, community school districts of New York City recently came up with a "57 Varieties" plan for mobilizing parent support. We include some of their more universally adaptable ideas that you can use for your computer project.

• Select a "Parent of the Month," someone who has assisted with programming in school, repaired a machine at no charge, or raised money at a cake sale for new software. In this way, you honor ten parents each school year.

• Establish a "Good Neighbor Day" by inviting people who live immediately around your school building for a tour of the building and some light refreshment.

• Recognize all your "computer volunteers" by holding a special "Thank You" assembly. The principal spoke at one such assembly and presented each parent-volunteer with a "byte" pin. The teachers' representative handed out carnations and pupils read salutory poems and stories that were composed and edited on the computer.

• Parents at a large middle school with several computers invited the PTA leadership of the feeding elementary schools for tea. After a tour of the computer room, the parents were told of the cost of the software and were invited to plan fundraisers for next year when the younger pupils would move up to the middle school.

• In another school, a "Computercard" is sent home to each parent of the child enrolled in the school's computer program. This is a regular postcard imprinted with a report on the pupil's progress in programming. Still another school mails home a mimeographed computer report card, along with a blank postcard addressed to the principal. The postcard is used by the parent to address any questions he or she may have about the computer project.

• A "Grandparents' Booster Club" was started in one school and now has been duplicated in neighboring schools. These retired people meet once a month at the school and are filled in on the latest computer happenings. They have committees devoted to fundraising, publicity, repairs, and software exchange—all to the benefit of the computer project.

The activities will generate a host of fundraising and morale-building activities on the part of the parents. Through them, the teachers and pupils in your school will feel encouraged to move ahead with renewed vigor.

10.8 SAMPLE PUBLIC RELATIONS CHECKLIST

Your computer project should not be a well-kept secret. Every school needs to develop a solid communications program aimed at informing the public and fostering support for its project. You may want to utilize the following public relations checklist, adapted from one used by the Millard Public Schools in Omaha, Nebraska, for guidance in this most critical area.

1. Efforts are made to acquaint new families with the computer project's curriculum and services:

   __before school begins   __during the school year

2. A newsletter is sent to parents:

   __occasionally   __on a regular basis

3. The principal is available to respond to parents' questions and concerns:

   __always   __frequently   __occasionally

4. Parents have opportunities to voice ideas and suggestions about the computer project through:

   __parent-teacher organization   __advisory committee
                  __informal gatherings

5. Appreciation for volunteer work connected with the computer project is expressed through:

   __notes   __social events or award ceremonies
                  __mention in newsletter

6. Before open house and/or curriculum night presentations about the computer project, teachers receive guidance on how to make effective presentations:

   __always   __frequently   __never

7. Teachers arrange special computer-related events to encourage parents to come to school:

   __frequently   __occasionally   __never

8. A computer course for parents and other members of the community is run:

   __frequently   __occasionally   __never

10.9 HOW TO MAKE PRESS RELEASES WORK FOR THE BENEFIT OF YOUR COMPUTER PROJECT

Would you like to get more of the good things about the school's computer project into the newspaper? You can orchestrate the handling and placing of news stories and items in your local paper. Here are some proven techniques for spreading the word:

1. Mail in "advance" stories of events related to your computer project. This practice can generate two stories: an announcement of the event and a follow-up on it. If you mail in your story early enough, an editor may send a reporter and/or a photographer to cover the story.

2. Season your releases. Be alert to timely opportunities for a story. Suggest computer-related gifts before Christmas.

3. Submit a column. Your weekly newspaper would probably welcome a regular column on computer news. Contact the editor and submit a trial column of about 500 words.

4. Send in fillers, brief items of one paragraph that newspapers use to fill out columns when longer stories leave gaps. Editors need many fillers and welcome local items. Send in short items about your computer project.

5. Update stories. Scan the papers daily for computer related news and follow up with how your school is meeting the challenge. If an article describes the nationwide surge in purchasing home computers, send in a story of how students in your school have designed their own video games or made money using their home computers.

6. Send in neatly typed, triple-spaced press releases. Be sure to include: what, who, when, and where. Here is a sample.

FOR IMMEDIATE RELEASE

Fairview Junior High School is holding a "Parents as Partners Night" in their newly opened Computer Laboratory. On Thursday evening, March 8, at 8:30, the staff of the Computer Department along with the pupil members of the Byte Club will thank the parents who have assisted them in setting up the Computer Lab. Refreshments will be served to all and awards will be handed out to parents who served as partners. The Computer Lab can be reached through the Lawrence Avenue entrance.

As you can see, a simple direct approach is all that is needed.

10.10 HOW TO TRANSLATE INITIAL SUCCESS INTO ADDITIONAL DOLLARS

Once your computer project is launched, you find yourself with the basic hardware and enough software for the first phase. You know, however, that this is hardly enough. You will soon need more money for several reasons:

- Money is needed for repair of equipment. The warranties don't last forever and service-call fees, even without charges for parts, can be substantial. Regular maintenance contracts are also expensive.
- Your students will soon be ready for new and greater challenges. Additional software as well as blank disks and cassettes will have to be purchased.
- The one, two, or three machines you started with will not suffice as additional students are plugged into the program.
- More sophisticated equipment will be needed as your pupil population grows in computer literacy and technique. Modems, printers, and other items will move from the "luxury" to the "necessity" category.

How do you raise these additional dollars? The best way is to build on your initial success. Call a meeting of the parents who have pupils presently in the computer program. Demonstrate or have the pupils demonstrate some of the skills they have acquired. Remember, if a picture is worth a thousand words, then the image of your own child handling the technology of tomorrow right before your eyes is worth ten thousand words!

Level with parents. Hand out a ditto sheet that details the cost of the computer equipment and supplies on hand and the cost of equipment and supplies needed next year. Emphasize the skills that the new equipment will give their children. After you are sure they understand how much money is needed and where it will be spent, let them organize their own fundraising projects. Once you have heated them up, let them raise their own steam. You should, of course, be available to guide parents and give them encouragement, but allow them to organize their own fundraising activities. Activities that generate funds from inside are: cake sales, Chinese auctions, raffles, 50-50 drawings, discount coupon books for neighborhood merchants, etc. Lucrative outside activities include candy sales, school photographs, stationery supplies, candles, flower bulbs, fruit cake, jewelry, novelties, etc.

Another way to generate enthusiasm is to offer computer training after school to adults in the community. The adult computer training would not necessarily prepare those who sign up for programming, but instead would give them a general understanding and awareness of the technology and its practical uses. More important, once these adults get "hooked" on computers they will become your active partners in translating the initial success of the project into more dollars.

At this stage of expansion, do not overlook the small and large businesses in your community, who spend money advertising in school and local newspapers. Offer them the opportunity to see how other businesses have stretched their limited advertising dollar by purchasing some supplies or equipment that bear their name and logo. Show them how the generous gestures of their peers have been mentioned in the school and town newspapers. Take them on a walking tour to see how 8 x 10 glossy photos of the actual presentations have been posted in the store window of competing shops. Share with them the glowing letters sent by the principal to previous donors, which are frequently displayed alongside the photos. Consider banks, pizza parlors, auto repair shops, bakeries, fast food restaurants—the list is endless. All these businesses want to attract young people and their parents. They will get a lot of mileage for every dollar they donate, especially if you help them. We have even seen plaques that read: "This Computer Lab has been equipped by the Lenox National Bank" or, laminated to a microcomputer, "Donated by Dr. and Mrs. John Russo."

Government sources are prone to lend support to projects that have already demonstrated a degree of success and are therefore low risk. Even after seed money has been spent, you can write proposals for state and federal grants that will generate additional dollars for your computer project. If your district does not have anyone with this kind of expertise, then contact a local community college, which is dependent on government and agency grants to keep its doors open. Persuade the community college to share its knowledge of funding sources. This will be easier to do if you first convince the school that you are not interested in competing with it in any area.

The manufacturers of computer equipment and supplies can sometimes be counted on to come across with some donated or "loan" items for schools with an admirable track record. Michigan schools received free from IBM equipment in a contract that required an explanation of how the free computers would be used. Salespeople of software can sometimes be convinced to let you "pilot" some new program for the district. In exchange for your trying the software and perhaps endorsing it, they will give it to you at cost or half price.

Finally, you may be able to do some small computer tasks for a fee for neighborhood groups. It would be understood that the fees paid would all be earmarked for the purchase of additional equipment for the school. Service clubs would appreciate a computerized membership list but do not want to buy a computer of their own. They might be happy to write your school a check for this service.

Doctors, lawyers, and other professional people in your community might be happy to do the same. Be sure to clear this line of action with your school board before accepting your first check.

10.11 SEVEN WAYS TO MAKE THE SCHOOL'S COMPUTERS BENEFIT THE COMMUNITY

Reaching out into the community-at-large will perform a public service, publicize your school, and enhance its image. Modify one or more of these seven ideas to suit your situation.

1. Your expensive hardware is probably never used after three o'clock or on a Saturday morning. Why not open the doors to the computer room at such times so that local citizens can try their hand at the equipment or actually take instruction? For a relatively modest fee, they can support the cost of a teacher at an hourly rate, plus the custodial fees.

2. Community agencies and non-profit organizations are always in need of up-to-date lists of residents and their addresses. Why not prepare mailing lists for these charitable organizations, alumni groups, and community members?

3. Bring in scout troops, youth organizations, and church groups of young people on a Saturday morning for an orientation to the computer room or for a refresher course. While these youngsters may not attend your school, the goodwill you will generate in the community will make it all worthwhile.

4. Provide the senior citizens in your community with a printout of all the available community resources. This would include such items as phone numbers of Medicare, contact persons at the Social Security office, and where to go for food stamps. The names of the senior citizens who volunteer for this exchange can also be passed along to Meals on Wheels and other special services.

5. Involve your local police and fire department by offering to have your computer prepare inventories of their equipment or personnel. You would be amazed at the additional security your school will receive as a result of your offer.

6. Offer post-graduate computer training or brush-up courses to your former students who are hired by local businesses. Employers can be told that if they hire the graduate of the local high school, you will make your computer facilities available to them for additional training.

7. Provide speakers and demonstrations for luncheon clubs and service organizations. These chalk talks or demonstrations will be welcomed by the program chairpersons of the local community groups. Your school will also benefit from the goodwill generated.

APPENDIX A:
Publications Specific to Educators

Write to each of the following publishers and request a free, sample copy of the magazine, newsletter, or journal it publishes. Not all will respond, so plan a visit to a well-stocked library to examine the various publications that do not arrive in the mail. Subscribing to at least two or three that seem best suited to your needs will prove a worthwhile investment.

AEDS Monitor. Educational Data Systems, 1201 Sixteenth Street, NW, Washington, DC 20036

Apple for the Teacher. c/o Ted Perry, 5848 Riddio Street, Citrus Heights, CA 95610

Apple in Education. 3413 NW 8th Avenue, Gainesville, FL 32605

Arithmetic Teacher. National Council of Teachers of Mathematics, 1906 Association Drive, Reston, VA 22901

Catalyst. Western Center for Microcomputers in Special Education, Inc., 1259 El Camino Real, Suite 275, Menlo Park, CA 94025

Classroom Computer Learning. (Formerly, *Classroom Computer News.)* 19 Davis Drive, Belmont, CA 94002

Collegiate Microcomputer. Rose-Hulman Institute of Technology, Terre Haute, IN 47803

Commodore: The Microcomputer Magazine. 1200 Wilson Drive, West Chester, PA 19380

Computer Town, USA! P.O. Box E, Menlo Park, CA 94025

Computer Using Educators of British Columbia Newsletter. Harold Brochman, 3264 St. Georges Avenue, North Vancouver, British Columbia V7N 1V3, Canada

Computers and Education. Pergamon Press, Maxwell House, Fairview Park, Elmsford, NY 10523

Computers and the Humanities. Pergamon Press, Maxwell House, Fairview Park, Elmsford, NY 10523

Computers and the Media Center News. 515 Oak Street, North, Cannon Falls, MN 55009

Computing Teacher. Department of Computer and Information Science, University of Oregon, Eugene, OR 97403

CUE Newsletter. Computer-Using Educators, P.O. Box 18547, San Jose, CA 95158

Educational Computer. M. Dundee Maples, P.O. Box 535, Cupertino, CA 95015

Educational Electronics. Electronics Communications, Inc., 1311 Executive Center Drive, Suite 220, Tallahassee, FL 32301

Educational Technology. 140 Sylvan Avenue, Englewood Cliffs, NJ 07632

Electronic Classroom. 150 West Carob Street, Compton, CA 90220

Electronic Learning. 902 Sylvan Avenue, Englewood Cliffs, NJ 07632

EPEI Report. EPEI Institute, Box 620, Stony Brook, NY 11790

ETC: Educational Technology and Communication. Subscription Department, Far West Laboratory, 1855 Folsom Street, San Francisco, CA 94103

Instructional Innovator. Association for Education Communications Technology, 1126 16th Street, NW, Washington, DC 20036

Journal of Computer-Based Instruction. Association for the Development of Computer-Based Instructional Systems, 8120 Penn Avenue South, Bloomington, MN 55431

Journal of Computers, Reading and Language Arts. Gerald H. Block, CRLA, Box 13039, Oakland, CA 94661

Journal of Computers in Mathematics and Science Teaching. P.O. Box 4455, Austin, TX 78765

Journal of Educational Data Processing. Ideas, Inc., P.O. Box 867, Soquel, CA 95073

Journal of Educational Technology Systems. Baywood Publishing Company, 120 Marine Street, Farmingdale, NY 11735

LOGO and Educational Computing Journal. Interactive Education Foundation, Suite 219, 1320 Stony Brook Road, Stony Brook, NY 11790

MACUL Journal. Michigan Association for Computer Users in Education, Wayne County ISD, 33500 Van Born Road, Wayne, MI 48184

Mathematics Teacher. National Council of Teachers of Mathematics, 1906 Association Drive, Reston, VA 22091

Micro-Scope. JEM Research, Discovery Park, University of Victoria, P.O. Box 1700, Victoria, B.C., V8W 2Y2, Canada

Microcomputer Digest. CEO Associates, 103 Bridge Avenue, Bay Head, NJ 08742

Microcomputers in Education. Queue, Inc., 5 Chapel Hill Drive, Fairfield, CT 06432

National Logo Exchange. Susan Thompson, Box 5341, Charlottesville, VA 22905

Oregon Computing Teacher. Oregon Council of Computer Education, Computer Center, East Oregon State College, La Grande, OR 97850

Rochester Computer Education Newsletter. The Computer Center, 671 Monroe Avenue, Rochester, NY 14618

School Courseware Journal. 1341 Bulldog Lane, Suite C, Fresno, CA 93710

SIGCUE Bulletin. Association for Computing Machinery, Special Interest Group on Computer Uses in Education, 1133 Avenue of the Americas, New York, NY 10036

Small Computers in Libraries. Graduate Library School, University of Arizona, 1515 East First Street, Tucson, AZ 85721

Teaching and Computers. 902 Sylvan Avenue, Englewood Cliffs, NJ 07632

Technological Horizons in Education (T.H.E. Journal). P.O. Box 992, Acton, MA 01720

Window (on disk only). Window, Inc., 469 Pleasant Street, Watertown, MA 02172

General Interest Publications
with Educationally Relevant Material

A.N.A.L.O.G. P.O. Box 23, Worcester, MA 01603 (specific to Atari® computer applications)

Apple Orchard. 910A George Street, Santa Clara, CA 95050 (specific to Apple computer applications)

Appleseed. Softside Publications, 6 South Street, Milford, NH 03055 (specific to Apple computer applications)

Byte. 70 Main Street, Peterborough, NH 03458

Call A.P.P.L.E. 304 Main Street, Suite 300, Renton, WA 98055 (specific to Apple computer applications)

Compute! 625 Fulton Street, Greensboro, NC 27403

Creative Computing. Box 789-M, Morristown, NJ 07960

Dr. Dobbs Journal. 1263 El Camino Real, Menlo Park, CA 94025

Home and Educational Computing. P.O. Box 5406, Greensboro, NC 27403 (specific to Commodore VIC-20 computer applications)

Infoworld. 530 Lytton Avenue, Palo Alto, CA 94301

Interface Age. 16704 Marquardt Avenue, Cerritos, CA 90701

Kilobaud Microcomputing. 80 Pine Street, Peterborough, NH 03458

Micro: The 6502/6809 Journal. P.O. Box 6502, Chelmsford, MA 01824

Microcomputing. P.O. Box 997, Farmingdale, NY 11737

Nibble. P.O. Box 325, Lincoln, MA 01773 (specific to Apple computer applications)

Pocket Computer Newsletter. 35 Old State Road, Oxford, CT 06483

Purser's Magazine. P.O. Box 466, El Dorado, CA 95623

Personal Computing. 50 Essex Street, Rochelle Park, NJ 07662

Popular Computing. 70 Main Street, Peterborough, NH 03458

Power/Play. Commodore Business Machines, Inc., 487 Devon Park Drive, Wayne, PA 19807 (specific to Commodore computer applications)

Softalk. Softalk Circulation, Box 60, North Hollywood, CA 91603

Softside. 6 South Street, Milford, NH 03055

Sync. 39 East Hanover Street, Morris Plains, NJ 07960 (specific to Sinclair computer applications)

TRS-80 Users Journal. P.O. Box 7112, Tacoma, WA 98407 (specific to the TRS-80™ microcomputer applications)

TRS-80 Microcomputer News. P.O. Box 2910, Fort Worth, TX 76113 (specific to the TRS-80™ microcomputer applications)

80 Microcomputing. Pine Street, Peterborough, NH 03458 (specific to the TRS-80™ microcomputer applications)

80 U.S. Journal. 3838 S. Warner Street, Tacoma, WA 98409 (specific to the TRS-80™ microcomputer applications)

APPENDIX C:
Larger, Educationally Oriented Organizations

Write to the following organizations and ask them for any literature describing their activities and for a listing of local affiliates that may be in your area. You will probably want to become a member of one or more such organizations, as they are an invaluable source of up-to-date information about educational computing.

Association for Computing Machinery, 1133 Avenue of the Americas, New York, NY 10036

Association for Educational Communications and Technology (AECT), 1126 16th Street, NW, Washington, DC 20036

Association for Educational Data Systems (AEDS), 1201 16th Street, NW, Washington, DC 20036

Association for the Development of Computer-Based Instructional Systems (ADCIS), Bond Hall, Western Washington University Computer Center, Bellingham, WA 98225

Computer-Using Educators, c/o Don McKell, Independence High School, 1776 Education Park Drive, San Jose, CA 95133

EDUCOM, P.O. Box 364, Princeton, NJ 08540

International Council for Computers in Education (ICCE), Department of Computer and Information Science, University of Oregon, Eugene, OR 97403

Library and Information Technology Association, American Library Association, 50 East Huron Street, Chicago, IL 60611

Microcomputer Education Application Network, Suite 800, 1030 15th Street, NW, Washington, DC 20036

Minnesota Educational Computing Consortium (MECC), 2520 Broadway Drive, St. Paul, MN 55113

National Videodisc/Microcomputer Institute, Utah State University, Logan, UT 84322

School Microcomputer Users Group of Alameda County (SMU-GAL), c/o Glenn Fisher, Alameda County Office of Education, 685 A Street, Hayward, CA 94541

Society for Applied Learning Technology (SALT), 50 Culpeper Street, Warrenton, VA 22186

Society of Data Educators, 983 Fairmeadow Road, Memphis, TN 38117

APPENDIX D:
Prime Sources of Funding

Adult Education—Grants to States. *Contact:* Director, Division of Adult Education, Department of Education, Washington, DC 20202. (202) 245-2278.

Appalachian Vocational and Other Educational Facilities and Operations. *Contact:* Executive Director, Appalachian Regional Commission, 1666 Connecticut Avenue NW, Washington, DC 20235. (202) 673-7874.

Apple Education Foundation (also known as the Foundation for the Advancement of Computer-Aided Education). *Contact:* Director, 20863 Stevens Creek Boulevard, B-2, A-1, Cupertino, CA 95014. (408) 255-3295.

Atari® Institute for Educational Action Research. Atari®, Inc., 1265 Borregas Avenue, P.O. Box 427, Sunnyvale, CA 94086. (408) 745-2000.

Bilingual Education—Title VII. *Contact:* Office of Bilingual Education, Department of Education, Reporters Building, Room 421, 400 Maryland Avenue, SW, Washington, DC 20202. (202) 245-2600.

College Library Resources. *Contact:* Education Program Specialist, Library Education and Postsecondary Resources Branch, Office of Libraries and Learning Technologies, Department of Education, R.O.B. #3, Room 3622, 400 Maryland Avenue, SW, Washington, DC 20202. (202) 245-9530.

Educational Research and Development. *Contact:* Office of Public Affairs, National Institute of Education, Department of Education, 1200 Nineteenth Street, NW, Washington, DC 20208. (202) 254-7150.

EXXON Education Foundation. 111 West 49th Street, New York, NY 10020. (212) 398-2273.

Financial Assistance to Meet Special Education Needs of Disadvantaged Children. *Contact:* Department of Education, R.O.B. #3, Room 3642, 400 Maryland Avenue, SW, Washington, DC 20202 (202) 245-3081.

Fund for the Improvement of Postsecondary Education. *Contact:* Office of Educational Research and Improvement, Department of Education, Washington, DC 20202. (202) 245-8091.

Handicapped Media Services and Captioned Films. *Contact:* Chief, Captioned Films and Telecommunications Branch, Office of Special Education, Donohoe Building, Room 4821, 400 Maryland Avenue, SW, Washington, DC 20202. (202) 472-4640.

Handicapped—Research and Demonstration. *Contact:* Chief, Research Projects Branch, Division of Innovation and Development, Office of Special Education, Department of Education, Donohoe Building, Room 3165, 400 Maryland Avenue, SW, Washington, DC 20202. (202) 245-2275 (Research); (202) 245-9722 (Model Programs).

Pacific Northwest Education Demonstration Projects. *Contact:* Pacific Northwest Regional Commission, 700 East Evergreen Boulevard, Vancouver, WA 98660. (206) 696-7771.

Science Education Research and Development and Resource Improvement. *Contact:* Division Director, National Science Foundation, 1800 G Street, NW, Washington, DC 20550. (202) 282-7786 (Educational Resources Improvement Unit); (202) 282-7900 (Development and Research Unit).

State Aid Programs for the Handicapped. *Contact:* Director, Division of Assistance to States, Office of Special Education, Department of Education, Donohoe Building, Room 4046, 400 Maryland Avenue, SW, Washington, DC 20202. (202) 472-4825.

Tandy TRS-80™ Educational Grants Program. Radio Shack Education Division, 400 Tandy Atrium, Fort Worth, TX 76102. (817) 390-3302.

Upper Great Lakes Education Demonstration Projects: *Contact:* Upper Great Lakes Regional Commission, Hawkes Hall, 2231 Catlin Avenue, Superior, WI 54880. (202) 696-7111.

Vocational Education—Program Improvement and Supportive Services. *Contact:* Division of State Vocational Program Operations, Office of Vocational and Adult Education, Department of Education, Washington, DC 20202. (202) 472-3440.

Vocational Education—Program Improvement Projects. *Contact:* Division of Research and Demonstration, Office of Vocational and Adult Education, Washington, DC 20202. (202) 245-9634.

W.K. Kellog Foundation. *Contact:* the Secretary, W.K. Kellog Foundation, 400 North Avenue, Battle Creek, MI 49016. (616) 965-1221.

APPENDIX E:
Software Catalogues, Directories
and Review Sources

Some of the following sources of information on educational software are free of charge; others are not. We suggest you send a letter on school letterhead to each address, with a statement such as: "Kindly forward a complimentary copy of (name of publication) or send descriptive literature and ordering information." You will quickly accumulate your own private library of much-needed information.

American Peripherals. 122 Bangor Street, Lindenhurst, NY 11757

Apple Journal of Courseware Review. Apple Educational Foundation, 20525 Mariani Avenue, Cupertino, CA 95014

Apple Software Directory—Education Volume. WIDL Video, 5245 West Diversey Avenue, Chicago, IL 60639

Atari® Program Exchange. Atari®, Inc., P.O. Box 427, 155 Moffett Park Drive, B-1, Sunnyvale, CA 94086

Book of Apple Software. The Book Company, 11223 South Hindry Avenue, Los Angeles, CA 90045

CIE Software News. Computer Information Exchange, Box 159, San Luis Rey, CA 92068

Commodore Software Encyclopedia. Education Department, 487 Devon Park Drive, Wayne, PA 19087

Courseware Report Card. 150 West Carob Street, Compton, CA 90220

Curriculum Product Reviews. 530 University Avenue, Palo Alto, CA 94301

Dvorak's Software Review. 704 Solano Avenue, Albany, CA 94706

Educational AudioVisual Software Catalogue. Educational AudioVisual, Inc., Pleasantville, NY 10570

Educational Instruction Systems Software Catalogue. 2225 Grant Road, Suite 3, Los Altos, CA 94022

Educator's Handbook and Software Directory. Vital Information, Inc., 350 Union Station, Kansas City, MO 64108

GAMCO Microcomputer Software. Box 310 P, Big Spring, TX 79720

Huntington Computing Catalogue. P.O. Box 787, Corcoran, CA 93212

Index to Computer Based Learning. Educational Communications Department, University of Wisconsin, P.O. Box 413, Milwaukee, WI 53201

International Microcomputer Software Directory. Imprint Software, 420 South Howes Street, Fort Collins, CO 80521

J.L. Hammett Software Catalogue. Hammett Place, P.O. Box 545, Braintree, MA 02184

K-12 Micromedia. 172 Broadway, Woodcliff Lake, NJ 07675

Marck Catalogue. Marck, Inc., 280 Linden Drive, Branford, CT 06082

Micro Center Catalogue. The Micro Center, P.O. Box 6, Pleasantville, NY 10570

Micro Co-op Newsletter. P.O. Box 432, West Chicago, IL 60815

Micro Learningware. P.O. Box 2134, North Mankato, MN 56001

Microcomputers Corporation Catalog. 34 Maple Avenue, P.O. Box 8, Armonk, NY 10504

Microdynamics Educational Systems Catalogue. 2360 S.W. 170th, Beaverton, OR 97005

Midwest Visual Equipment Catalogue. 65600 North Hamlin, Chicago, IL 60645

Peelings. P.O. Box 188, Las Cruces, NM 88001

Pipeline. Conduit, University of Iowa, Box 388, Iowa City, IA 52244

Reference Manual for Instructional Use of Microcomputers. JEM Research, Discovery Park, University of Victoria, P.O. Box 1700, Victoria, British Columbia, V8W 2Y2, Canada

Scholastic Microcomputer Instructional Materials. 904 Sylvan Avenue, Englewood Cliffs, NJ 07632

Scholastic Software Catalogue. Scholastic Software, 22 East Quackenbush Avenue, Dumont, NJ 07628

School Microware Directory. Dresden Associates, P.O. Box 246, Dresden, ME 04342

School Microware Reviews. Dresden Associates. P.O. Box 246, Dresden, ME 04342

Selected Microcomputer Software. Opportunities for Learning, Department L-4, 8950 Lurline Avenue, Chatsworth, CA 91311

Sharbeks Software Directory. 11990 Dorsett Road, St. Louis, MO 63043

Software Directory. Software Central, P.O. Box 30424, Lincoln, NE 68503

Software Review. Microform Review, 520 Riverside Avenue, Westport, CT 06680

Source for Educational Software. Canadian Software Distributors, Sault Ste. Marie, Ontario, Canada

Swift's Directory of Educational Software. Sterling Swift Publishing Company, 1600 Fortview Road, Austin, TX 78704

Texas Instruments Program Directory. TI, P.O. Box 53, Lubbock, TX 79408

TRS-80 Sourcebook and Software Directory. Radio Shack, 1600 One Tandy Center, Fort Worth, TX 76102

User's. 2520 Broadway Drive, St. Paul, MN 55113

VanLoves Apple II/III Software Directory. Vital Information, Inc., 350 Union Station, Kansas City, MO 64108

VMI Apple II Bluebook. Visual Materials, Inc., 4170 Grove Avenue, Gurnee, IL 60031

Queue Catalogues. 5 Chapel Hill Drive, Fairfield, CT 06432

80 Software Critique. P.O. Box 134, Waukegan, IL 60085

APPENDIX F:
Additional Sources of Information on
Educational Software and Microcomputer Use

There exist a number of information clearinghouses for educators interested in constantly updated information on uses of computers in schools. Write to them to find out how you can take advantage of the variety of services they offer.

MicroSIFT. Northwest Regional Educational Laboratory, 710 NW Second Avenue, Portland, OR 97204

Project EduTech. EduTech, Log AB, JWK International, 7617 Little River Turnpike, Annandale, VA 22003

Resources in Computer Education. Computer Technology Program, Northwest Regional Educational Laboratory, 300 SW Sixth Avenue, Portland, OR 97201

Talmis. Talmis Courseware Ratings, 115 North Oak Park Avenue, Oak Park, IL 60301

Technology Information for Educators. Far West Laboratory for Educational Research and Development, 1855 Folsom Street, San Francisco, CA 94103

Trace Research and Development Center for the Severely Communacatively Handicapped. 314 Waisman Center, University of Wisconsin, 1500 Highland Avenue, Madison, WI 53706

APPENDIX G:
A Sampling of
Educational Software Companies

Send away for catalogues from the following companies and you will have descriptions of some of the most popular and some of the best educational software packages on the market. Be sure to specify that you are interested in their "microcomputer software" catalogues, since many of the companies listed carry other products. Also, please note that this listing is just a representative sampling—there is a very large number of additional companies that publish software for educational use.

Addison-Wesley, 2725 Sand Hill Road, Menlo Park, CA 94025

Apple Computer Inc., 10260 Bandley Drive, Cupertino, CA 95014

Atari® Inc., 1272 Borregas Avenue, Sunnyvale, CA 94086

Avant-Garde Creations, P.O. Box 30160, Eugene, OR 97403

Bell & Howell, 7100 North McCormick Road, Chicago, IL 60645

Bertamax, Inc., Suite 500, 101 Nickerson Street, Seattle, WA 98109

Bolt Beranek and Newman, Inc., 10 Moulton Street, Cambridge, MA 02238

Brain Bank, 601 West 26th Street, New York, NY 10001

Cybertronics International, Inc., 999 Mount Kemble Avenue, Morristown, NJ 07960

Data Command, P.O. Box 548, Kankakee, IL 60901

Educational Activities, P.O. Box 392, Freeport, NY 11520

Educational Courseware, 10 Bay Street, Department 66, Westport, CT 06880

Edu-Ware Services, 28035 Dorothy Drive, Agora, CA 91301

Hartley Courseware, P.O. Box 431, Dimondale, MI 48821

Hayden Book Company, 50 Essex Street, Rochelle Park, NJ 07662

Krell Software, 21 Millbrook Drive, Stony Brook, NY 11790

Learning Company, 4370 Alpine Road, Portola Valley, CA 94025

Logo Computer Systems, Inc., 222 Brunswick Boulevard, Pte. Claire, Quebec, H9R 1A6, Canada

McGraw-Hill, 1221 Avenue of the Americas, New York, NY 10020

Micro-Ed Inc., P.O. Box 24156, Minneapolis, MN 55424

Micro Power & Light, 12820 Hillcrest Road, Dallas, TX 75230

Microphys Programs, 2048 Ford Street, Brooklyn, NY 11229

Micropi, Box 5524, Bellingham, WA 98227

Microsoft Consumer Products, 10700 Northrup Way, Bellevue, WA 98004

Milliken Publishing, Computer Department, 1100 Research Boulevard, St. Louis, MO 63132

Milton Bradley, Shaker Road, East Longmeadow, MA 01028

Minnesota Educational Computing Consortium, 2520 Broadway Drive, St. Paul, MN 55113

Muse Software, 330 North Charles Street, Baltimore, MD 21201

Program Design, Inc., 11 Idar Court, Greenwich, CT 06830

Random House, 2970 Brandywine Road, Suite 201, Atlanta, GA 30341

Reader's Digest, Educational Division, Pleasantville, NY 10570

Reston Publishing Company, 11480 Sunset Hills Road, Reston, VA 22090

Spinnaker Software, 215 First Street, Cambridge, MA 02142

SRA, 155 North Wacker Drive, Chicago, IL 60606

Sterling Swift Publishing, 1600 Fortview Road, Austin, TX 78704

TYC Software, 40 Stuyvesant Manor, Geneseo, NY 14454

Terrapin, Inc., 678 Massachusetts Avenue #205, Cambridge, MA 02139

T.H.E.S.I.S., P.O. Box 147, Garden City, MI 48135

APPENDIX H:
Major Sources of
Public Domain Software

A substantial amount of educational software is in the "public domain" and is therefore available to you at no cost or at a nominal fee (to cover the cost of copying and the media—disks or tapes—onto which it is copied). Although it is true that for some of it, "you get what you pay for," still, much of the public domain software is worthwhile and some of it is really quite good. If you can, visit a local microcomputer center to preview what is available (a good thing to do, when possible, before obtaining any software, by the way). You can make copies there if you bring your own blank disks or tapes.

The following sources should prove useful to you in tracking down educationally relevant, public domain software.

Catalog of Public Domain Software for the Apple. Apple Avocation Alliance, Inc., 721 Pike Street, Cheyenne, WY 82009

Commodore International Public Domain Educational Programs, reportedly available through Commodore computer dealers and Commodore Education Resource Centers

Oklahoma Educational Computer Users Program, Richard V. Andree, Mathematics and Computing Science, 601 Elm Street, Room 423, University of Oklahoma, Norman, OK 73019

Softswap. San Mateo County Office of Education & Computer-Using Educators, 333 Main Street, Redwood City, CA 94063

APPENDIX I:
Educational Computing Information Compendiums

We consider the following two compendiums a must for obtaining the most up-to-date, wide range of information about what is happening in the world of educational computing, at least in the United States.

"Directory of Educational Computing Resources," *Computer Classroom Learning*, 19 Davis Drive, Belmont, CA 94002

"Microcomputer Directory: Applications in Educational Settings," Monroe C. Gutman Library, Harvard University, Graduate School of Education, Cambridge, MA

APPENDIX J:
A Selected Listing of
Microcomputer Manufacturers

Apple Computer, Inc., 10260 Bandley Drive, Cupertino, CA 95014 (800) 538-9696

Atari®, Inc., 1265 Borregas Avenue, Sunnyvale, CA 94086 (800) 538-8547

Basis, Inc., 5435 Scotts Valley Drive, Scotts Valley, CA 95066 (408) 438-5804

Commodore Business Machines, Inc., 487 Devon Park Drive, Wayne, PA 19087 (215) 687-9750

Franklin Computer, 7030 Colonial Highway, Pennsauken, NJ 08109 (609) 488-1700

International Business Machines Corp., Educational Marketing, P.O. Box 1328, Boca Raton, FL 33432 (800) 447-4700

Radio Shack, 1600 One Tandy Center, Fort Worth, TX 76102 (800) 231-4717

Sinclair Research Ltd., One Sinclair Plaza, Nashua, NH 03061 (800) 543-3000

Texas Instruments, Inc., P.O. Box 10508, Mail Station 5849, Lubbock, TX 79408

Index

DEC 0 2 1988	DATE DUE	
FEB 0 1 1994		